MAINSTREAMING GUIDEBOOK FOR VOCATIONAL EDUCATORS

Teaching the Handicapped

Peter R. Dahl
Judith A. Appleby
Dewey Lipe

The American Institutes for Research
in the Behavioral Sciences

Olympus Publishing Company Salt Lake City, Utah

The work upon which this publication is based was performed pursuant to Contract Number 300-75-0345 with the Bureau of Education for the Handicapped, Department of Health, Education, and Welfare. Contractors undertaking such projects under Government sponsorship are encouraged to express freely their professional judgment in the conduct of the project. Points of view or opinions stated do not, therefore, necessarily represent official Office of Education position or policy.

Library of Congress Cataloging in Publication Data
Dahl, Peter R   1946-
    Mainstreaming guidebook for vocational educators.

    Bibliograpphy: p.
    Includes index.
    1. Handicapped children—Vocational education. 2. Mainstreaming in education. I. Appleby, Judith A., 1944- joint author. II. Lipe, Dewey, joint author. III. Title.
LC4019.7.D34   371.9'044   78-17113
ISBN 0-913420-78-6

Foreword

Our goal in writing this book was to give you a useful tool in serving handicapped students. We organized it around things you may have occasion to do in serving these students—establishing positive attitudes, assessing student capabilities and designing a program accordingly, eliminating physical barriers, and placing the student on the job.

The chapters of the book, while supporting one another, are designed so you can read them independently, thereby letting you, we hope, zero in on topics of pressing concern. We chose this organization, rather than one based on handicapping condition, for two reasons: (1) it parallels regular vocational education very closely, as good attitudes, a suitable program, a satisfactory physical environment, and successful placement are key factors in any first-rate program; and (2) it makes it easier, from the authors' end, to focus on how to capitalize on the capabilities of individual students, instead of on possible limitations associated with this or that handicapping condition. The latter point is emphasized repeatedly throughout the book in one form or another, and is vital to success with handicapped students. As you read the various chapters, ask yourself how you can use or adapt the techniques described to take advantage of the capabilities of the students with whom you deal.

Foreword

As you can see from the next paragraph, a great many people had a hand in the preparation of this book. The vocational educators among them have all found great reward from teaching handicapped students in their programs. We, and they, have every confidence that you will too.

We would like to thank the following persons who helped in the preparation of this book: Clarence Becker, Ralph C. Bohn, Ruth Brown, Al Burkhardt, Robert A. Cicchetti, Robert and Dorothy DeBolt, Emogene Driscoll, Helene Flolo, T. E. Freund, Joseph Gensiracusa, George A. Glaeser, John R. Gugerty, Ted Hawthorne, Robert M. Hendricks, Owen Hill, Charles Kokoska, Jerry Kuns, Ronald F. Linari, Kalisankar Mallik, Robert F. Mager, C. Carlyle Norment, Susan Phillips, James Raybourn, Eleanor Reynolds, Loren Schoof, Pearl Stephen, James Stott, Lloyd W. Tindall, Jose Vasquez, James R. Wallace, and Robert A. Weisgerber. Variously, they offered suggestions as to format, layout, and content; gave us access to photographs and drawings; provided examples included in the body of the book. Any shortcomings remaining in the book are exclusively the authors'.

We would also like to thank Irene Yurash for her careful work in preparing this manuscript for publication.

Peter R. Dahl
Judith A. Appleby
Dewey Lipe

Acknowledgments

In addition to those listed in the foreword, the following vendors supplied us with photographs. Their addresses are included here for the convenience of the reader. The authors cannot, of course, warrant or guarantee the suitability of any specific aids or devices, and nothing in this book should be so construed.

American Foundation for the Blind
15 West 16th Street
New York, New York 10011
Figures 6-25, 6-75, 6-28, 6-33

American Printinghouse for the Blind
1839 Frankfort Avenue
Louisville, Kentucky 40206
Figure 6-27

American Telephone and Telegraph Company
Services for the Blind
295 North Maple Avenue
Basking Ridge, New Jersey 07920
Figures 6-12, 6-13, 6-36

Brodhead-Garrett
4560 East 71st Street
Cleveland, Ohio 44105
Figures 3-10, 3-15, 6-5

Acknowledgments

Micon Industries
252 Oak Street
Oakland, California 94607
Figure 6-35

Telesensory Systems, Inc.
3408 Hillview Avenue
Palo Alto, California 94304
Figure 6-26, 6-30

The EdnaLite Corporation
200 North Water Street
Peekskill, New York 10566
Figure 6-21

Visualtek
1610 26th Street
Santa Monica, California 90404
Figure 6-29

Contents

1

Entering the Mainstream:
How and Why

INTRODUCTION

A handicapped individual's capabilities are much more important than that person's limitations. If a blind man can repair a telephone switching system, it does not matter that he cannot see the equipment. If a programmer can write a satisfactory program, it is of no importance that her hands must be supported by special braces while she does so. Handicapped people are teachers, businesspeople, technicians, scientists, craftspersons, writers, artists, and government officials. Indeed, it often seems that no sooner do you think of a job that a handicapped person *just could not do,* than you encounter a story about someone doing it.*

Handicapped people, like everyone else, deserve the chance to enjoy life and to make the most of their talents. While some of the most severely handicapped may have to

---

*Handicapped people themselves sometimes fall into this "just couldn't possibly" trap. A Canadian economist, himself blind, reported overhearing a conversation between a blind chemist and a blind lawyer. The chemist could not understand how the lawyer did his job, especially all that reading. For his part, the lawyer did not see how the chemist could do the dangerous things, such as pouring acid, that were part of his job. (Successful Disabled Persons International, Volume 2)

lead substantial portions of their lives in institutions, the great majority of handicapped people—including many with severe permanent disabilities—are quite able to participate in and contribute to mainstream society. Sometimes participation by the handicapped requires accommodation or adjustment. Sometimes making such adjustments or accommodations requires the intervention of specially trained professionals. Still, there is much that people whose primary training is not in rehabilitation, medicine, or some other specialized field can contribute. The purpose of this book is to help you as a vocational educator to extend your services to greater numbers of handicapped students in mainstream classes.

ISN'T REHABILITATION A SPECIALIZED FIELD? WHAT CAN THE LAYMAN DO?

Most of us would like to see the handicapped benefit more fully from the opportunities the mainstream of society has to offer, but doubt that we have much to contribute toward that end. There are, after all, specialists who have trained for years to work with those who cannot see or hear or walk or control their movements. What can a nonspecialist do that these specialists cannot? Is it not best to leave the training of the handicapped to such specialists?

Such questions are valid. Handicapped people do benefit greatly from the services of those specially trained to help them, and some aspects of training should be undertaken by such specialists or in cooperation with them. An interdisciplinary approach to assure a proper mix of services for the individual is recommended frequently in this book.

However, this book is about the mainstream of society and the entry of the handicapped into that mainstream. When the handicapped enter the mainstream, they do *not* enter a world populated by professionals trained specifically to serve them; rather, they enter the polyglot world of bus drivers, poets, teachers, carpenters, and engineers who have not received specialized training in working with handicapped people and who probably never will. Yet, people whose primary training is not in working with the handicapped are often able to use their expertise to help the handicapped enjoy the benefits of mainstream society. The following examples illustrate this point:

Chicago, Illinois Students at the Institute of Design prepared a booklet illustrating environmental barriers faced by people in wheelchairs and showing means by which these barriers can be overcome or eliminated.

Los Angeles, California Vocational educators at California State University, Los Angeles, conducted a joint program with special educators to train mentally retarded students in basic construction skills. Students built a frame tool shed with a cement floor as part of their training and are now working to renovate homes in deteriorating neighborhoods. In this case, two groups of professionals joined hands to do what neither could have accomplished alone.

Murray Hill, New Jersey Engineers at Bell Laboratories developed an electronic larynx which, when placed against the throat, allows a person without a larynx to speak.

St. Paul, Minnesota Neighbors added a large room to the house of a recently disabled man so that he could run his hobby shop without leaving home.

Petersburg National Battlefield, Virginia The National Park Service installed braille markers so that blind visitors could follow the course of the siege. Recorded descriptions of many key actions bring events to life for all who can hear and are especially useful to the blind.

New York, New York The American Broadcasting Company granted permission for same-day rebroadcast of a subtitled version of its evening news, thereby opening a previously closed source of information to the deaf.

Washington, D.C. The Congress of the United States, on behalf of all citizens, passed many bills affirming the national commitment to fair treatment of the handicapped in education, in employment, in recreation, and in gaining access to all other services to which they, as citizens, are entitled.

As you read these examples, you probably noticed that most of the contributions were made using skills that were not developed specifically to aid the handicapped. Design students are not primarily concerned with the handicapped, nor are vocational educators, Members of Congress or the electricians, carpenters, and others who modified the St. Paulite's house. Yet, as the examples show, people of each type can use their skills or position to make life more satisfying for handicapped people. In applying their skills, these people did not have to become experts in any of the specialties concerned with handicapping conditions. Rather, they were sensitive to the effect their activities could have in making life richer for the handicapped, and extended themselves to realize that effect.

An important related point is that specialists in working with the handicapped cannot themselves become knowledgeable in all areas in which a handicapped person might seek training. When it comes to auto mechanics, dental technology, or home economics, it is the special educator or the rehabilitation worker who is the layman and the vocational educator who is the specialist. As described below, handicapped people have succeeded in a wide variety of jobs. Vocational educators, through the training they can provide, hold the key to success in many of them.

SUCCESSFUL HANDICAPPED PEOPLE

What others can do for the benefit of the handicapped is only one side of the story. Handicapped people can, in turn, succeed on the job. In a recent survey Cook, Dahl, and Gale (1978) found over 300 jobs being performed by handicapped persons. Some of these are shown in Table 1-1 and illustrate the breadth of achievement among the handicapped population. Still, this list only scratches the surface. Publications of advocacy groups frequently print stories about successful handicapped people and any department of vocational rehabilitation can provide long and impressive lists of job placements.

Table 1-1
SOME JOBS AT WHICH HANDICAPPED PEOPLE ARE WORKING[a]

Area of Work	Job Titles	Handicapping Condition
Art	Advertising Layout Illustrator (commercial art)	Emotionally Disturbed Severely Health Impaired
Business Relations	Hospital Administrator Receptionist	Severe Health Impaired Cerebral Palsy
Clerical Work	Motor Vehicle Dispatcher Inventory Clerk	Paraplegia Quadriplegia
Counseling, Guidance, & Social Work	Employment Counselor Social Worker	Quadriplegia Cerebral Palsy
Crafts	Short-Order Cook Carpenter	Mentally Retarded Emotionally Disturbed
Education & Training	Secondary School Teacher University Faculty Member	Paraplegia Quadriplegia
Elemental Work	Welder Helper Baling Machine Operator	Mentally Retarded Mentally Retarded
Engineering	Tool Designer Architectural Drafting	Paraplegia Epilepsy
Entertainment	Radio Announcer	Paraplegia
Farming, Fishing, & Forestry	Scientific Helper	Quadriplegia
Investigating, Inspecting, & Testing	Real Estate Appraiser Medical Technologist	Severely Health Impaired Severely Health Impaired
Law & Law Enforcement	Patent Lawyer Tax Agent	Quadriplegia Paraplegia
Machine Work	Turret Lathe Operator Offset Press Operator	Multiply Handicapped Paraplegia
Managerial & Supervisory Work	Banquet Steward Dry-Cleaning Superintendent	Severely Health Impaired Quadriplegia
Mathematics & Science	Microbiologist Business Programmer	Paraplegia Quadriplegia
Medicine & Health	Psychiatrist Physical Therapist	Quadriplegia Severely Health Impaired
Merchandising	Farm Supplies & Equipment Sales Office Machine Sales	Quadriplegia Emotionally Disturbed
Personal Service	Cosmetologist Messenger	Cerebral Palsy Mentally Retarded
Photography & Communications	Dispatcher (police-radio) Transmitter Operator (radio & television)	Paraplegia Severely Health Impaired
Writing	Newspaper Editor Feature Reporter	Quadriplegia Cerebral Palsy

[a]More detailed information may be found in Cook, Dahl & Gale (1977). This listing is intended to show that handicapped people engage in a great variety of jobs. It does not begin to exhaust the vocations in which handicapped people are now succeeding.

It may be fairly argued that one goal of the American educational system has been to make available the full range of opportunities from which students could benefit. This goal can, perhaps, never be fully reached, but for some it has been less well approximated than for others. If the handicapped are to have available to them the full range of opportunities from which they can benefit—and that range is exceptionally broad—then those educational opportunities available to the nonhandicapped must also be made available to them. To open the full range of opportunities will require the careful blending of regular and special services, as it is both impractical and undesirable for special services to be developed that duplicate the bulk areas of training available to the general, nonhandicapped population. This provides a challenge and an opportunity for all educators as handicapped students increasingly enter the educational mainstream.

HOW MANY SCHOOL AGE HANDICAPPED PEOPLE ARE THERE? WHAT DOES VOCATIONAL EDUCATION HAVE TO OFFER THEM?

There are over 6 1/2 million handicapped children, aged 6 to 19, in the United States (National Advisory Committee on the Handicapped, 1976). Service to these students has been expanding in recent years. According to the National Advisory Committee on the Handicapped, 58% received educational services in 1976 as against about 40% in 1970 and 10% in 1950. This trend, which will surely accelerate under the impact of new legislation, will put new challenges before the educator. Handicapped students are now legally entitled to a free, appropriate public education, and to receive that education in the least restrictive environment commensurate with effective learning. In other words, they should be in the regular mainstream classroom whenever possible.

As these students enroll increasingly in regular programs, many of them will look to vocational education for the same reasons that nonhandicapped students do: to prepare for meaningful jobs. It is reasonable that they should do so. Not only do they have the *right* to enroll in appropriate programs, but handicapped people succeed at an exceptionally wide range of jobs, many of which can be entered following vocational training. Thus, vocational education has exactly the same thing—preparation for work—to offer handicapped and nonhandicapped students alike.

In addition, vocational education can help the student grow as an individual. A vocational student can gain self-esteem, experience the gratification of a job well done, and learn to work cooperatively with others. These outcomes are as critical for job success as the specialized skills gained. While handicapped students vary greatly in their life histories and experiences, it is still unfortunately true that a great many will have experienced an undue amount of rejection and failure. Vocational programs, because they are generally competency based and product oriented provide an excellent opportunity for genuine success and the confidence and pleasure that it brings.

WHAT IS MAINSTREAMING?

According to the National Advisory Council on Education Professions Development,

> . . . mainstreaming is the conscientious effort to place handicapped children into the least restrictive educational setting which is appropriate to their needs. The primary objective of this process is to provide children with the most appropriate and effective educational experiences which will enable them to become self-reliant adults. Within this objective, it is thought preferable to educate children the least distance away from the mainstream of society. Hence there is a heavy emphasis on movement into the regular classroom whenever possible. (National Advisory Council on Education Professions Development, 1976, p.7)

This definition, which is consistent with the provisions of recent legislation pertaining to the education of the handicapped as discussed below, requires the type of careful blending suggested above. As conceptualized here, "main-streaming" can be seen to encompass those services, adapted to the needs of the student, that can be delivered in the least restrictive educational setting possible. Thus, mainstreaming is a system of management intended to be sensitive to the needs of the handicapped student. The ultimate goal is to prepare the handicapped student for participation in the mainstream society.

At the same time, mainstreaming does not mean that every handicapped student must be placed in regular classes full time. The key is to select the most appropriate mix of regular and special services consistent with an individual's capabilities and limitations. Supportive services, supplementary instructional services, and part-time special class services will help the regular teacher to serve handicapped students more effectively if they are provided in those areas where the skills of the regular teacher, or the time that he or she has to devote to the handicapped student, do not suffice.

To be implemented most effectively, mainstreaming programs must also be sensitive to the needs of teachers and other staff. It benefits no one to place a student in a classroom lacking the proper equipment and directed by a teacher without the training or support to serve the student effectively. Thus, any mainstreaming effort must consider providing teachers with the appropriate training, equipment, and specialized support that they need to do their work effectively. The following chapters discuss practical steps you can take in these and related areas.

WHERE DOES MAINSTREAMING FIT IN THE LARGER SCHEME OF THINGS?

There is a national awakening to the potential of handicapped citizens to participate fully in mainstream society, which already is changing our physical, work, and social environments. This is manifested in many ways, for example:

- Ramps, curb cuts, reserved parking places, accessible restrooms, and lowered drinking fountains are now common sights whereas only a few years ago they were almost unknown.

- Employers are required not only to refrain from discrimination against the handicapped, but to make reasonable accommodation so that handicapped people have a fair chance to compete for jobs and promotions.

- Handicapped people form their own pressure groups to demand increased opportunities, strong regulations to implement their legal rights, and to have their full humanity recognized.

- The right of the handicapped to participate in publically supported programs, and to have access to public facilities is being increasingly recognized, and supported by legislatures and the courts.

In sum, handicapped people are increasingly dissatisfied with being shunted into society's byways; their right to participation is being recognized (and supported by law); and the ability of handicapped people to be active, successful, contributing members of society is becoming ever more apparent.

In line with this is greater participation in regular educational programs. As handicapped people participate increasingly in the mainstream of society, it is natural that they should ready themselves for that participation in the mainstream of education.

This is not to say, of course, that all is smooth sailing. Handicapped people are still prevented from participating fully in many activities by unnecessary attitudinal and physical barriers, archaic regulations, and ignorance. But the movement in society is in the other direction—it is a commitment for inclusion, and mainstreaming in education is a critical part of this movement.

WHAT DOES MAINSTREAMING MEAN FOR VOCATIONAL STAFF?

Essentially, it means new understanding of the needs of handicapped individuals and a wider range of skills.

Specifically, vocational staff will need to be able to carry out the following activities either by themselves or in cooperation with other professionals:

- Establish positive attitudes toward the handicapped.

- Assess the architectural accessibility of vocational facilities and determine needed modifications.

- Assess the capabilities and limitations of handicapped students in educationally relevant terms.

- Develop an individual educational program (IEP) on the basis of the assessment.

- Determine what special equipment and work station modifications are needed in the classroom.

- Place handicapped graduates in jobs.

Vocational educators will develop competence and self-confidence in dealing with handicapped students from skills developed through experience, additional in-service training, and the use of support services.

Vocational educators will not be alone in providing for the handicapped in regular classes. At the core of the mainstreaming movement is sweeping federal legislation—the Education for All Handicapped Children Act (PL 94-142) and Section 504 of the Rehabilitation Act of 1973 (PL 93-112). This legislation grants all disabled students ages 3 to 21 the right to a free public education in the least restrictive environment possible. It requires that programs and tests be modified as necessary for the handicapped. Public Law 94-482, the Education Amendments of 1976, likewise requires that handicapped students be assisted to study in regular vocational programs as much as possible. Thus, *all* educators will be responsible for meeting the mainstreaming challenge. And as a result, all educators will need to work together cooperatively to provide effective instruction for the handicapped.

A pressing need of vocational educators in serving the handicapped is the modification of existing programs. Such need is the focus of this book. Its contents can be conceived in the form of a pyramid (Figure 1-1) corresponding to the topics listed above. At the base is the general area of making ready for the inclusion of handicapped students. This comprises establishing attitudes favorable to including the handicapped in regular programs and making sure that vocational facilities are accessible to them. Next is the individual assessment process that provides the essential background information for building an appropriate program for that individual. It is a multidisciplinary process, involving the cooperation and expertise of many professional workers. The purpose of the multidisciplinary evaluation of the student is to work out the individual education program, or IEP—the next level of the pyramid. The IEP is a major requirement of PL 94-142, which stipulates that schools must draw up individual education plans for each handicapped student and that the plans must have parental approval. The assessment process and the IEP, in turn, provide the basis for modifying the curriculum to meet the identified needs of the handicapped student, including the acquisition of special equipment or modification of existing equipment as needed.

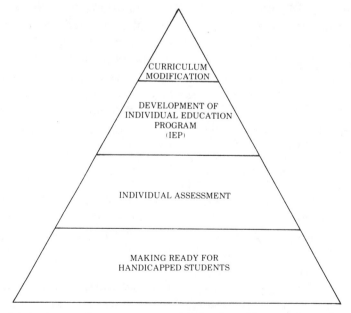

FIGURE 1-1. Service pyramid for handicapped students

AN ACTIVE MAINSTREAMING PROGRAM

The following example shows how one vocational program extends its services to handicapped students. This program serves a large number of handicapped students, doing so by enlisting the cooperation of vocational and special personnel. This provides an excellent model of what can be done; the approach you take should, of course, be tailored to the needs of your students, taking into consideration the circumstances in which your program operates.

BOCES of Nassau County, State of New York: A Case Study

BOCES of Nassau County is one of 47 Boards of Cooperative Educational Services in the State of New York, each serving a cluster of local school districts within a region. BOCES of Nassau serves 56 districts within the county.

More than 60 occupational education courses are available through BOCES as electives to all public high school students in Nassau County. The courses are offered in one-, two-, and three-year sequences and are designed to equip young men and women with salable skills. The nearly 6,000 students who currently select occupational education are bussed to the nearest area center for half of each day; they spend the remaining half in their high school pursuing a regular academic program.

Mainstreaming the Handicapped

Each year the occupational education area centers mainstream special needs students who number 10% of the student population. In order to make this a viable integration, BOCES obtains background information on each special needs student entering a program of occupational education.

When the Committee for the Handicapped, the Special Needs Guidance Counselor, and the Division of Occupational Education determine that the student is ready for entry into regular programs of occupational education and shows employability potential, an intake screening is set up. The participants of the intake meeting include the principal of the occupational education area center, local school personnel, the Occupational Education Special Needs Guidance Counselor, and the Coordinator of Special Needs Activities from the main office. The purpose of the meeting is to determine from all available data the readiness and potential of the student for participation in a regular program of occupational education. The data include:

1. psychological reports
2. achievement profiles
3. IQ test scores
4. anecdotal reports
5. written recommendations of qualified staff members
6. medical records and approval
7. school transcripts
8. parental approval
9. other pertinent data

The principal of the receiving BOCES area center is responsible for calling a case conference involving the receiving occupational education teacher, the guidance counselor, and the school nurse. These conferences are held for the purpose of informing the immediately involved staff of the special needs student's entrance into the program of occupational education. Through the intake screening and the material perused and discussed at such meetings, the occupational education teacher is better equipped to instruct the student while he or she is in the program.

To provide the individual student with a program that has a reasonable expectation of benefiting the student and providing a safe and healthy learning environment in the program for which the student is applying, the following guidelines are considered for enrollment into an occupational education program:

1. minimum age of 16 (consideration is given to special cases)

2. physical ability

3. intellectual competence

4. psychomotor and manual dexterity

5. level of emotional stability

6. student attitude and interest

7. student school and social adjustment

When the student enrolls in a program, it is the responsibility of the home district to formulate an Individual Education Plan as required by the Education of All Handicapped Children Act of 1975 (PL 94-142).

Representatives of both the home school district and the Division of Occupational Education meet periodically to evaluate both the efficiency of the screening process and the progress of the individual student referred to the occupational program. This process allows for the determination on a long-range basis of how to improve both the policies and procedures so that the eventual goal of gainful employment is more attainable for the individual.

Articulation of Occupational Education and Special Education

To provide an effective mainstream program, occupational and special education personnel must work cooperatively in the best interest of the individual. To this end and at the suggestion of the Superintendent of BOCES of Nassau, an interdivisional special education and occupational education policy meeting was set up in 1972 to formulate resolutions and a standard format for interdivisional cooperation in the development of career education opportunities for the handicapped. Meetings are held on a continuing basis, and the combined group is called the Coordinating Council. Coordinating Council members share their expertise to construct a program that is at once occupationally relevant and consistent with the students' capabilities and interests.

CHAPTER REFERENCES

Cook, Paul F., Dahl, Peter R., and Gale, Margaret A. *Vocational Opportunities*. Salt Lake City, Utah: Olympus Publishing Company, 1978.

National Advisory Committee on the Handicapped. *The Unfinished Revolution: Education for the Handicapped*. Washington, D.C.: U.S. Government Printing Office, 1976.

National Advisory Council on Education Professions Development. *Mainstreaming: Helping Teachers Meet the Challenge*. Washington, D.C.: National Advisory Council on Educations Professions Development, 1976

People-to-People, *Successful Disabled Persons International*. 6 Vols. Washington, D.C.: People to People, no date.

2

Developing Positive Staff and Student Attitudes Toward Mainstreaming

INTRODUCTION

Mainstream education naturally arouses questions and doubts in the minds of both the handicapped and non-handicapped individuals involved. When those doubts and concerns reflect false beliefs or negative feelings, they represent attitude barriers to the progress of handicapped students. This chapter presents steps toward eliminating those barriers by establishing sound beliefs and a positive orientation regarding handicapped students in mainstream education.

The word "attitude" is used in a great many contexts with a wide range of nuances. For our purposes we will place some boundaries on the meaning and give our usage a practical orientation. In this chapter the term attitude will mean simply the tendency to act for or against the interests of a handicapped student in a given situation. This definition of attitude applies as well to the handicapped, themselves, as to the nonhandicapped.

A variety of attitudes are represented in concerns commonly expressed by students, school staff, and parents. Those attitudes range from optimistic to discouraging, as shown in the following examples:

1. Handicapped Students' Attitudes

   - "Will teachers and students feel awkward around me? Will they seriously doubt whether I can succeed in school and in a job?"

   - "I know what career I want and I'll work as hard as anyone to get the training I need and to get a job."

   - "In the past people have treated me as if I were not human. I don't expect that to change in the future."

2. Vocational Teachers' Attitudes

   - "I already have enough problems dealing with students who can't read or are discipline problems. I don't need a whole new set of problems."

   - "Handicapped students may get hurt or cause other students to get hurt on the equipment."

   - "I know I could accommodate a student in a wheelchair but I would have to learn how to provide for a blind student."

3. School Administrators' Attitudes

   - "My teachers and staff understand each student's strengths and limitations. This is true of all students, both handicapped and nonhandicapped. We treat each student as an individual with a unique set of needs and assets."

   - "Handicapped students will cause too much congestion in our narrow hallways. Our insurance rates will surely go up."

4. Parents' Attitudes

   - "There will have to be someone with my son all the time. Otherwise, who will look after him."

   - "The special education teacher understood my daughter and the class was small enough for her to receive individual attention. What will become of her when she is herded in with everyone else?"

- "My son will have to learn how to succeed in competition with nonhandicapped people and I believe he has the capacity and drive to do it."

Attitudes are not always expressed in words; nevertheless, they are pointedly and powerfully communicated. Positive attitudes are expressed in actions that help handicapped students achieve success in school. Negative attitudes inhibit success, either by direct action or indirectly through lack of action. Because the impact of attitudes on handicapped students' progress in school can be profound, it is important to know how to shape attitudes to be helpful rather than harmful. This chapter describes how attitudes develop, what influences them to change, and the impact of various attitudes on success in school. Attitudes of parents, students, teachers, and other school staff are discussed in separate sections of this chapter.

THE FUNCTION AND IMPORTANCE OF ATTITUDES IN MAINSTREAMING

How Do Attitudes Toward the Handicapped Develop?

Many of us have known individuals who were crippled by war or by an accident. Maiming of the body may be associated with acts of heroism, with fortuitous events that were particularly unlucky for the person who was harmed, or with bad judgment and poor decision. Our aesthetics may influence our attitudes especially toward handicaps that involve visible disfigurement. Isolated encounters with handicapped individuals may color our attitudes. We may have avoided communicating with a deaf or blind person because we did not feel like putting forth the extra effort required or were afraid of embarrassing ourselves or the handicapped person. Consequently, our attitudes form gradually from direct experiences with the handicapped and also indirectly by cultural stigma, religion, beliefs about the beauty and function of the human body, literature, well-known personalities such as Franklin D. Roosevelt, and many other sources.

Many of us have not had a close association with blind, deaf, paralyzed, speech impaired, retarded, or other handicapped individuals. Attitudes that have not been tempered by much direct experience with handicapped individuals tend to generalize to all persons of a given handicap. For example, we may lump all blind students together in a descriptive classification of detached, aloof, nonconforming, disheveled, and generally inept. Based on limited direct experience with the handicapped we would probably differentiate our attitudes fairly adequately between handicapping conditions but we may not adequately differentiate our attitudes toward individuals with the same handicap.

For most of us, our attitudes toward the handicapped are not good or bad nor right or wrong. Rather they are too general and undifferentiated. Our beliefs and emotions regarding the handicapped have not been refined and tuned to the individual differences between handicapped persons. Because our attitudes are expressions of our beliefs and emotions, they are integral to our personalities and they do not change suddenly in response to simple directives. When they do change, they seldom do a complete flip-flop unless in response to an overwhelming emotional and intellectual experience. Thoughts and feelings evolve slowly as we acquire more accurate and more detailed information and as our expectations are either confirmed or disconfirmed through personal relationships with handicapped individuals.

It should be clear then that an attitude does not refer to a carefully planned course of action. It refers rather to a spontaneous tendency to act one way or another. The tendency is determined by the accumulated beliefs and feelings that are triggered by a given situation. We cannot change our attitudes precipitously simply because we cannot command sudden shifts to occur in our beliefs and feelings; however, we can choose the direction that our attitudes will develop and choose the experiences that will shape our attitudes. In other words we can plan and direct our attitude development.

What Attitudes Most Benefit Mainstreamed Handicapped Students?

This question concerns attitudes of the handicapped themselves as well as of parents, teachers, and other important persons in a handicapped individual's life. It seems to be most helpful to describe attitudes as processes, with examples, rather than as states of mind. The many positive attitudes that have been associated with successful achievement by handicapped students may be capsulized in four processes:

- High expectations relevant to capabilities
- Abundant praise for progress
- Occasional prodding, scolding, or even angry admonition, *as necessary* to get the handicapped youth on track
- Relaxed sense of humor

The first and last processes apply to both the handicapped and the nonhandicapped. Praise and admonition are effective processes when used by those nonhandicapped individuals who are important in the life of a handicapped person.

High Expectation

High expectation refers here to a goal based upon what the handicapped individual *potentially can do.* This does not mean to ignore the handicap because that could prove both dangerous and cruel. To treat a blind student no differently from a sighted student could pave the way to injury or isolation. High expectation does mean having a long-range goal such as living in an apartment; holding a job; living a productive independent life; learning valuable skills; and making a contribution to society. There may be substantial barriers to be overcome before achieving any of these goals but the vision of the goal is never forgotten. The following is an example from the DeBolt family which has eight adopted handicapped children.

FIGURE 2-1. Karen DeBolt assembling toys in the family workshop. Her sisters, Wendy and Twe, are in the background. (Courtesy Robert and Dorothy DeBolt)

Karen who was adopted at age six by Dorothy and Bob DeBolt was born without arms or legs. When she came to the DeBolt family she had learned to use prosthetic hands (hooks) and legs and crutches. (See Figure 2-1.) From the very first day in the DeBolt family she was expected to surmount barriers on her own, as shown in the following excerpt from *19 Steps Up the Mountain* (Blank, 1976).

> Bob carried Karen from his car, up the front porch steps to the door. Dorothy opened it. Bob placed Karen on the threshold step. He wanted to give her the chance to walk into her home. The only barrier to her entering the house was a 3/4-inch doorsill. There seemed to be an unspoken agreement among all members of the family who were standing to welcome her in a smiling group on the front porch: Karen was going to take that step into the house on her own.
>
> She leaned her left shoulder against the door jam for balance. She moved her right crutch over the

sill. After sliding her shoulder forward about an inch, she raised her left crutch and moved it across the sill. Then she tried to drag her feet over it. She couldn't. She broke into a sweat. She wore an uneasy, fixed smile. She swiveled in her bucket and simultaneously pushed upward on her crutches. Several children began urging her with, "Come on, Karen, come on," and "You can do it—a little more!" Dorothy couldn't breathe.

Karen hunched a little, pushed again, and dragged her feet to the other side of the threshold. The children cheered. Karen's black skin was gleaming with sweat, and her eyes were bright with pride. (Blank, pp. 105-106)

Karen clearly showed a high degree of self-esteem, motivation, and sheer grit that all handicapped youth do not have. These qualities spurred her on to many new achievements:

At the hospital Karen had used a fork and spoon with handles that were curled to make them easier to hold between her hooks. The DeBolts had left them at the hospital, convinced that Karen could learn to use conventional utensils.

The two hooks on each hand were lined with smooth rubber and held closed by a heavy rubber band. Karen could open the hooks by moving her shoulder, pulling a cable that separated the two prongs of each hook. She eagerly tried to use the household's utensils, but her effort sent knife, fork, and food flying across the table: the handles kept slipping between the hooks. Bob solved that problem by lining Karen's utensils with heavy abrasive tape, the kind used on the floors of industrial plants to prevent slips on spilled oil. The tape increased friction, enabling Karen to control firmly the angle of her knife and fork. She had never used a knife at the hospital—an aide had always cut up her food—and it took her several weeks to acquire the knack as she went from cutting a fried egg to vegetables, then hamburger and firm meats.

Her skill with the hooks increased virtually every day. Her drawing and writing improved. She peeled hard-boiled eggs and oranges. She learned to hold a slice of hard-boiled egg so precisely that her hooks neither allowed the slice to fall nor squashed the delicate yolk. After one failure she could hold an ice cream cone without cracking the fragile cone.

She loved to help Dorothy in the kitchen. "Karen, would you give me a hand with the potato salad?"

"Sure, Mom."

"Now, look, dear, this gadget is called a potato peeler. Watch me. See how it peels that skin right off."

No toy could have given Karen more joy.

She also learned how to help with the preparations for an omelet. Dorothy cracked an egg on the edge of the bowl and dropped the contents into the bowl. Karen tried it. On her first attempts she squeezed the egg too hard and both egg and pieces of shell fell into the bowl. Then she held the egg too loosely and it slipped from between the hooks and broke on the counter. Finally she got it right—the correct pressure to retain the egg and the correct force to crack it. Then she pulled apart the shell and dropped the contents into the bowl. After finishing all the eggs with great concentration, she looked up at Dorothy, a broad smile on her face. Dorothy hugged her.

Karen became so adept with her hooks that the other members of the family lost sight of the fact that they were not hands. When Sunee and Melanie wet their fingers to pick up cake and cookie crumbs, Karen automatically ran her tongue over her hooks so that the crumbs would adhere to them. Once Sunee swung swiftly toward Karen after Karen had accidentally slammed a door on her hooks. "Does it Hurt?" Sunee asked with deep concern. "Is it bleeding?" The two girls looked at each other for a moment, then began laughing. (Blank, pp. 124-125)

The DeBolt's expectations for Karen were that she learn

to do those things that able-bodied children learn as part of their normal development of competency. Evolving competency builds self-esteem. Karen was not only learning to carry her own weight in the family, she was a contributing member. The DeBolt's high expectation for Karen is, of course, coupled with ready assistance to help figure out how to solve problems that arise. But, underlying their assistance in problem solving, their creating of new opportunities for Karen to learn, and their spontaneous encouragement is their unquestioned expectation that Karen *will achieve* each goal.

Abundant Praise for Progress

Giving students praise for progress is an essential skill that every teacher learns to perfection. The only difference in applying that skill with handicapped students is that smaller achievement steps may warrant acknowledgment and praise because of the considerable effort required. A teacher normally would not praise a student for going to the proper work station; however, for a mildly retarded student this might be a significant achievement.

The example below concerns 4 1/2 year old Sunee, another DeBolt child, whose legs are paralyzed. The example describes this support, encouragement, and praise offered by Sunee's teenage brothers, Tich (pronounced Tuck) and Anh (pronounced On), and by her mother, Dorothy. Tich and Anh, also paralyzed below the waist, modeled stair climbing for Sunee as well as verbally instructing her.

Each day Sunee practiced the steps. It was slow, exhausting work. It took a week for her to climb three steps. Tich coached her along, and Ahn stood behind her most of the time to break her fall if she lost her balance and toppled backward. Then her determination eliminated fear, and she told Anh that he didn't have to protect her. Dorothy was cooking one day when she heard a crash in the front hall. She ran in and saw Sunee sprawled across the bottom step of the staircase. "I'm all right, Mommy," Sunee assured her. She checked to see that her leg braces were locked in the straight position (leg braces are hinged at the knees to allow a sitting position), grabbed the baluster and pulled herself upright. Her face was set. She began her climb again. On reaching the fifth step she raised a crutch and beat the step several times in anger. Then she looked at Dorothy and said, 'Tomorrow that step won't make me fall."

About three months after her arrival Anh knocked on the door of Dorothy's bedroom and said, "Mom, we wanna show you very important thing. Sunee has surprise for you."

Dorothy went to the second floor landing. Tich and Sunee stood at the bottom of the staircase. Sunee began struggling up the stairs. Sometimes she lost her grip on the banister, but she didn't fall. After the exertion of climbing four or five steps, she stopped to catch her breath. But she hoisted and heaved and willed herself up those nineteen steps. It took her twenty-five minutes. When she reached the second floor landing, Dorothy grabbed her and hugged her and exclaimed "I'm so proud of you. So proud."

"Then why are you crying Mommy?" Sunee panted.

"They're happy tears, Sunee."

Sunee licked her cheek and said, "Yes, they taste happy."

Then Dorothy hugged Tich and Anh. They were grinning, bursting with a sense of achievement. Dorothy stepped back from them and said, "You guys are something else." (Blank, pp. 35-36)

Admonition

The barriers confronting the handicapped are not always apparent to a stranger who does not know a particular handicapped individual's fears and doubts that have accumulated from past experiences. The example below is again from the experience of Sunee learning to climb the 19 steps in the circular staircase to the second floor. The hardest part was negotiating the first step.

On the first morning of the Christmas school holiday sixteen-year-old Tich motioned four-year-old Sunee toward the foot of the stairs. He was all business. She was all apprehension. "You learn climb stairs," Tich announced. "No big deal. You listen. You watch. Okay. Now, put left hand on railing like this and reach under with fingers and grab this thing"—the baluster. "Get good grip. Hang one crutch on right shoulder like this. Now put right crutch on step. Now you pull with left hand on railing and push up with right arm on crutch. See? I go right on to step."

Sunee tried it. The pull-push action required both technique and strength. She was carrying the additional burden of one-fourth of her own weight in braces and corset. "I can't do it," she cried. "It's too hard."

"We try again tomorrow," Tich said.

Occasionally Dorothy or Bob watched the lessons, standing in the entrance to the kitchen or sitting in a chair in the front hall. Neither ever said a word, and usually both pupil and teacher were oblivious to their presence.

After five or six attempts Sunee still couldn't mount that first step. Tich said, "Okay, Sunee, what's the matter?"

"I can't do it."

"Why you can't?"

She was silent.

"Why?"

"I'm afraid."

"Of what?"

"Falling."

"You no be afraid. I right behind you."

When several more sessions passed without any progress, Tich changed his approach. "You don't try hard enough," he admonished.

"I do. I just can't get up there."

Tich's voice hardened and he leaned toward Sunee's face, saying, "Don't tell me you can't! I have crutches and braces same as you." He slapped his knuckles against her lower abdomen, producing a dull thump on her plastic corset. He rapped the front of his corset. "See? Just the same. I don't wanna hear you can't do it. Don't wanna hear it! Now you do it! You do what I do. You do it right now!"

Sunee obediently turned to the step. Pulling and pushing, straining and grunting, she heaved herself to the first step. She turned her head to Tich; tears were running down her cheeks. "There!" she yelled angrily.

Bob quietly rose from his chair and slipped back into the kitchen. Tears were on his cheeks also.

Later Tich told Bob, "Sunee make that first step."

"Great. Took some doing, huh?"

"Not too much." (Blank, pp. 34-35)

Relaxed Humor

Humor is spontaneous, that is its nature. Sometimes funny things happen that involve a person's handicap. Being relaxed enough to allow yourself to laugh spontaneously is usually experienced as a tremendous relief by the handicapped person. It also relieves the tension felt by the nonhandicapped individuals involved in a situation that could be awkward or embarrassing for a handicapped person.

Sometimes truly ludicrous things happen that defy a person not to laugh. The incongruity of the situation creates the humor. Such was the case with Karen's arms:

One day Karen and Sunee were playing on the porch with Yup-Yup, and they asked Dorothy to put the dog's chain on Karen's hook so she could hold and pet the animal. Dorothy did so and went back to work at her desk in the bedroom when she suddenly heard great shrieks. She looked out and there was Karen lying on her back on the cement porch—both her arms off. When Dorothy reached her, Karen was laughing uproariously as she explained that Yup-Yup's chain had gotten caught in her hook. Dorothy looked around—and there was the dog running down the walk with Karen's arms. And Dorothy stood there yelling, "Come back with Karen's arms!"—and wondering what the neighbors thought went on around there. (Blank, pp. 123-124)

Someone may see potential humor to be created such as the double meaning for Karen to say, "Look Mom, no hands!" Melanie saw such potential for Karen in the following situation. Melanie said:

"Hey, Karen, while your legs are off I have an idea." She ran into the kitchen for a shopping bag. She ran back and inserted Karen into the bag. Only her head showed. Then Melanie marched with the bag from room to room, proclaiming, "Look what I bought at Safeway. They were having a big special on them today." Karen's laughter rang through the house. (Blank, p. 133)

A similar but unplanned situation occurred some time later:

One afternoon Dorothy heard a commotion in the first-floor bathroom and ran to it. Anh was supporting himself on one crutch, his back against the toilet tank to maintain his balance. His weight also was on the tank lever, causing a slight flow of water. He was leaning down into the bowl, his left hand under Karen's armpit, grimly trying to pull her out. Only her head and neck showed above the seat. She was staring desperately up at Anh, yelling, "Don't flush, don't flush!" The scene was so unexpected and unimaginable that Dorothy burst into laughter. As she pulled Karen out of the bowl Anh admonishingly said, "Not so funny to fall in toilet." (Blank, pp. 133-134)

ATTITUDES OF PARENTS

By the time students enter vocational classes their attitudes have been shaped by thousands of interactions with their parents. The influence of their parents contributes much toward their becoming optimistic, energetic, striving personalities or hopeless, defeated, lethargic persons, or perhaps angry, aggressive, defiant individuals. The interactions of disabled students with their parents are often confounded by the impact of the handicap upon the parents. The initial shock of learning about the abnormality may be followed by guilt, resentment, pity for the child, self-pity, anger, resignation, and many other negative attitudes and emotions. The parent's own reactions obviously affect the way they deal with the child.

Many parents decide that they cannot handle the situation and they give up the child for institutional or foster home care, as was the case with J. R. DeBolt. J.R. is paralyzed from the waist down and blind but was most severely handicapped by the attitude of well-intended foster parents and institutional staff who cared for him until age 10 when he was adopted. J.R. had proven his intelligence by mastering braille but had not been taught how to care for himself. At mealtime his meat was cut for him. He had not been encouraged to develop the strength and coordination needed to get out of his wheelchair and walk with the aid of braces and crutches. He had spent most of his hours day dreaming and waiting for things to happen to him.

J.R. learned to cut his own meat at his very first meal in the DeBolt family; however, it took many months to attain the desire and drive to achieve independence. He often lapsed into day dreaming rather than asserting himself in the affairs of the family. His exercises to stregthen arm and hand muscles were token attempts to please his parents rather than sweat producing effort to achieve greater mobility for himself. His parents worked hard to help J.R. acquire motivation to improve himself. The following is an example of that effort:

> J.R. rolled his chair into the front hall, parked near a side table, and slid down from the chair. He groped under the table and found the 5-pound barbell. Slowly and lackadaisically he raised and lowered the weight. He recognized Bob's fast steps down the staircase and said, "Hi, Dad."

"Hi, J.R." Bob watched for several seconds, then said, "J.R., what are you doing?"

"I'm exercising!"

"Is it hard?"

"Not very."

"It's got to be hard or it isn't exercise." Bob's tone was edged with anger. "Do it fast. Do it until that barbell feels as if it weighs a ton—then keep on doing it. You've got to build up those muscles. It'll take strain and sweat. All your brothers and sisters did it, and so can you. Not one of them could climb the nineteen steps in that staircase when they arrived. Now they all can without any trouble. That's your goal, J.R. Those steps are this family's Mount Everest. But you won't be able to conquer it if your mother and I have to keep reminding you to exercise properly. What do you think about when you lift that weight?"

"Nothing."

"Think about standing up on crutches and braces. Think about walking. Think about climbing those steps. Remember, you're going to walk for your own sake. You have to want to do it because it's going to make your life better. Not Mom's. Not mine. Yours. Do you want to sit like a damn lump in that chair for the rest of your life?"

"No." J.R.'s face was expressionless.

"We can't get you out of that chair, J.R. We can't wish you out of it. And you can't daydream your way out of it. Only determination and work on your part will do it. Understand?"

"Yes, Dad."

His voice softening, Bob said, "I'm talking to you like this, J.R., because we care about you. You're our son. We love you." He paused. "Now pick up that weight and when I come back I want to see sweat." (Blank, pp. 160-161)

When J.R. had surmounted the incredible barrier between the wheelchair and his walking on crutches and braces, he went on to learn how to climb the 19 steps to the second floor. At that point he revealed in words something of the profound change in motivation that he had achieved:

> "You know what, Mom? Every time I think of those people who tell me I can't do something, I want to tell them, 'That's a dirty lie.'" (Blank, p. 234)

J.R. surmounted formidable barriers to self-sufficiency largely because his parents were able to envision what J.R. could learn to do. The achievement of such a vision is a major accomplishment for many parents. They often must first work through their own disappointment and bitterness over having been "burdened" with a disabled child. Then they must work through their pity for the child and their inclination to do too many things for him or her. Finally, they must run the risk of incurring the child's anger toward them, and worse, the risk of receiving the wrath of their friends when they place demands upon their handicapped child.

When a disabled student produces evidence of success in a vocational class, for some parents that success will provide a first ray of hope that their child may actually, some day, be self-supporting. In the more extreme cases it may lift a great burden of worry about the future. When this happens, the parents become a powerful ally of the vocational teacher in furthering the accomplishments of the student.

The remainder of this section on parental attitudes describes how and why some negative attitudes develop. It also presents some examples of noteworthy parental objectives. Finally, it discusses how parents can assist the vocational teachers to enhance the success of their child in vocational classes.

What Are Some Reasons for Negative Parental Attitudes Toward Their Handicapped Children?

Some bizarre accounts have emerged about handicapped children being hidden by their family in a back room away from possible public encounter. The abhorence of the public toward some handicapping conditions was felt so greatly by parents in these extreme cases that they simply could not cope openly with the situation. Especially in cases of congenital handicaps, parents were likely to blame themselves. They would hide the baby rather than show it off as most new parents do. The hiding became a way of life; and, as the infant grew up, it became harder and harder for the parents to cross the barrier to give their child public exposure. Consequently, the child was doomed to a life of isolation and vegetation.

Such an extreme reaction, while rare, is instructive of the kind of adjustment that is often required of parents of handicapped children. Some handicaps such as blindness or paralysis, which are apparent to an onlooker, draw attention to the family when in public. This makes the family not just the center of attention but often the stimulus for curiosity, maudlin pity, and even revulsion. In addition to adjusting to the stigma, the family members have to deal with their own feelings, whatever these might be. At the very least they must resolve their disappointment over not having a "normal" child. Beyond this are often the special dreams that they feel are shattered due to the disability. Regardless of how well or how poorly they resolve their emotional response and reorient their expectations, there is the ever present reality of having to learn how to rear a handicapped child. Some handicapped children require considerable attention and care that the parents may not have been prepared to give.

It isn't surprising that not all parents of handicapped children measure up to the demands of their situation. Some do not resolve their resentment and their negative feelings may be communicated to the child in hundreds of subtle ways. Others openly reject their child by frequently complaining about the extra work, expenses, disgrace, and whatever other problems the child "caused." Still other parents genuinely love but overprotect and overindulge the child. In the latter case, ironically, it is having to live with a spoiled kid that leads to the parents' resenting the child.

Some handicaps pose a unique problem to parents. Parents of a blind child may fear being suspected of having a social disease. Parents of a retarded child may be tempted to push the child beyond the limits of his or her ability in hopes that the child may pass as "normal." In some cases parents may fear that their child will be dependent upon them for life and after they die there will be no one to care for their handicapped son or daughter.

No parents should be prejudged as having a negative attitude toward their handicapped child. Many parents have achieved an objective point of view about the handicap. They have learned how to provide security without overprotecting the child and instilling an emotional dependency upon them. In many cases parents have overcome significant barriers in their own attitudes in the process of learning how best to think about and deal with their child's disability. In any case, whatever the parent's attitude may be when their adolescent enters vocational training, it is likely that they have had to grapple, however successfully or unsuccessfully, with a pretty basic trauma in their feelings about and aspirations for their offspring.

What Are Some Noteworthy Objectives of the Parents of Handicapped Boys and Girls?

Dozens of such objectives could be given. Here are presented three that are also highly pertinent to vocational education staff.

1. Teach the child to share responsibilities.
2. Teach the child how to receive pay for goods produced or services rendered.
3. Develop skills and talent.

The DeBolt family, from which the following examples are taken, in a sense was an unplanned family. In other words, Bob and Dorothy DeBolt decided that they wanted each additional child only at the time when they learned the child wanted a home. They did not experience the shock and disappointment that biological parents experience; but they did have to learn how best to care for and teach each new addition to their family.

Sharing Responsibilities

Each child, including the able bodied and the disabled, does household chores. A typical morning's assignments are made by Dorothy, as follows:

"Wendy and Phong did the dishes yesterday. So this morning—let's see—how about you, Lee, rinsing the plates and tableware and you, Sunee, putting them in the dishwasher. I'll do the pans. Karen," she added, "please sweep the floor."

Lee rolled her wheelchair parallel to the sink, then pulled herself out of the seat and perched on one arm of it. Hanging on with one hand, she rinsed the dishes with the other and handed them to Sunee. Sunee, propped on one crutch and leaning against the dishwasher door, put them in the racks. Meanwhile Karen, her eyes gleaming with determination, grasped the tall broom handle halfway down its length in her hooks and swung the bristles in awkward arcs over a muffin crumb by Twe's chair. Finally, on the fourth pass, she caught it. (Blank, pp. 19-20)

Paying for Goods and Services

When kids contract to mow lawns, baby sit, or deliver newspapers, they discover the relationship between dollar and work as well as develop a self-image as a contributing member of society. These are valuable career lessons and preparation for vocation training.

Tich and Anh DeBolt, both paraplegic teenagers, took a paper route that included climbing steps to four floors of one apartment house and five floors of another. Seeing the value of this experience, the DeBolts, along with the Chapman family, developed a kind of cottage industry where all their children could work for pay making toys. The shop includes a power band saw, power sanders, and power drills which the older children operate. Wages vary according to the level of responsibility and skill the children exhibit. Original design toys are produced under the DeBolt/Chapman Wood-N-Wonders trademark and are sold in toy stores around the country. The toys are sold on the competitive market and no mention is made of their being produced by handicapped persons. (See Figures 2-2 and 2-3.)

The handicapped and nonhandicapped children share *all* responsibilities including stamping the outline on the wood, cutting out the pieces on the bandsaw, drilling holes for axles and smoke stacks, sanding, assembling, and soaking in mineral oil. The work is closely supervised by adults and quality control is strictly maintained. The shop equipment and furniture are painted in bright colors coordinated with the bright colors of the children's crutches.

Developing Skills and Talent

Stated another way, this objective is to help handicapped youth shine at what they like and do best. Many disabled youth reveal special musical or artistic talent. Karen plays marimba; Sunee plays piano; Twe sings perfect pitch in French, Vietnamese, and English. These talents had to be identified and encouraged but they have advanced to a level where the group has performed in public including on television. All of the children have intellectual, mechanical, or artistic capabilities that have evolved as areas in which they strive for perfection and in which they achieve considerable self-esteem.

The main point of this objective is its emphasis upon what the person can do. Not only does this remove attention from the disability, it is a major stride in creating a place for the handicapped individual in the mainstream. All of us, as we live and learn, become more adept at avoiding situations that emphasize our weaknesses and work our way into positions where we can use our skills to best advantage. We feel best about ourselves and others enjoy us most when we are relaxed and performing well. When Karen plays the marimba, the music is exquisite and her exuberance contagious. Her handicap doesn't seem like a handicap at all.

How Can Parents Help Their Disabled Sons or Daughters Progress in Vocational Classes?

Because the objectives of vocational education classes correspond so closely to the most important goals that many

Figure 2-2. Wood-N-Wonders ™ workshop where DeBolt and Chapman children perform all stages of manufacture including operation of power equipment.

FIGURE 2-3. Twe and J.R. DeBolt, both blind, are assembling wheels and axles for various Wood-N-Wonder™ truck models.

parents have for their handicapped children, those parents typically become enthusiastic supporters of the vocational teacher and the vocational program. Their involvement, in turn, can be very helpful to the teacher and extremely helpful to the student. These parents help in the following ways:

- They help the student make the transition into mainstream vocational education. They bring their son or daughter to school, make introductions to teachers and staff, and convey an optimistic attitude to the student.

- They meet the vocational teacher, ally themselves with the teacher's program and learn about the program.

- They maintain communication and visit from time to time. They follow the student's progress.

- They help their daughter or son solve problems that arise and provide rewards for evidence of success in achieving milestones.

- They provide encouragement if the going gets difficult.

ATTITUDES OF STUDENTS

The severity of the handicap has been found in several studies to have very little relationship to handicapped individuals' attitudes toward themselves and others. Very severely handicapped individuals may have basically positive attitudes and less severely handicapped persons may be quite negative in their outlooks. Jim Wallace is wheelchair bound and has little use of his hands, yet his attitude is positive and his range of activities amazingly large. Because of congenital deformity of his joints, Jim has to perform many manipulations with his mouth. (See pictures in Chapter 6.)

He reported in an article for *Rehabilitation Gazette** that his mother and father were naturally disappointed when the doctor told them he was severely handicapped. But, they decided to make the best of it and raised him as normally as possible He went on to describe his boyhood and school experiences, as follows:

> Childhood days were happy. I can remember sitting on the floor for hours playing with my building blocks and other toys. When I couldn't do what I wanted with my right hand, which was the best one, I would lean over and use my mouth. I became very good at playing marbles with my tongue instead of fingers.
>
> I had no trouble attending public and high schools. I enjoyed school, especially associating with the able-bodied students. The young people were fantastic in helping me around the schools. In high school I had to travel from classroom to classroom so I had a desk built that would fasten to the wheelchair. The kids would throw their briefcases and books on my desk and away we would charge down the halls or the guys would grab the chair and hoist me up or down the stairs.
>
> (*Rehabilitation Gazette*, Vol. 18, p. 6)

Attitudes of able bodied students toward handicapped students can usually be steered in a positive direction if the disabled students' attitudes are positive and if the teacher does some of the steering. This section on students' attitudes discusses how such a positive orientation may be achieved.

What Attitudes Inhibit Success in Mainstream Vocational Education?

Attitudes of handicapped students that can create problems for themselves in mainstream vocational education include:

---

*The *Rehabilitation Gazette* publishes articles of interest to the disabled and their associates. The *Rehabilitation Gazette* can be ordered by writing to 4502 Maryland Avenue, St. Louis, Missouri 63108. The price of $5.00 to nondisabled and $3.00 to disabled. (Excerpt reprinted courtesy of the *Rehabilitation Gazette* and Mrs. Jones Wallace.)

- Anxiety about entering a new situation
- Low self-esteem
- Lack of self-confidence
- Fear of failure
- Shyness, lack of assertion

These attitudes could represent nonhandicapped as well as disabled students; and, the solutions that teachers have found that work for able-bodied students will work as well for the handicapped.

Handicapped students generally are more keenly aware of their limitations than are other adolescents; therefore, they may be cautious, reserved, and just plain careful. Nevertheless, they have the same concerns that nonhandicapped students have when entering a new class, meeting new people, and not knowing what will be expected of them. Their greatest problems will be:

- Breaking the ice
- Dealing with awkward, stiff, or uncomfortable responses of others
- Dealing with alienation
- Dealing with situations that make them appear ignorant, clumsy, or inept

Breaking the Ice

Some pointers about getting to know handicapped individuals may go a long way toward minimizing potential negative attitudes of a disabled student.

1. Relax
2. Attend to the person, not to the handicap
3. Be your natural self
4. Offer help when requested
5. Offer help that is natural, without being overprotective

6. Avoid prejudging an individual as either courageous or helpless

Dealing Comfortably with Handicapped Students

When asked what situations made them most aware of their handicap, adolescent blind students designated social encounters more often than they did physical situations that require sight. The impact of contacts with other people is strongly felt by students who have other handicaps as well. Since the classroom is a social situation, chances are that it will heighten the handicapped student's self-consciousness regarding the disability. Sunee's experience was, "When you have a handicap they look at you and look at you and look at you" (Blank, p. 168). To the extent that the handicapped student has learned to manage anxiety and respond in a relaxed way with peers and elders, that initial self-consciousness will quickly dissipate. However, if the disabled student is aloof, detached, or withdrawn, the social barrier will persist as potentially anxiety arousing and otherwise disruptive of the learning process.

School staff who feel relaxed, secure, and comfortable in their relationships with handicapped students set an example for the other students and also clear the way for the disabled students to let down their guard and turn their attention instead to succeeding in class. The state of being relaxed and comfortable, however, does not occur instantaneously. It takes time to get to know and achieve rapport with any person. For this reason it is essential for a vocational education teacher to learn about a handicapped student's abilities and limitations and to meet the student personally before the student enters the class.

Curiosity of other students regarding a given student's disability can best be dealt with openly. With the handicapped student's permission, the teacher might explain something about the cause of the handicap, the physical impairment, and, if there is a prosthesis, how it works. If the handicapped student doesn't mind, other students may be allowed to examine braces, hearing aid, wheelchair, or parts of the handicapped person's body that might be a source of curiosity. Just the simple act of the teacher's touching the handicapped student while explaining functions and dys-functions will do much toward overcoming barriers of doubt and natural reservation on the part of other students.

Avoiding Embarrassment and Alienation

The kinds of alienation that can develop include ignoring the student, teasing, ridiculing, and, in extreme cases, beating up the handicapped student. Students with communication difficulties including blind, deaf, and speech impaired are ones most likely to be isolated and ignored. Mildly retarded students are ones most likely to be teased, ridiculed, or otherwise abused. Any handicapped student who has learned to be quiet and stay in the background is likely to be overlooked and not develop friendships with other students.

The solution to avoiding embarrassment and alienation is not in avoiding failure. It is unrealistic to expect students to venture into new skill areas and not fail from time to time in their early attempts. They are expected to be awkward at first but to improve with practice. It is important for handicapped students, as for any students, to learn how to handle failure. One simple, but very effective, approach of vocational educators is to monitor what students say to themselves. Words can significantly influence attitudes and behavior, especially words and phrases that students say over and over to themselves. Following are some examples of helpful and harmful phrases:

Harmful	*Helpful*
I can't do that.	I can't do that *perfectly, yet.*
I can't do anything right.	I didn't do *this thing* right.
I did it all wrong again.	I did it wrong again. I'd better figure out what I need to *do differently,* to do it better.
I don't want to try that, I'd just make dumb mistakes.	It will be hard, and I will make mistakes *at first.* I can do what I have to do: if I keep trying.

The old saying "as a man thinketh, so is he" is particularly true of handicapped students whose self confidence is often made tenuous by their departure from the norm. All who work with them must take special care to keep up their coverage.

Vocational teachers are in a position to be particularly effective in correcting such negative thinking. When a student says negative things out loud to himself, the teacher can say that such statements simply won't be tolerated in that class and then give the student an acceptable statement to replace the damaging one. Acceptable statements are accurate, specific to the situation at hand, and realistically optimistic.

The teacher can also set the stage for failure experience by saying that students are not expected to do something perfectly or even well the first time but that they are expected to try and they are expected to improve. Similar statements do much toward taking the embarrassment out of clumsy first attempts. Without the embarrassment, the teasing and ridicule are less likely to start. Also, under these conditions, timid students are more likely to take the risks involved in class participation.

Sometimes problem situations have already developed outside of class and are simply perpetuated in class. One student may already have become the brunt of comments and jokes. Once a shy, weak, or mildly retarded student has been thus singled out, it is difficult to alter the situation. Often it takes some rather creative and practical action on the part of the targeted student and school staff. One sound principle to keep in mind is that when the consequences of bullying become aversive, bullying typically ceases.

How Can Handicapped Students Be Prepared for Mainstream Vocational Education?

The blending procedure for mainstreaming handicapped students has not worked. This procedure is simply to schedule a handicapped student into a mainstream class without discussing it with anyone and hoping that the student will blend in and go unnoticed. The student does get noticed, though, either immediately or when a problem arises. The flaw in this approach is that the necessary preparation to accommodate the student does not begin until after the educational process has already broken down. This is unfair to both the teacher and the student.

Some transitional steps prior to the first day of class can make a world of difference in the success of a handicapped student. Two examples of effective transition are given below. One is a transition program for groups of handicapped students and the other is an individual transition approach.

Group Transition

Five Area Centers of the Board of Cooperative Education Services (BOCES) serves 56 school districts throughout Nassau County, New York. The BOCES Division of Occupational Education and the Division of Special Education have been guided largely by common sense, insight into human desires and needs, and trial and error in their development of a transition program for handicapped youth. They took advantage of a one-hour period between the morning and afternoon shifts, when the Centers are closed for teacher preparation. They set up Midday Programs of Occupational Exploration for handicapped students who were considering entering the program. Since the Centers ostensibly were closed anyhow, they had maximum flexibility in activating any of their 42 occupational education programs depending upon the needs of a particular group of handicapped students and particular teachers' willingness to participate. Teachers were paid for their extra effort, which included:

1. Attending a general orientation session for vocational teachers who elected to participate in the Midday Exploration Program

2. Visiting the home school to meet the teacher and tell the students about his or her occupational field

3. Writing a lesson outline for each midday session in that occupational field (The number of sessions in most cases ranged between 9 and 12 for a given

occupational area. The outlines were used by "sending" teachers in preparing the kids for the experience)

4. Conducting the sessions

Any one group of handicapped students would usually participate in the sessions for each of 5 to 10 occupational fields. By that time students have become well acquainted with the occupational education program and no longer are concerned with "breaking the ice." They have also had enough experience usually to alleviate their fear of appearing ignorant, clumsy, or inept. Another extremely important outcome is that teachers who elect to participate learn to relax with and to develop friends with handicapped individuals in class. Consequently, when the handicapped students enter mainstream vocational education in the Center, the teacher already has established a warm, cordial relationship with them which automatically provides an example for other students to imitate. That example may be a significant influence in overcoming the alienation barrier.

Individual Transition

The San Jose [California] Regional Vocational Center serves six school districts and offers 25 instructional programs. Counselors discuss the programs with handicapped students and their parents, obtain information to supplement the file received from the sending school, and then make tentative program suggestions. They are actually counseling the students for potential employment. The choice of instructional program is bassed primarily upon the student's chances of getting and holding a job in a given field.

"Alice," a mildly retarded student, and her parents had chosen the occupation of cook. The Food Services instructor knew the job market well and, after discussing job possibilities with Alice and her parents, decided this was a feasible goal and worth checking further. He knew that if Alice succeeded in his course, she would have a good chance of being hired as a preparation cook for one of the local supermarket chains.

For each job the instructor has done a complete task analysis. For Alice he pulled out those skills that she could learn and clustered them as closely as possible to the requirements of preparation cook. The instructor likes to put each student through as much of the curriculum as possible in order to identify skill potentialities that may otherwise be missed. Nevertheless, by having a specific attainable goal to start with, Alice and her parents were greatly reassured that the mainstream vocational education venture would be successful.

What Aspects of Mainstream Vocational Education Are Most Rewarding to Participants?

The Center for Independent Living (CIL) in Berkeley, California, went to City Hall and *won* its fight to continue operating its computer training project on the fourth floor of a downtown building. At issue was a fire safety ordinance. In their appeal to have an eviction order overturned, CIL Deputy Director Judy Heumann argued that "as disabled individuals we have worked very hard to remove from the public the image of persons with disabilities as being hopeless, helpless cripples. Yet the fire department contends that if there are more than five or six persons who are labeled by the state as being non-ambulatory then the code that must be applied is that which is applicable to hospitals and other institutions. The implication once again is that we are unable to take responsibility for ourselves" (*The Independent,* Spring 1977, Vol. 3, No. 4, p. 6; reprinted courtesy of the Center for Independent Living, Berkeley, California).

The question of protecting handicapped individuals at the expense of their freedom to choose for themselves is critical to the goals of independent living. The tendency to overprotect is deeply ingrained in our laws as well as in our attitudes. This is true in other "advanced" countries as well; for example, in Britain an elevator was deleted from plans for a second story theater. Elevators had been included to provide access for the handicapped; however, the fire protection requirements ruled that an elevator could not be counted upon as a means of escape and the court ruled that fire protection regulations could not be subordinate to access requirements of the disabled (*National Center for a Barrier Free Environment Report,* Nov./Dec. 1976).

Protection of the handicapped is noble but overprotection is pernicious. The line between the two is sometimes very hard to determine. The profound value of mainstream vocational education will be realized as vocational educators resist the tendency to overprotect and instead allow their handicapped students freedom to take risks. This involves some risk on the part of the teacher, namely, risk of censure and risk of being blamed if a handicapped student gets hurt. The alternative for the handicapped, in the words of Michael Williams, is "growing up tight." Michael grew up with cerebral palsy. To this was added the psychological handicap of growing up overprotected, as he describes below:

> When you grow up with cerebral palsy, chances are you grow up isolated—first in a padded cell of parental protectiveness, then in special schools that have been so thoughtfully provided for you by the state, and finally, and most completely, by your own fears.
>
> Peer group pressures played little part in my development. When I was subjected to it, I was usually snatched from it as if from a flame. Once, when I was about four, I was playing in a sandbox with a friend. I was hogging the shovel and my friend decided to give me an object lesson in the art of sharing. He snatched the shovel from my hand and hit me over the head with it, cutting me rather badly.
>
> From that point on my mother took over management of my alter ego. Whenever I entered a new area of experience, my mother always would pave the way for me. I always let her. After all, it was so much easier than doing it myself. I couldn't talk, she was very articulate. She always said the things I would say (*The Independent,* Spring 1977, p. 19; reprinted courtesy of the Center for Independent Living, Berkeley, California).

Michael's parents both died within a period of six months
and he was on his own for the first time:

> Well, I spent the first six months of my "indepen-
> dence" holed up in a five room house which I now
> owned, listening to rock music and dancing a
> furious and concerted dance until I fell over in a
> heap. It wasn't a very creative period. I tried to
> spice up my ennui via a lukewarm suicide attempt,
> complete with music by Leonard Cohen on the
> stereo. All I succeeded in doing was to prove poor
> intentions make poor art.

The profound value of mainstream vocational education
for handicapped students is the legitimate avenue it
provides to independence. By mixing with the mainstream of
their peer group, handicapped students identify, assess, and
develop their strengths relative to that group. Their
performance is evaluated against the same standards as all
students and consequently, success is truly earned.

The earned part of a success experience is critical.
Earned success means that standards have not been lowered
for a handicapped student. The tasks may be chosen
selectively for a handicapped student as they were in the
case of Alice. Unless speed of completion is part of the
performance criteria, handicapped students, as any students,
would be allowed reasonable time to perform at their best.
But, when the performance is rated, it must be rated on the
same scale as that of the other students in the class. By the
rules of fair play, no student should be privileged nor
handicapped by the evaluation criteria used. No disabled
students should be handicapped by use of conventional
classroom procedures that unnecessarily exclude them from
access to information and skill training. Neither should they
be privileged by being given a high rating for inferior work.
Such a privilege will prove to be a handicap in the long run.

An aspect of mainstream vocational education for handicapped students that often goes unmentioned is the
rewarding experience it provides for teachers and for
able-bodied students. The inspiration of witnessing someone
succeed in spite of horrendous barriers is the most obvious.

Another benefit for teachers stems from disabled students' acute awareness of their limitations. At the adolescent stage, any awareness at all of even some limitation is often experienced with thankfulness by teachers who have to deal with those students. Another benefit for able-bodied students is the model of problem solving provided by many handicapped students. As one "quad" of 25 years recommended for his handicapped cohorts, "If you can't use your hands, use your head. Don't depend on others to do your thinking for you. Keep thinking, thinking, thinking, looking, and testing new ideas, new approaches—seeking new solutions . . ."(*Rehabilitation Gazette,* 1975 p. 3) Thinking as a means of solving problems can serve as an extremely valuable model for able-bodied adolescents.

ATTITUDES OF TEACHERS, ADMINISTRATORS, AND OTHER STAFF

The prospect of having one or more handicapped students in class naturally arouses questions and concerns. A food-service instructor might ask, "How can I possibly explain subtle aspects of baking to a deaf student. Some points just can't be made in writing." Another instructor may feel personally insulted that anyone would suppose a mentally retarded student could succeed in that instructor's trade. Other concerns are that the extra work required will be humanly impossible to do. Questions about legal rights of the handicapped, safety and liability factors, setting realistic goals, and many others spring to mind.

Some staff may feel caught in the vise of a double bind. On the one hand is the law which requires fair and equitable treatment of handicapped students in the mainstream of American education. On the other hand, staff may feel that they are already overworked. When they think about the many barriers to be surmounted, mainstream vocational education of handicapped students may seem more like a burden than an opportunity.

If school staff view mainstream vocational education of handicapped students as an unwanted burden, then they will be little inclined to make it work. If, instead, they see it as a manageable task with benefits for everyone concerned, then they will likely apply their energy and creative talents to make it succeed. The purpose of this section is to discuss how positive staff attitudes may be established on sound beliefs such that *everyone* concerned will benefit.

How Can the Concerns of School Staff be Met?

The first step in establishing positive staff attitudes is to respond with understanding to staff questions and concerns. The most concerned staff, of course, would be teachers. They must deal with handicapped students on a day-to-day basis. Responses to teachers' questions and concerns need not be definitive, but they should deal directly with the uncertainties, doubts, anger, or whatever is at the heart of staff comments. The following are some typical issues and suggested responses.

Overload

Teachers, in addition to being experts in their trade, are expected to know how to teach required skills effectively and to control recalcitrant or abrasive students. They are already required to be miracle workers of a sort. There is a limit beyond which more strain would cause the currently functioning system to start to break down. Teachers who already feel they are taxed to the limit would naturally resist a surge of new work.

Mainstream education of handicapped students need not disrupt the instructional process nor increase the tax on teacher energy. There are several reasons for this. One is that handicapped students would not be placed in a class situation where they could not be accommodated. Vocational teachers, counselors, special education teachers, and other school staff who might be involved with the students should carefully consider and agree upon class placement. Another reason that handicapped students need not cause an overload of work for teachers is that considerable resources and several individuals with needed expertise are typically available or can be obtained to help the handicapped students and vocational teachers. A third reason is that advance preparation for both the students and the teacher often helps the transition of handicapped students into mainstream vocational education to go smoothly.

Safety

A concern that disabled students will jeopardize their own or others' safety is sometimes expressed by school staff. The response to this concern is that all students, including those who are handicapped, are required to follow safety rules and to continuously be conscious of possible danger to other students. Neither handicapped nor any other students should be placed in unnecessarily hazardous situations. Careful thought and good judgment will be used in deciding what is a hazardous situation for any given individual.

Stigma

The fear that handicapped students will stigmatize a vocational program is simply unfounded. The many examples of high achievement of even severely handicapped individuals should dispel this fear. In the case of mentally retarded students, for example, it is not necessary for them to achieve the goal of apprenticeship in a trade. A more limited set of objectives may be selected as appropriate for a given student in order to provide that student with marketable skills. Alice's training at the San Jose Regional Vocational Center to become a preparation cook is an example of this.

Priorities

The argument has been raised that preference should be given to "regular" vocational education students rather than deflecting precious time and effort to serving handicapped students. This point reflects a distorted view of mainstream vocational education of handicapped students. The law in this regard simply states what most vocational educators already accept; that is, handicapped students are themselves "regular" vocational education students as a matter of rights. The manifestation of those rights now is a matter of highest priority.

What Are the Basic Sound Beliefs on Which to Establish Positive Attitudes?

After the staff's immediate concerns have been resolved, some dormant myths about certain handicapping conditions may emerge to impede the mainstreaming process. A myth is a generalization that may be untrue and even damaging to a given individual. The limitations and capabilities of each handicapped person are unique. It is essential to get to know each handicapped person individually in order to acquire an accurate understanding of how that student will best be able to succeed in school. Below are some common myths that constitute attitude barriers to successful mainstream vocational education of handicapped students.

Blind and Visually Impaired

Teachers might assume that all instruction of blind and visually impaired students would have to be oral. They might think that blind students have to be taken or led every time they need to change location. Staff might also think that blind students would have to be watched constantly, especially where there are power tools, hot stoves, or dangerous chemicals with which the students might hurt themselves or others.

The fact is that many visually impaired people can make use of residual vision under proper circumstaces. A person is legally termed blind and is eligible for government assistance if optimum vision in the better eye is 20/200. Factors other than visual acuity and type of visual impairment are also very important in determining the capabilities of a particular individual. These include age of onset of blindness, amount of practice and level of skill of the individual in learning new physical surroundings, whether or not the individual has learned braille, and other factors.

Blind persons usually have fewer accidents than the general population. Some blind persons develop facility in getting around independently both in and out of buildings. The best procedure for communicating course information to a particular blind student would be determined in conjunction with specialists who had previously worked with that student.

Deaf and Hearing Impaired

It is an erroneous belief that all communication must be written for deaf or hearing impaired students. Some hearing impaired students are able to hear sounds within a limited range of pitch. Many deaf students have learned to lip read by the time they enter vocational classes. Lip reading for some students is facilitated by pantomine, limited sign language, and finger spelling. These can readily be learned by school staff who are intrigued by such means of visual communication.

One of the greatest problems in working with deaf students is a psychological one associated with this *inconspicuous* disability. Even when a staff member knows that a particular student is hearing impaired, it is easy to forget because the disability is not visually apparent. Actions of the student may seem rude or inappropriate, such as not responding when spoken to. Deaf students may tend to avoid spoken communication by checking things out for themselves rather than asking someone else, even when the latter would be more courteous if not considerably easier for a person of normal hearing. Whenever a student is labeled as rude, that label can become a barrier to productive staff/student relationships.

If a student's actions that result from hearing difficulty are interpreted as evidence of a personality problem, than a stigma may develop. For example, staff might assume that deaf students hear what they *want* to hear and purposefully ignore the rest. This notion might be embellished by the belief that if they really wanted to hear they would try harder. Staff must remind themselves from time to time of a student's hearing loss in order to avoid a natural tendency to connect the problem unnecessarily to some psychological dimension.

Cerebral Palsy and Multiple Sclerosis

These two disabilities are considered together here because both involve impairment of the central nervous system and affect control of voluntary movements such as walking, speaking, and writing. Multiple sclerosis may also affect seeing and hearing. Myths associate these disabilities with mental retardation, emotional disturbance, or even contagious virus. Neither cerebral palsy nor multiple sclerosis involves any of these aspects.

These disabilities are at the opposite extreme from deafness in that they are profoundly apparent. Individuals who manifest awkward gait and involuntary movements may arouse fear and invoke prejudice on the part of persons who have not become accustomed to these "unusual" behaviors. Michael Williams, in his article "On Growing Up Tight," said that he felt like Frankenstein because many people reacted to him as if he were.

Students with cerebral palsy or multiple sclerosis will represent the same range of intelligence and emotional stability as their able-bodied counterparts. Most of them, of course, will fall within the normal range. Because staff may previously have associated facial distortion and awkward or clumsy movements with severe mental retardation, it is especially important to look behind the facade to identify the capabilities and assess potential for developing skills.

Paraplegia and Quadriplegia

The predominant myth here is that spinal cord injuries, especially neck injuries that cause paralysis of all four limbs, destroys any possibility of productive activity. Quite the contrary is true in fact. Quadriplegics are enabled to control their wheelchairs and perform a considerable range of manipulations by using various devices now available. Scott Luebking, after an accident left him quadriplegic midway through his college career, went on to graduate and receive his Phi Beta Kappa key. He then entered the computer science program at University of California at Berkeley. Ed Roberts, a respiratory polio quad since age 14, was appointed Director of the California State Department of Rehabilitation. Roberts uses a portable respirator, motorized wheelchair, and mouth stick. Many, many more examples could be included here.

Mental Retardation

Academically slow school-aged youth are anathema to many educators. The primary myth associated with mentally retarded youngsters is that they will frustrate the teacher at almost every turn and that teachers will find very little in terms of student progress to reward even massive teaching time and effort. The myth is that slowness is equated with inability to learn at all and that the attention span of mentally retarded individuals is a matter of seconds, at most. The fact is that the attention span of mentally retarded students is no shorter than that of anyone who is expected to learn something that is completely beyond that person's capability. Mentally retarded young men and women can maintain their attention and succeed at tasks that are within their respective levels of ability. Of course, a cooperative and supportive learning environment helps, as it does with any student.

Individual differences among mentally retarded youth are great. When given tasks that they can learn to perform at the criterion levels required, mentally retarded students do not appear different from any other students. In the Food Services example given earlier, the instructor explained procedures slowly and carefully to the group of his better students so that Alice had a reliable model to imitate. He disciplined the pair that included Alice by the same standard of conduct that he disciplined all his students.

In some settings it may be appropriate to group several mentally retarded students together on a project and let them work at their own pace. This was done as an experimental project at the San Gabriel Valley Training Center work site in LaPuente, California. Ten mentally retarded men aged 13 to 36 whose I.Q.s ranged from 30 to 70 were given the job of constructing a 20 x 30 storage shed according to blueprint plans. The concrete floor took 4 1/2 weeks to complete, but it passed building inspection. The next concrete floor they built only took 1 1/2 weeks. This, or a similar group project approach, when successful, is highly rewarding to the group participants and might also serve to identify potentially marketable skills.

What Can Staff Do To Help Establish A Positive Atmosphere for Mainstreaming?

Uncertainty and apprehension among both handicapped students and school staff will likely be overcome only gradually at first, then increasing in rate of speed as momentum builds up. The first efforts at getting the momentum started are the most crucial. Success will be determined in large measure by how effectively tact and good judgment are applied.

Role of Administrators

Administrators set the tone for instruction and learning not so much by their formal policy statements as by their own attitude and by the kinds of details they attend to. The particular details that would have impact in establishing a positive atmosphere for mainstreaming include:

- Personally welcoming handicapped students who are new to the school

- Attending to communication channels among staff members who will be responsible for a particular handicapped student

- Arranging for the introduction of handicapped students to the other students with whom they will be associating

- Dealing openly and in a relaxed way with the other students' curiosity about the disability

- Communicating warmth and respect for the handicapped student

- Contacting outside agencies such as the State Department of Education and arranging for necessary consultation and assistance

Counselors/Special Education Teachers

The titles of counselors or special education teachers may not exactly fit the titles of pertinent staff in a given setting; however, the critical role referred to here is responsiblity for individual students as opposed to groups or classes. The two general functions of counselors and special education teachers in establishing a positive learning atmosphere are: (1) orientation and (2) follow-through. Orientation is necessary for teachers in regard to specific students and for students in regard to the school or center. Follow-through includes assessment of progress during the term and post-term action such as advancement to further training or job placement.

The specific contributions of counseling and special education staff include:

- Obtaining medical, educational, and social information concerning individual students
  - their capabilities, skills, talents
  - possible problems
  - kinds of personal assistance received in prior educational settings
- Presenting information to vocational teachers
- Arranging the initial meeting between vocational teacher and the student and the students' parents
- Planning for the students' first experiences in class
- Following the progress of the student by periodically checking with the teacher

CHAPTER REFERENCES

Blank, J.P. *19 Steps Up the Mountain: The Story of the DeBolt Family.* Philadelphia: J.B. Lippincott Company, 1976.

Wallace, J. Avocations: Club Work and Hobbies. *Rehabilitation Gazette*, Vol. XIX, 1976, pp. 6-7.

Laurie, G. A Compendium of Employment Experiences of 101 Quadriplegics. *Rehabilitation Gazette*, Vol. XVIII, 1975, pp. 2-23.

Williams, M.B. On Growing Up Tight. *The Independent*, Vol. 3 No. 4, Spring 1977, pp. 18-19.

You *Can* Fight City Hall. *The Independent*, Vol. 3 No. 4, Spring 1977, p. 6.

The Reasonable Cost of Reasonable Accommodation. *Report*, May/June 1976, p. 3. A publication of the National Center for a Barrier Free Environment.

San Jose Regional Vocational Center, San Jose, California

Board of Cooperative Educational Services (BOCES) of Nassau County, Division of Occupational Education, Salisbury Center, Westbury, New York

3

Eliminating
Architectural Barriers

INTRODUCTION

A building, by its very design and construction, demands certain capabilities on the part of the person using it. To see this, ask yourself the following questions about a building you know well: How much force must be applied to open a door? Is it necessary to walk to get around the building or to use restrooms, drinking fountains, and other typical fixtures, or could a person in a wheelchair do so? How high must a person step to ascend a flight of stairs? How well must a person be able to see to avoid obstacles? How well controlled must movements be to use door handles, water faucets, locker latches, and other items that must be pulled, pushed, lifted, twisted, or pressed? How high or low must a person be able to reach to use such items at all? How acute must vision be to read room signs, exit signs or warning signs for dangerous areas? How acute must hearing be to respond to fire alarms and other warning devices? The answers to these questions and to others like them define the demands placed on a user by a building. For the non-handicapped individual, the particular answer to any of these questions is usually not very important: serious problems will arise only if a door is terribly heavy, a sign tiny, or a latch bafflingly complex. For the handicapped, on the other hand, the particular answers are vital; they can mean the difference between using a facility readily and using it only with extreme difficulty or not at all. When the demands are severe, an architectural barrier results.

Having said this, we should also point out that many handicapped people are quite adept at getting about in a world not designed for them—they have had a lot of practice, after all—and will be able to use a facility even if some architectural barriers exist within it. This is, of course, an individual matter in which handicapped people vary greatly. In a sense, you can "eliminate" barriers by taking advantage of the ingenuity, determination, and experience of many handicapped individuals. The balance of this chapter will help you identify those features of a facility that make demands that handicapped people find difficult to meet and to lessen those demands. The balance of the chapter will:

- familiarize you with some of the architectural barriers faced by handicapped people

- provide key questions to ask when you assess a planned or existing building for architectural barriers

- show some ways of designing facilities so that they are free of architectural barriers

TYPES OF ARCHITECTURAL BARRIERS PRESENT IN VOCATIONAL FACILITIES

Vocational facilities may present barriers to handicapped persons in four main areas:

1. Getting to the building—entering the grounds from bus stops, parking lots, or passenger unloading zones.

2. Entering the building—approaching and opening doors, and passing through the doorway.

3. Negotiating the building once inside—moving safely between sections of the building and from floor to

floor, reading signs that indicate the purpose of a room, avoiding hazardous areas, perceiving warnings, and exiting quickly in an emergency.

4. Using fixtures, appliances, study areas, and other items integral to the building—using libraries, study carrels, drinking fountains, rest rooms, equipment storage areas, light switches, and other items commonly utilized while on campus. Tools and machines may also present barriers; such barriers and their removal are discussed in Chapter 6.

The problems stated above are so obvious that almost anyone could arrive at them by applying common sense. Still, such barriers can discourage handicapped students who might otherwise take part in programs in which they could succeed. Aulger and Woodson (1975) and Frank (1975), respectively, conducted thorough studies* of selected facilities used by the San Diego County, California, Regional Occupational Program and the Wisconsin Vocational, Technical, and Adult Education System, that identified barriers in each of these areas. Highlights of their results are reported below to illustrate problems likely to be found in vocational facilities.

Getting to the Building

Seven facilities were examined by Aulger and Woodson; all but one presented barriers to the orthopedically impaired person seeking to reach the building. Barriers included: inconveniently located parking areas, parking areas with no stalls set aside for the handicapped, unramped curbs, rough pavement between parking lots and buildings, and excessive distances and sharp grades between passenger unloading zones and the buildings. Even when parking lots or

---

*These studies were undertaken in cooperation with the districts involved, with the intent of improving opportunities for the handicapped by identifying problems and developing solutions for them. They are reported here to illustrate typical problems encountered, and should not be construed as criticism of the districts; the opposite should be construed.

unloading zones were located near buildings, it sometimes happened that the entrance nearest the parking lot could not be used by some handicapped people, requiring them to take roundabout paths to accessible entrances.

Entering the Building

Aulger and Woodson also found serious problems facing the handicapped student who made it to many of the buildings. These were primarily problems for students in wheelchairs who might confront raised doorsills, steps, or narrow doorways, depending on the facility. In addition, excessive force was required to open doors at three of the facilities, presenting problems for the frail as well as those in wheelchairs. A related problem noted by Frank was the frequent absence of adequate signing to indicate which of several entrances was accessible. Such signing, including the clear indication of access routes from parking lots to accessible entrances, is particularly important in older buildings with several entrances, only one or two of which have been remodeled for accessibility.

Negotiating the Building Once Inside

Doors and doorways presented substantial problems to handicapped persons who gained access to buildings according to the Aulger and Woodson study. Most serious were doorways too narrow to permit a wheelchair to pass through, doorknobs that were more difficult to use than lever-style handles, and emergency exit doors that required excessive force to operate. A related problem regarding the nature and locations of signs indicating room function was noted by Frank in many of the facilities he examined. Classroom and laboratory door signs often did not have raised or engraved letters that could be felt by the blind; moreover, signs were often mounted directly on doors rather than on walls, presenting the danger that someone might open the door from the other side striking a blind person while the latter was feeling the sign. Elevators examined by Frank universally lacked floor indicators that could be distinguished by touch, and controls were frequently placed too high to be easily reached by a person in a wheelchair. Frank found that emergency egress presented problems for those with severe hearing impairments as well as for the orthopedically impaired as warning signals rarely included a visual component such as bright flashing lights (in addition to the house lights) to augment the typical bells, buzzers, or sirens.

Using Fixtures, Appliances, Study Areas and Other Items Integral to the Building

Both the Woodson and Aulger, and Frank studies uncovered many barriers in this area. Rest rooms frequently lacked stalls wide enough to accommodate a wheelchair; particularly uncommon were stalls roomy enough to allow the door to be closed for privacy. Other rest room facilities related to hygiene and grooming such as sinks, towel dispensers, and mirrors were often constructed or placed so that their use was difficult for persons in wheelchairs. Other standard items related to personal convenience, comfort, and safety were often placed poorly for those in wheelchairs; fire extinguishers, telephones, and drinking fountains were frequently too high. Study carrels and work stations in media centers and laboratories were frequently found to be inaccessible to those in wheelchairs in Frank's study, generally because of inadequate leg clearance.

Source of the Barriers and the Importance of Overcoming Them

The barriers described above and others like them result from architectural planning or equipment specifications that did not take the handicapped into consideration. Thus, vocational facilities examined in these two studies would have to be modified before handicapped students could take courses offered in them. That these facilities be modified is of great practical importance as they house many programs in which handicapped students can succeed. This point was emphasized by Aulger and Woodson who assessed the physical requirements of six occupations in which instruction was offered at the facilities they examined—small appliance repair, keypunch operations, lens grinding and polishing, machine engraving, medical transcription, and advanced office occupations. Their assessments, conducted in cooperation with the instructors in each field, showed that all of these programs offered bona-fide training and placement opportunities to some handicapped students who would be kept out or substantially inconvenienced because of barriers present in the facilities in which the programs were housed.

This is not to suggest, of course, that all handicapped persons could participate fully in each of these programs, for such is not the case. The point is, rather, that a handicapped student who *could* benefit might be prevented from receiving instruction from a willing teacher only because of the facility in which instruction was offered.

ASSESSING A VOCATIONAL FACILITY AND MAKING IT ACCESSIBLE

In trying to assure accessibility, three basic questions arise: What barriers does a building present? What can be done to eliminate the barriers? How much will it cost to eliminate the barriers and who will pay the costs? The examples and procedures suggested below should help you to find answers to these questions.

The Assessment Team

The assessment team should include persons of the following types:

1. *Someone familiar with the identification of architectural barriers and ways of overcoming them.* This person should be responsible for making sure that the assessment is undertaken systematically and thoroughly and that options are suggested so that the most practical modification can be chosen for the particular facility.

2. *Faculty or staff members who will be affected by any changes that are made.* Faculty and staff cooperation is

needed if handicapped students are to be served. Therefore, their involvement at all stages of facility and program planning is crucial; nobody likes to have changes imposed by another. Moreover, some facility modifications may create new problems that someone not thoroughly familiar with the instructional program would not suspect. For example, a fire extinguisher placed low enough to be reached by a person in a wheelchair might be in danger of being blocked by carts or dollies that are frequently moved about the shop. Faculty and staff can make sure that new problems are not created while solving old ones.

3. *Someone able to estimate the approximate cost and effort required to make the suggested changes.* For planned facilities, this should be the architect and a representative of the contractor. Often, features that would be very expensive as modifications to an existing structure can be incorporated at little or no additional cost in a new building. In the case of existing facilities, this team member should be someone experienced at construction cost estimation.

Conducting the Assessment

The overall purpose of the assessment is to lead to whatever changes are necessary to serve handicapped students. Thus, the procedures used should be directed at eliciting the involvement of faculty and staff, as well as arriving at technically satisfactory means of overcoming whatever barriers are identified. The steps below will help you to achieve both purposes. In carrying out these steps, particularly Steps 2, 3, and 4, be sure to comply with state and local building codes. The standards suggested in subsequent sections for your use in assessing a facility and recommending changes were developed following a review of many of the best sources currently available. We are confident that the suggestions are sound, but cannot guarantee that they satisfy all building codes.

1. *Enlist the cooperation of faculty and staff of the facility to be assessed.* Begin by consulting with faculty and staff about the nature and purpose of the assessment, and solicit

their concerns related to the nature of the facility or to the instructional programs offered at the facility that should receive special attention in the evaluation. Insofar as possible, schedule the assessment to avoid conflict with classes. This will not only prevent disruption of instruction, but will also allow faculty and staff to participate more fully.

2. *Develop a plan for conducting the assessment.* Determine the questions to be asked during the assessment and the sequence in which various portions of the facility are to be evaluated. The questions suggested in the balance of the chapter constitute a good list to start with, and the sequence in which they are presented will often prove satisfactory. The suggestions about desirable features that follow each question provide standards that you can use when checking the facility; you may find it helpful to convert these standards into checklists to use in examining the facility. The suggestions made by faculty and staff of the facility should, however, be used to modify these lists as some questions may not be relevant to a given facility and others that are relevant may not be on the list. As a final step, assign duties to each member of the evaluation team, specifying what portions of the building or grounds each person is to assess, and the role that each person is to fill during the assessment.

3. *Conduct the assessment.* Systematically assess the facility for barriers in accord with the plan. Record the locations of any barriers discovered and photograph or sketch the barrier as needed for clarity.

4. *Make recommendations for eliminating the barriers.* Consult with special educators, rehabilitation counselors, and faculty and staff of the facility to set priorities for action and to arrive at practical means to overcome any barriers uncovered. A note of caution here—handicapped people can often get along well in a world not designed for them; therefore, some of the standards suggested below may not have to be met before handicapped students can be enrolled, even though they may still serve as long-term goals. Special educators and rehabilitation personnel will be able to help you decide which modifications *must* be made immediately if

handicapped students are to be served and which can be done without for the time being. Staff of the vocational facility may be able to contribute greatly to overcoming many barriers, as the skills needed to overcome many of them are within their domains of expertise. They will often be able to suggest the most economical ways of remodeling a rest room or constructing a ramp; remodeling may make a practical, worthwhile learning experience for students in some of the programs.

A Note on the Law

Regulations issued pursuant to PL 93-112, the Rehabilitation Act of 1973, describe the steps that are legally required to assure program accessibility. Basically, the regulations make the following requirements:

- No otherwise qualified handicapped person can be excluded from participation in a program merely because facilities are inaccessible (Section 84.21).

- Facilities must be examined for physical accessibility to determine if each program or activity is available to the handicapped. This does not necessarily mean that each and every facility be accessible, but that each program or activity from which a handicapped person might benefit might be accessible. Also discussed are strategies that can be employed to ensure program accessibility such as building modifications, reassignment of classes from inaccessible to accessible rooms, and home instruction; timeliness for implementation; and the development of a transition plan. (Section 84.22)

- New construction (including alterations of existing buildings) must be done in a way that assures accessibility for the handicapped. This requires that, as a minimum, the standards of the American National Standards Institute regarding accessibility be met (see the list of references at the end of this chapter). (Section 84.23)

ASSESSING BARRIERS TO GETTING
TO THE FACILITY

This section presents key questions for use in assessing parking areas and access routes to buildings from parking areas. The discussions following these questions include standards that you can use in assessing a facility.

The suggestions about desirable features reflect an ideal that you may not always find possible to attain in practice. Consultation with special educators and other professionals who serve the handicapped frequently, together with common sense and good judgment, should allow you and staff of a particular facility to decide which features most need to be altered, how, and in what order of priority.

Parking Areas

Parking area design is of particular concern to the orthopedically handicapped who drive their own cars or who ride with classmates. The questions below are also relevant for passenger drop-off zones for those who do not drive themselves. Consider the following when assessing parking areas:

1. *Are parking places provided for the handicapped?* Such spaces should be 12-1/2 feet wide to allow doors to be fully opened when a vehicle is parked in the next space. They should be clearly marked with the international symbol of access and they should be located as close as possible to an accessible entrance.

2. *If a curb surrounds the parking lot, is there a well-placed, well-designed ramp to allow the person in a wheelchair to move from the parking lot to the walkway leading to the building?* A ramp is well placed if it can be reached from handicapped parking places without entering traffic aisles and without moving behind parked cars. The ramp should also be well marked and should be placed along a convenient route of travel between the parking lot and an accessible entrance. Care should be taken so that the ramp cannot be blocked by cars or other obstructions. A well

designed ramp, preferably of the "curb-cut type," rather than one that projects into the parking area, should rise no more than one inch in 12 (an 18.33% slope), be a minimum of 40 inches wide, and have a tactile warning device such as plantings, railings, or grooves in the surfacing material which should be placed near the entry to alert the blind to the presence of the ramp.

3. *Is the parking lot surface suitable for persons in wheelchairs and for those on crutches?* The surface should be smooth and level while providing good traction, for example, by using broom-finished concrete. Potholes, gravel, and other loose and uneven surfaces should be eliminated or repaired. Drain gratings with openings large enough to trap a wheel or to admit a cane or crutch should be replaced. (Crossed half-inch bars spaced three fourths of an inch apart are generally satisfactory.) In addition, parking lot and ramp surfaces should be kept clear of leaves, rocks, and other debris.

4. *Is parking lot lighting adequate for night use?* Lighting should be sufficient to reveal any debris that may be present along the path from the parking space to the ramp leading out of the parking lot. This is particularly important for those on crutches and for those with poor coordination who may stumble or fall if they step on rocks or other loose objects. The sign indicating the location of the ramp out of the parking lot should also be clearly illuminated, as should the walkway leading to the building.

Route from the Parking Area to the Buildings

The parking area questions reflected the concerns of the orthopedically handicapped almost exclusively. Their concerns are again reflected here, but the questions also consider the blind and visually impaired. Consider the following when assessing access routes:

1. *Are the slope of the walkway and the walkway surfaces satisfactory for persons on crutches or in wheelchairs?* Walkway slopes of 3% or less are best, but 5% is satisfactory if level rest areas are provided every 30 feet. (If absolutely

necessary because of the terrain, more severe slopes—up to 8.33%—can be used for short distances. Try to avoid anything over 5%, but if steeper slopes must be used, the specifications for ramps discussed under *Entering the Building,* below, should be followed in regard to railings and level rest areas.) The surface should be smooth, provide good traction, and should be kept free of debris. If a walkway is laid in sections, as is the case with concrete, the transition from one section to another should involve a change in height of less than one-half inch; larger rises can block wheelchars or can trip the blind or poorly coordinated.

2. *Is the walkway wide enough to handle the expected traffic?* Standard wheelchairs range from 25 to 30 inches in width and are a little over 40 inches long; some motorized models are considerably longer. Most authorities recommend a minimum width of 48 inches for a walkway, assuming one-way wheelchair traffic. If two-way traffic is expected, or if large numbers of persons not in wheelchairs are to use the walkway as well, widths of at least six feet are preferable. If only modest amounts of two-way traffic are expected, compromises can be made. For example, the walkway can be 48 inches in most sections, with wider turnouts (that can double as rest areas) spaced along the way. If turns must be executed, five foot square level areas should be provided for this purpose.

3. *Are walkways adequately marked and lighted?* A sign should indicate the direction of travel to an accessible entrance, and additional signs should be posted at any points at which the walkway intersects with another to indicate the path that the handicapped person should take. As with parking areas, lighting should be adequate to allow the detection of any obstacles that may have found their way onto the walkway. For the blind, the edges of the walkway should be clearly marked by a surface easily distinguishable from the walkway surface by touch. Shrubbery, grass, railings, and curbs are among the items that can serve this purpose.

4. *Most blind and many ambulatory orthopedically handicapped people prefer steps to long walkways when both*

are available. Are stairways on the approach to the building satisfactory? Stairs should be designed with risers of moderate height, nosings that will not trip those with uncoordinated movements and rails that are easily grasped and that do not constitute a hazard to the blind. Figure 3-1 shows the basic configuration of a satisfactory stairway; more detailed specifications and illustrations regarding stair and handrail design are given under *Assessing Barriers to Entering the Building,* below.

5. *Is there adequate protection against the elements?* What constitutes adequate protection varies greatly as a function of local climate. A satisfactory walkway in San Diego where it seldom rains and never snows might be wholly inadequate in Chicago where it does both frequently. Possible solutions for inclement weather include covered walkways, very close-in parking spaces, or special permission for very close-in parking in otherwise restricted areas on foul days.

Barrier Free Building Access: An Example

Figure 3-1 shows the application of many of the standards discussed above in the modification of a hypothetical existing building. It attempts to show how good sense was applied by those who planned the modifications. For example, the ramp from the parking lot to the walkway is wide enough to allow two-way wheelchair traffic and to accommodate fairly heavy one-way traffic at the start and end of the school day. The placement of the concrete barriers to prevent cars from blocking the route from parking places to ramp shows a creative use of a standard item to assure that a person in a wheelchair does not have to enter traffic lanes. The walkway is not suitable in rain or snow, but handicapped students can park near the service entrance and use it in bad weather. Finally, because the walkway must cross a stream—in practice, a drainage ditch is more likely—stop curbs and railings were installed to prevent wheelchairs from going over the edge and to warn the blind that they are approaching the bridge. As a general principle, stop curbs and railings should be installed whenever the walkway goes by a hazardous area.

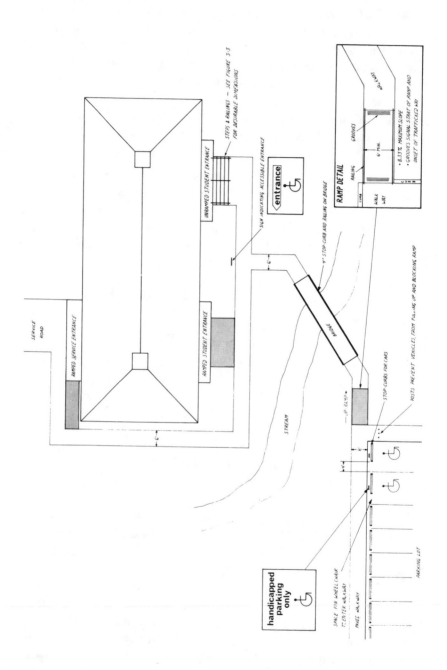

FIGURE 3-1. A building with accessible approaches.

ASSESSING BARRIERS TO ENTERING
THE BUILDING

Steps that are difficult to ascend, doors that are hard to open, and doorways that present obstacles to passage give rise to entry barriers. The questions below bring out many of the details that you should consider when assessing plans or existing facilities to identify and eliminate entry barriers.

Steps and Ramps

As noted above, many blind and ambulatory ortho-pedically impaired people prefer steps to ramps; steps, of course, are impossible for those in wheelchairs. Thus, a building should have both, if possible, or a ramp if only one is possible. Consider the following when assessing steps and ramps:

1. *Can the building be designed to eliminate the need for entry steps or ramps altogether?* The easiest way to solve a problem is to keep it from arising in the first place. In new construction, designs that place entrances at the level of the walkway leading to the building serve this purpose. Regrading the approach to bring it up to the level of the door can have the same effect in remodeling projects, but it is not always practical.

2. *Are ramp slope, width, and surface satisfactory? Are there enough level rest areas given the slope of the ramp?* The lower approach to the ramp should have a level straight run of at least five or six feet. The ramp itself should have a slope of not more than 8.33%. For slopes up to 5% a level rest area at least 4-1/2 feet long should be included every 30 feet; for slopes from 5% to 8.33%, rest areas should be provided every 15 feet. As with walkways, ramps should be at least 4 feet wide, but the width actually chosen depends on the amount of traffic expected. A non-skid surface should be provided for traction, and consideration should be given to maintaining usability during bad weather. A porch to keep off rain and snow is the best solution, although overhanging eaves may suffice in climates where rain and

snow are rare, while electrical ice melting systems may be desirable where snow is likely to drift onto the ramp and form icy patches. (Porches, extended eaves, and ice-melting equipment are nice to have, but expensive. The need for them can be greatly reduced if snow is removed quickly before ice can build up and if someone is standing by to give a helpful push up when the ramp becomes slippery. In any case, the absence of these features is no reason to keep a handicapped student out.) Figure 3-2 shows a sample ramp arrangement. Note that level areas are provided wherever a turn is required. Minimum dimensions for one-way traffic are shown in the figure.

3. *Does the ramp have adequate safety features?* Handrails should be present on each side of the ramp if the slope exceeds 5% or if there is a drop-off at the edge of the ramp. Railings should be 32 inches above the ramp surface; railings should extend 12 inches beyond the ramp at the top and bottom. Stop curbs, two inches high, are desirable along those edges of the ramp that do not abut a wall. As a convenience to the partially sighted, the edges and sloping portions of the ramp can be colored brightly to contrast with other pedestrian areas to signal drop-offs and changes of grade. Safety features are also illustrated in Figure 3-2.

4. *Are stairways designed for safe and easy use by the visually impaired and the ambulatory orthopedically handicapped?* Steps should have vertical or slanted risers. Open risers and squared nosings are particularly apt to trip people and should be avoided; inserts can be used to modify such stairs to remove the hazard. Risers should not exceed 7 inches, although 5 inches is preferable; treads should be 11 to 15 inches long. For the visually impaired sharply contrasting riser and tread colors add a margin of safety, particularly if the tread color also contrasts with that of the floor leading up to the stairway. There should be a railing on at least one side of the stairway, although it is better to have a railing on each side, particularly if there is extensive two-way traffic. The rail should be 32 inches above the front edge of the riser and should extend 18 inches beyond each of the top and bottom steps. Figure 3-3 shows satisfactory stair designs.

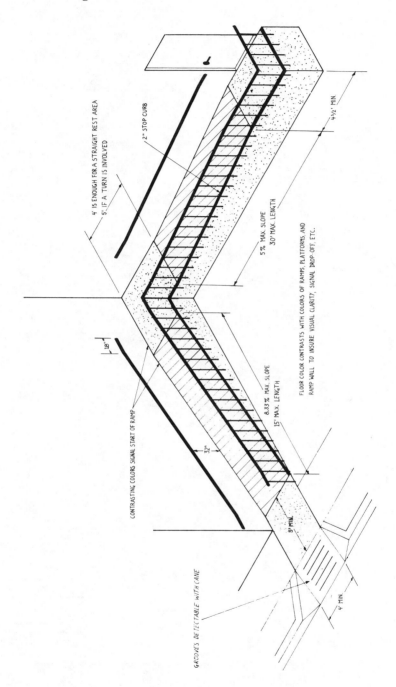

FIGURE 3-2. Desirable ramp dimensions and features.

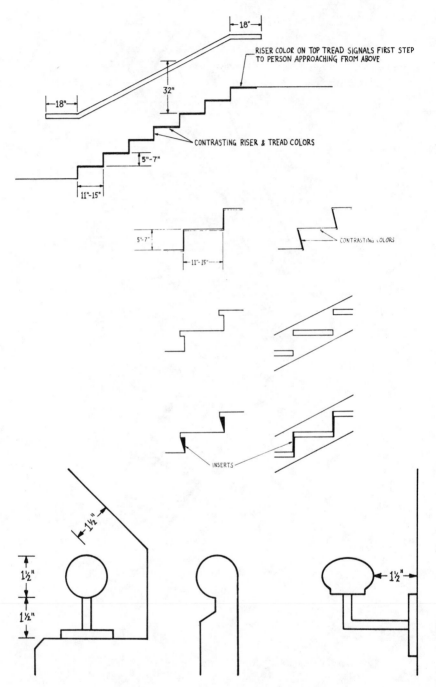

FIGURE 3-3. Stairs and stairways.

Doors and Doorways

Barriers to the orthopedically impaired may result from the physical structure of doors, their placement, or obstacles such as sills and mats over which a person must pass to go through the doorway. Consider the following when assessing doors and doorways:

1. *Can a door be opened with one hand in a single effort, or is excessive strength or manual dexterity required? Are other physical features of the doors satisfactory?* Doors should not require more than eight pounds of pressure to open, and lever handles should be used instead of doorknobs as the former require less strength to operate and are easier to grasp. Levers should be three feet above the floor for easy reach. Glass doors must have a smooth kick plate that reaches at least eight inches above the floor (12 inches is preferable) to receive the impact of the wheelchair footrest. Other doors that do not have a smooth surface should be similarly equipped to facilitate pushing by the wheelchair user, and to prevent the door from becoming dented or gashed. It is desirable for doors to have windows in them to allow users to see activity on the other side. This is particularly important to prevent someone from opening the door and striking a blind person standing nearby. To be usable by those in wheelchairs, the window should extend from 40 to 55 inches above the floor, inclusive. Figure 3-4 shows suitable doors and fixtures.

2. *Are doorways wide enough and are they free of obstructions?* Doorways should be at least 32 inches wide to allow passage of a wheelchair. At least one side of a double door should be 32 inches wide so that only one door has to be opened to permit passage. Abrupt rises over 1/2 inch, such as may be caused by doorsills, doormats, and the like should be eliminated or ramped as they can block a wheelchair. Other items, such as gratings and automatic door rails can also make wheelchair maneuvering difficult and *may* make it hard for a cane or crutch user to get firm footing. Each case must be judged separately, and satisfactory grate surfaces and automatic doors are available. Indeed, pressure

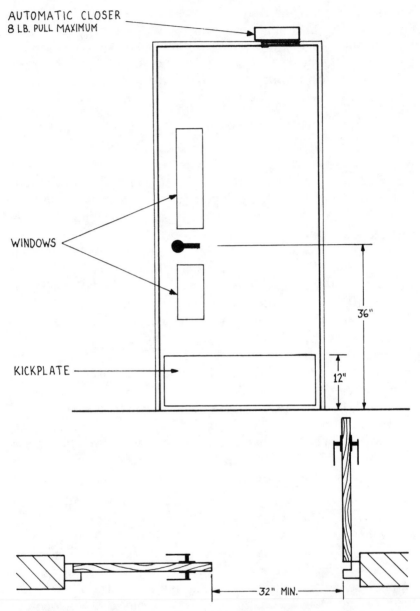

FIGURE 3-4. Doors and doorways. (Top drawing from *An Illustrated Handbook of the Handicapped Section of the North Carolina State Building Code* by Ronald L. Mace, edited by Betsy Laslett. Courtesy North Carolina Department of Insurance.)

activated doors that move on overhead rails or that swing open are the best for the orthopedically handicapped. The former are preferable, however, as swinging doors are a hazard to the blind.

3. *Is there adequate maneuvering room next to the door?* A level platform at least five feet square should be provided on each side of the door. This platform should be placed so that it extends at least one foot beyond the base of each jamb. Successive doors should not be placed closer than 6-1/2 feet apart to provide adequate maneuvering room if one or both doors open into the vestibule. If both doors open out, there is no problem (Figure 3-5).

ASSESSING BARRIERS TO NEGOTIATING THE BUILDING

Such barriers fall into two major categories: problems encountered in traveling between rooms, and problems in getting about in a room once it has been reached. This section discusses these two types of problems in turn.

Travel Between Rooms

The standards for entry steps, ramps, and doorways already discussed apply equally within the building. This section discusses elevators, elevator controls, and signing with attention given to the needs of the orthopedically impaired, the visually impaired, and the blind.

1. *Are there accessible routes for the physically handi-capped within the facility?* Routes within the facility should have smooth, level surfaces that provide good traction. Doors along the route should be designed for easy opening as described above, and adequate maneuvering room should be provided before all doors. Modest changes in level (a flight of only a few steps into a recessed cafeteria, for example) can be ramped as described above. It is often impractical to install ramps between stories, both because of the space required and the physical demands placed upon users of long ramps. Thus, elevators are usually necessary in multi-story

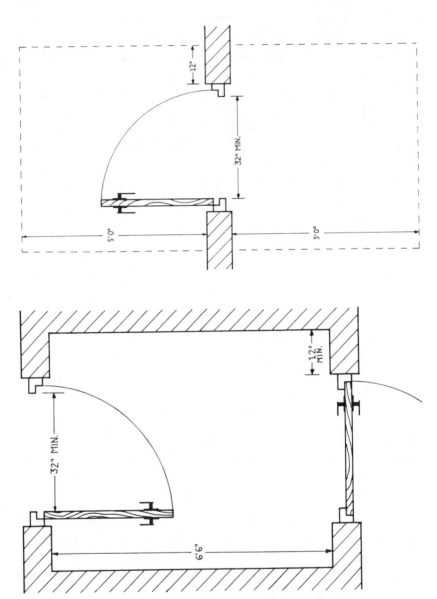

FIGURE 3-5. Adequate Maneuvering room by doorways.
(From *An Illustrated Handbook of the Handicapped Section
of the North Carolina State Building Code* by Ronald L.
Mace, edited by Betsy Laslett. Courtesy North Carolina
Department of Insurance.)

buildings. Elevators should be at least 5 feet 4 inches square to allow a wheelchair user to pivot about to face the door. If others are to use the elevator at the same time, more space will be required. Elevator control buttons should be no higher than 5 feet above the floor, and emergency telephones and alarm buttons should be within easy reach. Figure 3-6 shows a well configured elevator for the physically handicapped. Also shown are appropriate labels for the blind and visually impaired.

2. *Are routes for the physically handicapped conveniently located and adequately marked?* It is not always practical to make all possible routes within a building accessible. This is particularly true in two or three story school buildings where it may be possible to have only one elevator, but in which there are several stairways. If possible, the elevator should be located to minimized backtracking along the route from classrooms and shops to auditoriums, cafeterias, restrooms, and other frequented areas. Signs should be posted to indicate accessible routes to various parts of the building and to emergency exits.

3. *Are rooms, elevator controls, hazardous areas, and emergency equipment adequately labeled for the blind and visually impaired?* Room labels should have characters 1-1/2 to 2 inches high, raised or indented 1/8 to 1/16 of an inch, so that they can be easily read by touch. (Braille labels can be used, but they are strictly for backup; only about 10% of the blind read braille.) Signs should be mounted at a standard height, ideally 5 feet above the floor. Similarly, elevator buttons should be labeled with numerals that can be identified by touch, and a raised numeral can be attached to the inside jamb to indicate floor. The visually impaired can be greatly aided by oversized signs indicating room function, floor, or the location of emergency equipment. Such signage adds an attractive touch in new buildings or in extensive remodeling projects. Elevator labels are shown in Figure 3-6. Doors to stairways, furnace rooms, auto shops, traffic lanes, and other dangerous areas should have distinctively knurled handles (Figure 3-7). Stairways themselves may have contrasting risers and treads as shown in Figure 3-3.

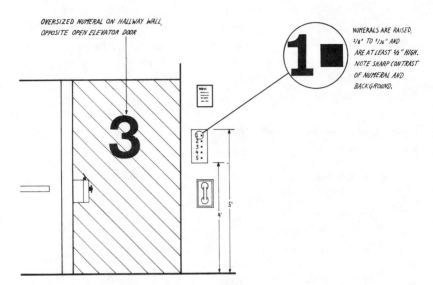

FIGURE 3-6. Elevator with accessible controls

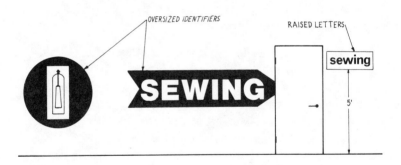

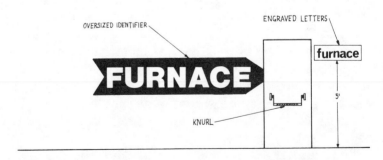

FIGURE 3-7. Labels for the blind and visually impaired.

4. *Are passages free of protruding or overhanging objects that may be a hazard to the blind or visually impaired?* Properly trained blind and visually impaired people seldom crash into things, particularly in buildings with which they are familiar. Nonetheless, protruding objects should be removed, relocated, or signaled as much as possible. Overhanging signs can be raised, fire extinguishers placed in niches, and water fountains recessed into alcoves. The last item presents a difficulty; if the alcove is narrow, people in wheelchairs will not be able to reach the fountain. A solution that meets the needs of both groups is to lay tile around the fountain that contrasts in texture and color with the floor in the passage. This will serve as a "warning track" for those with visual handicaps and will not interfere with the wheelchair user. In existing buildings, recessing is usually too expensive, but it is a practical approach in designing new facilities. Figure 3-8 shows common hazardous objects and safe repositioning.

5. *Do warning systems have visual as well as auditory components?* Most fire alarms and other warning devices use a bell or buzzer. Warning systems should include flashing lights, or other visual signals to alert the deaf.

Routes Within Classrooms, Shops and Other Student Areas

This section discusses how safe, well located routes can be established for the orthopedically and visually impaired student in the classroom. This section also offers suggestions for cafeteria design and assembly seating to make each type of room usable by the orthopedically impaired.

1. *Is there adequate maneuvering room in classrooms and shops for those in wheelchairs or on crutches?* School hallways are so wide that they almost always provide adequate maneuvering room. Laboratories and shops, however, may not be laid out in a way that gives the orthopedically handicapped enough room to move between work stations or from work areas to storage areas. Paths three feet wide are required for straight travel by both

wheelchair and crutch users. More room is needed for turning. Figure 3-9 shows the room needed by the wheelchair user making 90° turns, 180° turns, three-point turns, and full pivots. Figure 3-10 shows how this information can be used in assessing maneuvering room in a laboratory. If maneuvering space is adequate for a wheelchair user, it is, of course, enough for someone on crutches. In assessing maneuvering room, remember to consider obstructions such as protruding vises, other students, stools, and portable tool chests in your measurements. To be functional, a passage should be wide enough for a wheelchair when such common obstructions *are in place*. Note, too, that not every possible passage in the lab has to be negotiable in a wheelchair. It is only necessary that the student be able to move from his or her work station to storage areas and equipment. Common sense in work station assignment can minimize the need for equipment rearrangement.

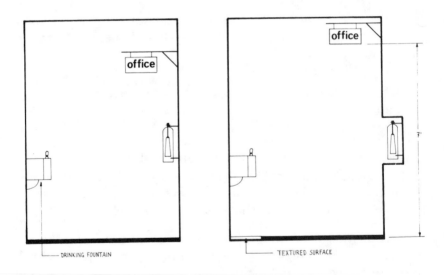

FIGURE 3-8. Relocation of hazardous items in passages. (From *Accessibility Modifications* by Ronald L. Mace. Redrawn courtesy North Carolina Department of Insurance.)

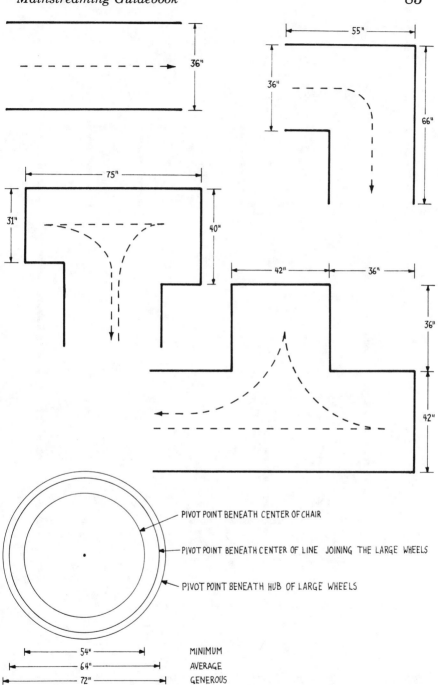

FIGURE 3-9. Wheelchair maneuvering room.

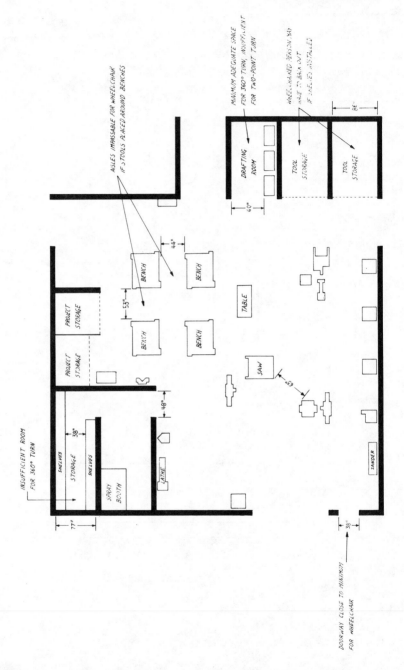

FIGURE 3-10. Maneuvering room in a cabinet making and millwork shop. (Courtesy Brodhead-Garrett.)

2. *Are routes within shops and classrooms safe for the blind and visually impaired?* Blind and visually impaired students will be able to negotiate almost any environment as well as their sighted peers if they are properly oriented to the location of items in the room during the first few days of class. They will be no more likely to blunder into power equipment, hot stoves, moving vehicles, and the like than anyone else. If anything, their safety records are likely to be superior. The following features, already included in many shops for general safety purposes, are a great help for the blind or visually impaired: high traction surfacing on paths between machines—this provides a tactile cue to the blind; and safety zones painted a color that sharply contrasts with the rest of the floor around equipment that only the operator or instructor are allowed to enter—this provides a cue to those with residual visual ability. These features are illustrated in Figure 3-11. Blind students are also quite able to use other cues that exist in the shop. For example, the blind person can learn that the line defined by the edge of a bench leads to a storage cabinet, or that the power sander is a foot or so beyond the crack in the floor. During orientation, an aide experienced in helping the blind learn to negotiate their surroundings will be able to assist the blind person identify cues in the room and learn to negotiate using them.

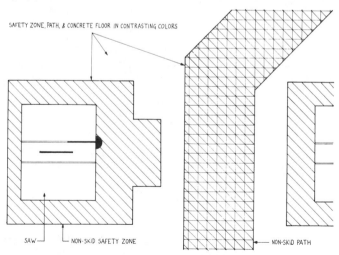

FIGURE 3-11. Safe paths through a shop.

The suggestions already made related to labeling and to the removal of overhanging and unnecessarily protruding objects also apply when similar situations arise in the classroom or shop. Objects that must protrude, such as vices and free-standing tool cabinets need not be removed as the blind person will learn to avoid them. If such objects are moved, the blind person should be told so that he or she will not encounter a surprise obstacle. Similarly, tool carts, dollies, and the like should not be left in aisles as they too can constitute surprise obstacles.

3. *Are commonly frequented public areas on campus accessible to the physically handicapped?* Most schools have cafeterias, auditoriums, and other areas where students frequently gather. These and other public areas should be accessible if physically handicapped students are to participate fully in school activities.

Figure 3-12 shows a cafeteria food service line with adequate space for passage. Ideally, cafeteria display cases should be designed so that a person in a wheelchair can conveniently grasp food passed from behind the counter. The student shown in the figure has the reach of an average adult (24.5 inches from the shoulder) and is capable of full-arm extension; thus, the pictured student could grasp an object if the server leaned over the case with it. Many people in wheelchairs are unable to extend their arms fully. For their convenience, lower cases can be installed, or front panes of some cases removed to lessen the reach required. If such modifications prove impractical because of expense, or if they conflict with local health regulations, a friend can accompany the person in the wheelchair to obtain hard-to-reach items. The presence of adequate maneuvering room within the balance of the cafeteria can be assessed using the standards discussed for classrooms and shops above; 5.5 feet from table edge to table edge is generally enough to allow passage between tables when chairs are in place.

Auditoriums should have level parking spaces for wheelchairs in several rows, if possible. The configuration of existing facilities will greatly affect the number of rows in which wheelchair seating is possible. Factors to be considered include: access to the row—must steps be negotiated within the auditorium?; cross-aisle width—will others be able to get past the wheelchair once it is in position?; will the wheelchair user be able to swing aside to let others pass?; would a wheelchair in certain locations constitute an obstruction under local fire regulations? Figure 3-13 shows an auditorium which incorporates several solutions to the wheelchair seating problem. Also shown is "staggered" seating which results in additional leg space for an aisle seat in each row. Such an arrangement is needed by persons wearing leg braces as these orthoses are locked in a stiff-legged position for walking and are released only after the wearer is seated; 18 to 24 inches are required in front of the seat for the person to sit down before the brace is unlocked.

Other areas where students congregate should also be examined for accessibility. The questions suggested throughout this chapter should provide guides for most circumstances that may arise.

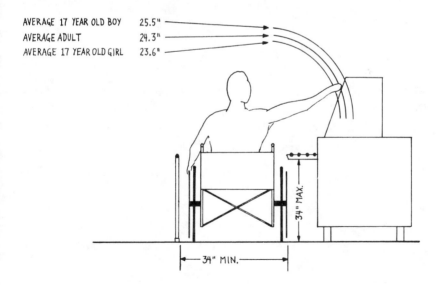

AVERAGE 17 YEAR OLD BOY 25.5"
AVERAGE ADULT 24.3"
AVERAGE 17 YEAR OLD GIRL 23.6"

34" MAX.

34" MIN.

FIGURE 3-12. Cafeteria food service line. (Adapted from *An Illustrated Handbook of the Handicapped Section of the North Carolina State Building Code* by Ronald L. Mace, edited by Betsy Laslett. Courtesy North Carolina Department of Insurance.)

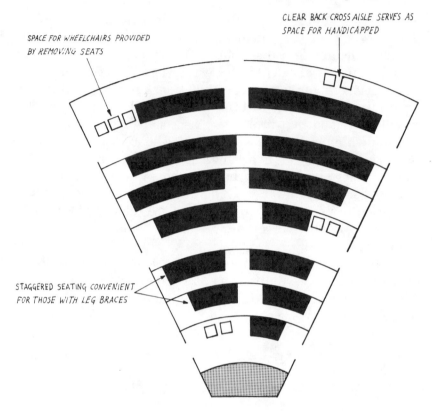

FIGURE 3-13. Auditorium seating. (From *An Illustrated Handbook of the Handicapped Section of the North Carolina State Building Code* by Ronald L. Mace, edited by Betsy Laslett. Redrawn courtesy North Carolina Department of Insurance.)

ASSESSING BARRIERS TO USING FIXTURES, APPLIANCES, STUDY AREAS, AND OTHER ITEMS INTEGRAL TO THE BUILDING

This section identifies common problem areas in using general-use items found in most vocational facilities. The next chapter discusses problems in using specific work-related tools and equipment. This section is not exhaustive, but the variety of problems identified should help you to see others that are similar.

Work Stations and Study Carrels

Some work stations in a laboratory or shop and some tables or study carrels in a resource center should be designed to accommodate the orthopedically impaired. Potential problems fall into two major classes—difficulties in reaching the work surface or storage areas, and difficulty in manipulating objects that are part of the work station.

1. *Are work surfaces and storage areas within reach of the physically handicapped?* Figure 3-14 shows a study carrel and a work station that are generally satisfactory for wheelchair-using adults of average height who enjoy full use of their arms and torsos.

The table measurements shown for the study carrel are critical. At least 29 inches are necessary between the floor and the bottom of the table top to clear the arm rest and 21 inches are required from the wall to the forward edge of the table top to allow the user to wheel close to the work surface. The 31 inch high work surface is suitable for most users.

The work station is shown without a kneehole because some vocational fields demand work surfaces with the strength provided by a "supporting wall." In such cases, a space should be provided beneath the bench, as shown, to accommodate the footrest during turns. The 32.5 inch high work surface is satisfactory for most, but shelf height or depth may have to be adjusted for those who are shorter, or whose reach is restricted. The best heights for a given student can be found by trial and error the first few days of class.

In many cases, the ideal heights shown in Figure 3-14 can be achieved through simple modifications of existing furnishings. For example, blocks can be put under table and carrel legs; bookcases or racks with adjustable shelves can be used; stationary shelves that are too high or low can be left vacant; and wooden inserts can be used to make shelves shallower. In other cases, problems can be avoided by the

92

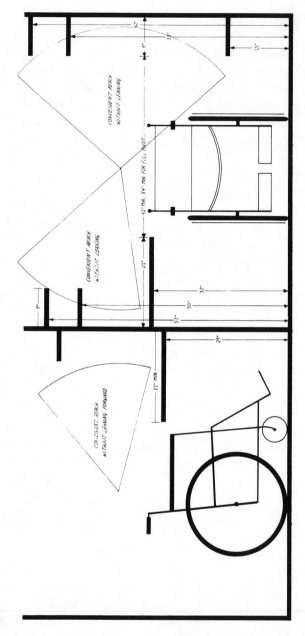

FIGURE 3-14. Study Carrel and Work Station Dimensions. (After Humanscale 1/2/3 by Neils Diffrient, Alvin R. Tilley and Joan C. Bardagjy; designed by Henry Dreyfuss Associates.)

careful selection of standard equipment.* (For example, many drafting tables have powered height adjustment mechanisms which are exceptionally covenient. Similarly, drafting tables that have legs on either end are preferable to center pedestal models, particularly if crosspieces connecting the legs are placed where they will not interfere with a wheelchair.)

2. *Are work station fixtures within reach and easy to use?* Faucets, spigots, gas jets, electrical outlets, switches, and other items in the work station should be within reach and easily manipulated. Similarly, handles and latches on drawers and cabinet doors should be easy to operate. Figure 3-15 shows a work surface configuration that places a variety of items well within the range of easy reach for most users. Figure 3-16 also shows some good and bad examples of controls, handles, and latches. In general, well-designed handles and other fixtures are those that can be grasped with a single gross movement, and which can be operated with a single pull or push, not requiring powerful or precise movements of the fingers nor rotation of the wrist. Poorly designed controls are usually easy to replace with more suitable, readily available items, as discussed in the following chapter. Similarly, it is often easy to reposition or modify poorly located fixtures. Most vocational centers have faculty members who can easily make such modifications or who could allow students to make them as a class exercise.

Restrooms

Three types of problems often limit restroom accessibility—difficult entryways, hard to use toilet facilities, and unusable hygiene and grooming fixtures.

1. *Are restroom entryways negotiable in a wheelchair?* Doors and doorways should meet the standards discussed above, and adequate maneuvering room should be available inside the restroom door. The latter often presents a problem

---

*This is a general strategy that is very useful in tool and equipment selection. It will be discussed in more detail in the next chapter.

FIGURE 3-15. An electronics work station with controls accessible to most wheelchair users. Lower drawers are out of reach for some. (Courtesy Brodhead-Garrett Company)

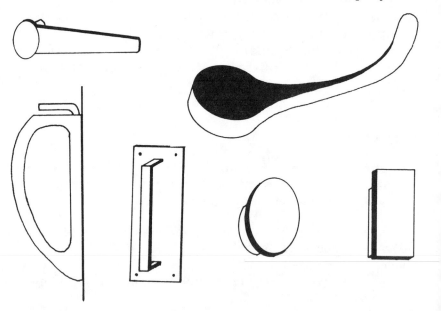

FIGURE 3-16. Desirable controls: levers and simple full handles.

as successive doors or walls and partitions as are frequently installed for modesty purposes leaves inadequate maneuvering room for those in wheelchairs. The successive door problem was shown in Figure 3-5. If insufficient maneuvering space is available in the vestibule (78 inches if one door is to open into the vestibule), then one door can be removed or remounted so that they both swing out from the vestibule.

The need to make sharp turns in insufficient space is also a frequent problem. Figure 3-17 illustrates one such problem and shows accessible entryways. The drawings of accessible entryways show minimum dimensions in commonly encountered situations; most problems can be solved by some variation of these.

2. Are toilet facilities usable by those in wheelchairs? Each restroom should have at least one stall that is usable by physically handicapped persons. Figure 3-18 shows a sample toilet compartment, including desirable fixture heights. Note that wall mounted toilets are superior to pedestal models as they can easily be mounted with the seat 20 inches above the floor and because they generally provide more room below the bowl thereby allowing closer wheelchair approach. If pedestal models are already in place, the seat height can be raised the approximate two inches usually necessary by inserting a "filler ring" between the bowl and the seat.

3. Are fixtures for hygiene and grooming usable by those in wheelchairs? Figure 3-19 shows satisfactory sink and towel dispenser design and placement. Note that all dispensers, switches, outlets, and the like are 40 inches or less above the floor, that the mirror is long enough to be used both by standing and sitting individuals, that the faucet has a level control for easy operation, and that the pipes leading to and from the sink are insulated and are mounted high enough not to interfere with a close wheelchair approach. Pipe insulation is necessary because many wheelchair users lack sensitivity in the legs and may be badly burned if they come into contact with hot pipes that they cannot feel.

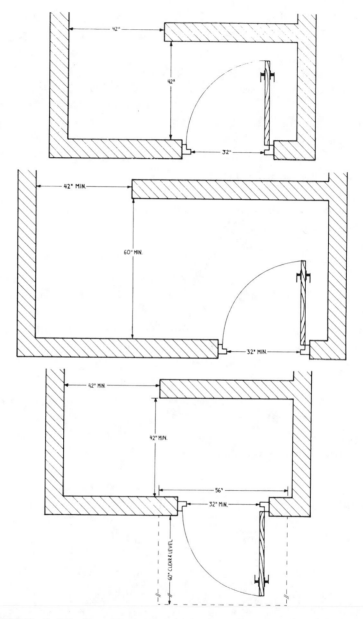

FIGURE 3-17. Restroom entryways. (From *An Illustrated Handbook of the Handicapped Section of the North Carolina State Building Code* by Ronald L. Mace, edited by Betsy Laslett. Redrawn courtesy North Carolina Department of Insurance.)

Other Items

Vocational facilities usually include a host of objects that the student may have occasion to use. These include light switches, emergency alarms, vending machines, telephones, and drinking fountains. Such items should be located where they can be reached by students in wheelchairs, and should have easily manipulable controls.

1. *Are items that must be manipulated within reach?* Items that must be manipulated include light switches, fire alarms, window pulls, fire extinguishers, and any other like items. Such items should be positioned so that they are no more than 40 inches above the floor, and so that they can be approached directly by the wheelchair user without elaborate maneuvering.

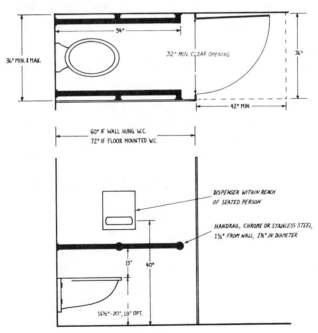

FIGURE 3-18. Accessible toilets. (From *An Ilustrated Handbook of the Handicapped Section of the North Carolina State Building Code* by Ronald L. Mace, edited by Betsy Laslett. Redrawn courtesy North Carolina Department of Insurance.)

2. *Are drinking fountains usable by the physically handicapped?* Figure 3-20 shows a satisfactory drinking fountain design. Note that the fountain has a squared bottom allowing the user to drive up close. Note, too, that the fountain has a lever handle for easy use. Such handles should be included on all fountains as ambulatory orthopedically-handicapped persons may have difficulty operating button or pedal activated mechanisms.

3. *Are telephones usable by the handicapped?* Telephones for use by those in wheelchairs should be mounted so that the highest working part is no more than 48 inches above the floor and so that there is a 27 inch clearance beneath the cabinet. For the hearing impaired, telephones with adjustable volume headsets are a great convenience. Such sets should be clearly marked, and instructions for volume adjustment should be provided. Accessible telephones are also shown in Figure 3-20.

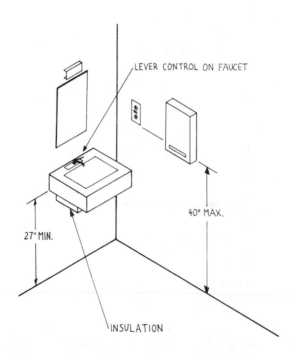

FIGURE 3-19. Hygiene and grooming facilities.

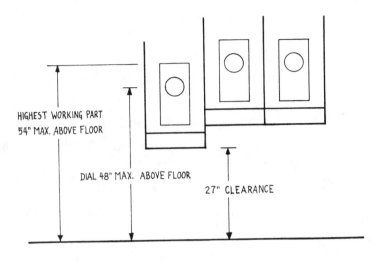

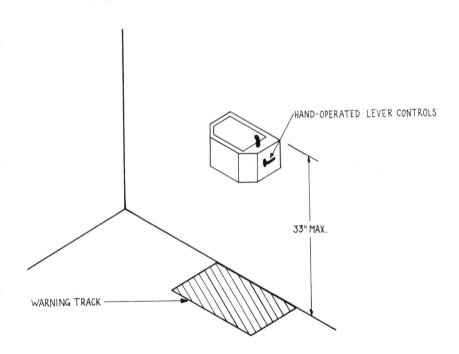

FIGURE 3-20. Telephones and water fountain.

RESOURCES

The following resources were used extensively in the preparation of this chapter. They provide excellent additional resources.

Comprehensive Introduction to the Field

Goldsmith, S. *Designing for the Disabled*. London, England: Royal Institute of British Architects, 1967.

Contain Checklists for Assessing Vocational Facilities

Aulger, A.A. and Woodson, W.E. *A Pilot Study of Selected ROP Curricula and Facilities to Determine Their Appropriateness and Accessibility for Orthopedically Handicapped Students*. San Diego, California: Department of Education, San Diego County, 1975.

Frank, K. *Architectural Barriers to Physically Disabled Persons in Wisconsin's Vocational, Technical, and Adult Education System*. Menomonie, Wisconsin: Center for Vocational, Technical, and Adult Education, University of Wisconsin—Stout, 1975.

Especially Useful for Assessing Buildings, Entrances, Interiors, and Fixtures

American National Standards Institute. *American National Standard Specifications for Making Buildings and Facilities Accessible to, and Usable by, the Physically Handicapped*. New York: American National Standards Institute, 1961.

Mace, R.I. *An Illustrated Handbook of the Handicapped Section of the North Carolina State Building Code*. Raleigh, North Carolina: North Carolina Department of Insurance, 1974.

Mace, R.I. *Accessibility Modifications: Guidelines for Modifications to Existing Buildings for Accessibility to the Handicapped*. Raleigh, North Carolina Department of Insurance, 1976.

Especially Useful for Assessing Workstations

Diffrient, N., Tilley, A.R., and Bardagjy, J.C. *Humanscale 1/2/3*. Cambridge, Massachusetts: The MIT Press, 1974.

Especially Useful for Assessing Outdoor Areas

U.S. Department of Housing and Urban Development. *Barrier Free Site Design*. Washington, D.C.: U.S. Government Printing Office, 1976.

4

Assessing the Individual Handicapped Student

INTRODUCTION

Background information about each student is essential if vocational educators are to build appropriate programs for the handicapped. The process of obtaining this information is called *individual vocational assessment.* (Other commonly used terms for this process are *diagnosis* and *evaluation.*) Considerable disagreement exists about what should constitute this process and how it should be defined. For purposes of this book, it is:

1. a comprehensive process conducted over a period of time,

2. involving a multidisciplinary team approach,

3. with the purpose of identifying individual characteristics, and education, training, and placement needs,

4. which provides educators the basis for planning an individual's program,

5. *and* which provides the individual with insight into his or her vocational potential.

Individual vocational assessment should be a continuous, on-going process rather than strictly a one-time activity. Although a concentrated period of assessment typically occurs, the student needs to be re-evaluated frequently as he or she progresses through the various stages of vocational preparation. The student should be reviewed for gains and improvements in each of the assessment areas, with the ultimate goal of minimizing the need for special services.

Vocational assessment for mainstreaming must involve the cooperation and expertise of many professional workers—vocational educators, special educators, general educators, psychologists, medical doctors, social workers, and rehabilitation personnel. Because mainstreaming, ideally, will be accomplished within a system based upon a continuum of educational and support services, ranging from total education within a regular classroom for the mildly handicapped to highly specialized services outside of the public school system for the most severely handicapped, various personnel along the continuum need to be involved in the assessment process. Vocational assessment is not the specialty domain of anyone, although a vocational counselor probably comes closest. In the secondary setting, the special education teacher (with knowledge of jobs in industry and procedures followed in the world of work) may assume the role of vocational counselor and serve as the coordinator of all services. In the postsecondary setting, a state vocational rehabilitation counselor or a rehabilitation workshop counselor may assume this role (Brolin, 1976).

The purpose of vocational assessment is not to serve as a selection and classification process but rather to aid educators in identifying and providing for each student's particular needs. Assessment can reveal problems and needs that are remediable or modifiable, and these should form the basis for special services, training, or treatment. Moreover, while assessing a handicapped individual, it is essential to pay attention to the assets, or potential assets, that every individual possesses in some measure so that the program staff and the student can facilitate their development and use.

Before an individualized educational program can be designed, individual characteristics, problems, and needs related to occupational goals must be identified. Then the assessment team must try to determine just how these characteristics will influence the student's chances of achieving his or her goal. Obviously, this is not a simple task. The person's physical, emotional, and intellectual characteristics, personal values, aptitudes and interest, self-concept, and motivational reinforcers are all influential factors. As many of these factors as possible should be identified so that program staff can adequately plan for student achievement of an occupational goal.

Assessment, then, provides information to staff for planning individual programs. This is important, but the process should go one step further. It should provide the individual with insight into his or her vocational potential. To do this, it is imperative that the student be actively involved in the assessment process. Like counseling, which is itself an integral component of the process, assessment is something that one does *with* a student and not *for* or *to* him or her. While program staff and parents can and should assist the student in making a realistic career choice, it is ultimately a decision that the student must make.

THE ASSESSMENT PROCESS

As mentioned earlier, vocational assessment should be a continuous, on-going process. Typically, however, a concentrated period of "formal" assessment occurs at entry into the vocational program. Such an assessment should consist of:

1. a personal interview with the student;
2. the collection of background information gained through school records and supplemental reports;
3. psychometric and basic skills testing;
4. work sample assessment; and
5. behavioral observations.

The Personal Interview

An individual background interview should be held with the student for the purpose of establishing rapport; determining the student's interests and tentative career goals; and obtaining specific biographical data regarding medical, social/psychological, educational, economic, and vocational factors. (It is best to note biographical data as they come up during conversation rather than to pursue them in detail. The student may not know all the details and thereby feel tense by not being able to answer the questions.)

If the student has already developed strong vocational interests and abilities through exploratory or pre-vocational courses, field trips, resource speakers, or career guidance classes, the results of the interview and, indeed, the entire vocational assessment process will be enhanced. Of course, all information and data obtained from this interview must be treated with confidentiality.

Collection of Background Information from School Records

A wealth of background information on the student can be obtained from school records and reports, supplemented by discussions with the individual, parents, and various professionals. The most difficult task, however, is deciding which of all this information is pertinent to planning an appropriate vocational program. The following types of assessment data should be considered: medical, psychological, educational, and social.

Medical Data

Because doctors do not prepare medical reports in a form readily usable for planning vocational programs, vocational educators should review documents and ask questions of professionals that focus on their planning needs. Specific areas of concern to vocational educators include:

1. Student's general health—any conditions that need medical attention and monitoring and that will affect

his or her ability to attend and maintain a job; work situations that should be avoided as a result

2. Student's physical abilities—extent of physical strength; any limitations to lifting, bending, carrying, etc. and how they will affect any employment considerations

3. Student's visual ability—any need for glasses; any type of visual work that should be avoided; any evidence of perceptual problems and, if so, how they can be corrected; prognosis

4. Student's general motor coordination—any problems in walking and, if so, how they can be corrected; hand and finger dexterity; any kinds of jobs that medical professionals feel would be impossible as a result of poor coordination

5. Student's level of linguistic functioning—any specific speech and language deficiencies and, if so, how they can be corrected or worked around

6. Student's hearing ability—any hearing problems and, if so, how they can be corrected or worked around; implications for vocational programming (Brolin, 1976)

If existing documents and medical reports do not provide adequate and up-to-date information, school officials should initiate arrangements for any further medical examinations. If the student is an eligible Department of Vocational Rehabilitation client, the examinations can often be underwritten at DVR expense.

Collected medical information can be summarized in checklist form (see Figure 4-1) in which the individual's physical capacities are noted in relation to job demands.

Psychological Data

Specific psychological test data found in the student's records may be of limited value. In recent years, formal testing of the paper-and-pencil variety has come under severe criticism when used with handicapped students. Such tests have been criticized for their lack of content validity and lack of appropriate norms or reference groups. Another limitation is the testing medium itself. For example, if learners had difficulty reading an arithmetic problem on an aptitude test, perhaps the test provided an indicator of reading ability instead of numerical aptitude. The most

---

FIGURE 4-1

JOB DEMANDS AND PHYSICAL
CAPACITIES APPRAISAL*

DIRECTIONS FOR COMPLETING FORM: Indicate the capacities of the student in the column to the left of the job factor, using the symbol 0 (zero) if the capacity for meeting the activity or working condition is absent or negligible and an X if there is partial or limited capacity. For the Job Demands columns, rate each occupation (using a 1, 2, or 3) in terms of its demands—high, moderate, or low—for each job factor in which the handicapped student's capacity is absent or limited. (Physical capacities required for a particular job classification can be obtained from the *Dictionary of Occupational Titles* and *Supplements.*) If this capacity or working condition is a requirement of the job, mark it with an X; if not, mark it with a 0.

The completed form provides a list of factors that are requirements of the job and for which the handicapped individual has limitations—those factors marked 0 or X in the Student Capacities column and X in the Job Demands column. The presence of such factors does not necessarily or automatically rule out the occupation being considered. At this point, more detailed evaluation should be attempted. There may be specific jobs in the occupation for which factors are not important, the job may be easily modified to change or adapt the requirements so the handicapped individual can meet the job demands, or special assistive devices may allow the worker to perform otherwise impossible tasks.

---

*From Patterson, 1971. Reproduced courtesy Harper & Row Publishers, Inc.

Figure 4-1 (continued)

Student Capacities	Job Factors: Working Conditions	Job Demands		
		Job 1	Job 2	Job 3
	Lifting			
	Carrying			
	Pushing			
	Pulling			
	Climbing			
	Balancing			
	Stooping			
	Kneeling			
	Crouching			
	Crawling			
	Reaching			
	Handling			
	Fingering			
	Feeling			
	Standing			
	Walking			
	Treading			
	Sitting			
	Turning			
	Talking			
	Hearing			
	Smelling			
	Near Vision			
	Far Vision			
	Depth perception			
	Color vision			
	Inside			
	Outside			
	Extreme cold			
	Extreme heat			
	Sudden temperature change			
	Humid			
	Wet			
	Dry			
	Noise			
	Vibration			
	Cluttered floors			
	High places			
	Moving objects			
	Hazardous machinery			
	Danger of burns			

Figure 4-1 (continued)

Student Capacities	Job Factors: Working Conditions	Job Demands		
		Job 1	Job 2	Job 3
	Electrical hazards			
	Explosives			
	Fumes			
	Odors			
	Toxic conditions			
	Dust			
	Poor ventilation			
	Poor lighting			
	Variety of duties			
	Repetitive work			
	Fast pace of work			
	Following specific instructions			
	Exacting performance			
	Meeting emergencies			
	Competitive work			
	Working alone			
	Working around others			
	Working with others			

significant criticism has been the inadequacy of test results for suggesting appropriate teaching methods or materials; often tests cannot be readily translated into useful information that the teacher can use in planning or sequencing instructional experiences (Phelps, 1976).

Nonetheless, properly used tests are able to provide valuable information that needs to be considered along with all other background information on the student when planning an individual program. When reviewing test results, it is important to:

1. recognize the limitations of the specific test;
2. know exactly what behaviors, aptitudes, etc. the tests are measuring;
3. be sure the test is valid for persons with the student's particular handicapping condition;
4. use the results in a prudent and reasonable manner.

Psychological assessment should focus on three specific

areas of an individual's work personality: intelligence, personality, and perceptual-motor skills. A psychologist should be consulted regarding which tests are appropriate for the particular student. The psychologist can also be of assistance to vocational educators in assessing the individual's skills, in pinpointing intellectual and personality strengths and weaknesses, and in recommending modifications for vocational programs.

Educational Data

Educational data should be assessed in terms of the student's academic ability for job placement. Some jobs require high academic ability, others do not. However, a certain level of ability is required to care for one's everyday affairs. Educational assessment data include transcripts (credits and grades), standardized achievement test results, attendance records, lists of competencies or other performance records, work experience records, and job progress reports.

In assessing the academic potential of handicapped students, it is especially important to judge each student as an individual and not as a representative of a particular category such as educable mentally retarded or hearing impaired. For example, reading levels for the educable mentally retarded generally range from the 2nd to 6th grade levels. While 60% of the seriously hearing impaired possess a reading level of 5th grade or less, the general range is from about 2nd to 10th grade or higher. The individual differences of reading ability among students with a particular handicap are obviously great enough to affect seriously potential job placement—thus, the concern for assessing each student as an individual (Szoke and Vest, 1975).

Motivation and maturation are also factors that must be taken into consideration when interpreting educational achievement results. Such consideration can, for example, assist in preventing a mildly retarded student who is highly motivated from being placed in an unchallenging position and in becoming underemployed, which might occur if academic ability were the sole criterion for job placement.

Care must also be taken in interpreting grades and standardized test results for the physically handicapped who are mentally able. Time lost from school, for example, because of illness or the nature of the physical handicap itself may adversely affect grades, reading level, or other measures of academic achievement. Similarly, a physical disability can slow down the test-taking process and lower scores artificially.

In reviewing educational data and in talking with school personnel, vocational educators should seek the following types of information:

1. Nature of student's past educational program—comments of regular and special school personnel

2. Student's reaction to school—behavior, interpersonal relationships, motivation

3. Student's academic achievement and interests—level of academic achievement in various subjects; subjects liked and disliked; any occupational interests or pursuits

4. Student's learning style—most effective teaching techniques; type of reinforcement needed

5. Student's academic potential—need for and possible benefit from remedial academics; possibility of coordinating remedial academics with vocational program

6. Any student academic limitations of importance in future life functioning (Brolin, 1976).

Social Data

Assessing social data involves evaluating the student's social skills, ability to care for personal needs, and ability to use leisure time wisely. Such data will likely be in the form of anecdotal statements written by school personnel and will typically concern the relationship of the student with his or her peers and authority figures, personal hygiene, reports on family background, and teacher's comments on a student's aggression or submissiveness in the classroom. Such information is highly confidential and only parents and appropriate professional personnel should have access to it. Procedural safeguards guaranteed by law include confidentiality of information relating to each individual and assurances that all assessment procedures accurately reflect the individual's performance in the area being assessed rather than his or her impairment or racial or cultural background.

Social data are also of a highly subjective nature and special precaution is required in using them. Although social data may be of some assistance in assessing the student's social maturity and citizenship, *work attitudes and behavior as observed and objectively rated during the vocational evaluation process or in a prevocational laboratory setting may be a more reliable indication of the individual's social readiness for employment* (Szoke and Vest, 1975).

In reviewing social data and in talking with social workers and vocational counselors, vocational educators should seek the following types of information:

1. Student's general family situation—for example, accepting, rejecting, helping, stable, overprotective

2. Student's involvement in family activities

3. Extent of student's self-help skills required for activities of daily living

4. Extent of student's interpersonal relationships— friendships and extent of meaningful relationships

5. Student's use of leisure time and other avocational activities—appropriate utilization of spare time

6. Student's potential for living independently in the community

7. Student's level of ego strength—ability to face obstacles, frustrations, crises, and other occurrences that adults must face; any indications of future problems with self-confidence or self-concept

These, then, are the basic types of information that may be found in school records or supplemental records—medical, psychological, educational, and social. In addition to the information they provide, school records or other reports also indicate areas for further psychometric and basic skills testing.

Psychometric and Basic Skills Testing

Psychometrics may be defined as the use of standardized tests to measure personal interests, intelligence, eye-hand coordination, dexterity, and manipulative skills. While such tests may provide insight into a student's vocational assets and liabilities, as mentioned previously caution must be used in the selection of these tests and in the interpretation of the test results. Nevertheless, the appropriate use of standardized tests does have its place in the total vocational assessment process. Complete reliance on subjective impressions or on the trial-and-error method of enrollment practically at random in vocational classes or a similar selection of work samples or work experience stations can be inefficient and discouraging. Properly used standardized tests, supplemented if needed by locally developed basic skills tests, are valuable tools in the evaluation process. While they may serve as guides for the elimination of certain occupations as being outside the realm of probable attainment for a particular student, they should even more importantly be used as positive indicators of potential success in a specific occupation or occupational cluster (Szoke and Vest, 1975).

Responsibility for determining the tests to be used should rest with a multidisciplinary selection committee. Membership of the committee might include a vocational evaluator, a career guidance counselor, a vocational adjustment counselor, and a school psychologist. Additional representation might include a psychologist, vocational counselor, or vocational evaluator of a nearby rehabilitation center or local DVR office; and a psychologist or rehabilitation counselor from a nearby college or university.

The selection committee should also determine the number and type of basic skills tests (for example, business arithmetic, change making, tool knowledge) to be purchased or developed locally. Local development of tests should be the joint responsibility of the vocational and special education staffs.

A large selection of tests is not necessary for most school-administered assessment programs. In general, one or two tests for each of the following categories is adequate: personality, interest, aptitude, dexterity, and basic skills. Comprehensive programs serving students with a wide range of handicapping conditions and ability levels may need a larger potential test battery, although only one or two carefully selected tests in each area would be administered to any given student.

Work Sample Assessment

The handicapped person who has been sheltered and overprotected during his or her developmental years has not typically had hands-on experiences from which he or she can make logical vocational choices. In some cases, the handicapped person's disabilities have slowed academic achievement and because of low reading ability and the anxiety caused by taking reading and writing tests, he or she may have done poorly on standardized paper-and-pencil tests, making additional methods of vocational assessment essential.

Work Samples

Work samples are a relatively popular development in vocational assessment over the last several years, due in part to the growing awareness that other methods may be inadequate for evaluating the work potential of many handicapped people.

A work sample is a close simulation of an industrial task, a business operation, or an occupational area. It can be as simple as stamping envelopes or as complex as operating a keypunch machine. It may be completed in 10 or 15 minutes or require 3 to 5 hours to complete. Usually the work sample is normed on workers in industry doing the actual work.

Work samples emphasize performance rather than

verbal skills and, hence, are more effective with students who have low verbal abilities. Work samples can provide practical hands-on experience in a number of occupations in a relatively short time—the student likes it or dislikes it—and because of their work relatedness, they tend to create less anxiety than a paper-and-pencil test (Birch, 1976).

The Work Sample Evaluation Process

While the student does the work sample, a vocational evaluator observes him or her and records observations on explicit behavior factors, performance factors related to the *Dictionary of Occupational Titles,* and indications of interest.

When the work sample is completed, the evaluator scores it to determine how well the student has performed relative to others who have taken the sample and relative to the norm of workers in industry doing the actual work. This process is repeated for each work sample. Each day the evaluator summarizes the results of all work samples done that day, in terms of the student's behavior, interest, and performance.

After all work samples are completed, the evaluator summarizes his or her daily observations and meets with the student for a feedback interview in which they discuss the student's reactions to the work sample process, work samples the student especially liked or disliked, the student's estimate of his or her own behavior and performance, the student's actual behavior and performance, and the student's reaction to this information.

Synthesizing the work sample records and the feedback interview, the evaluator prepares a comprehensive work sample evaluation report which is sent to the student's counselor. The report includes information on physical appearance, communication, behavior in interpersonal situations, worker characteristics, learning and comprehension, discriminatory abilities, and manipulative skills. The report also presents recommendations for appropriate areas of employment and/or training for the student and supportive services that may be needed.

Work Sample and Classroom Tryout: A Case Study

The following case study (Birch, 1976) shows how work samples and classroom tryouts are used together to arrive at a student's vocational objective. A 20-year-old male student attended the Gateway Technical Institute in southeastern Wisconsin. At the time of evaluation, he had arrested hydrocephalus with a repaired spina bifida. (Hydrocephalus is a collection of excess cerebrospinal fluid in the brain; this excess fluid presses the brain against the skull creating the potential for causing brain damage. Spina bifida is a failure of the spinal column to close.) The spinal column of this student was surgically closed and the fluid pressure relieved. However, at the time he was referred to the Gateway evaluation program by the Wisconsin Division of Vocational Rehabilitation, he was working in sheltered employment doing assembly work. He was depressed and apathetic. Referral indicated an IQ score of 78. His educational development was also hindered.

When the student expressed a liking for arithmetic, he was given a Wide Range Achievement Test that showed his reading to be at the 5th grade level and his arithmetic at the 6th grade level. During evaluation he completed a variety of work samples including office and sales work, cooking and baking, and assembly work. Although slow in his work, he performed above average in quality.

He did not like assembly work, and cooking and baking were out because of the standing and walking required. Office work, however, was possible. As a result, he was allowed to try out two types of calculators and was given classroom tryouts in typing and calculator operation. In both cases, the instructor reported favorably. The outcome was to identify a one-year Account Clerk training program as a future goal, to be preceded by remedial work in reading and arithmetic, and with the recommendation that he get his General Educational Development diploma. Gateway Technical Institute was able to provide all of these services within its vocational-technical adult program.

Because of the student's low reading ability, he went through work samples and classroom tryouts rather than interest tests.

Locally Developed Work Samples

A battery of work samples of sufficient variety to assess various manipulative and intellectual capacities may be compiled or developed locally. They may include simple mechanical comprehension (for example, repair of a frayed appliance cord) and tasks evaluating the ability to use basic hand tools, conduct petty cash transactions, price and/or inventory items typically found in a grocery store, care for pets, or collate and perform simple clerical tasks. Ideas and directions for the preparation of homemade work samples may be found in a number of evaluation manuals available from rehabilitation agencies.

Work samples, however, like psychometric testing, should only be a part of the total vocational assessment process. In addition to their advantages, they do have major disadvantages which include the problem of validity and reliability due to the inevitable subjectiveness of the evaluation and the difficulty of establishing norms with which to compare the individual's performance with that of others; the expense and time necessary to develop them; the difficulty in developing enough representative samples to cover all the major occupations; and the problem of work sample obsolescence in a rapidly changing society (Szoke and Vest, 1975).

Commercial Work Samples

Commercial work sample batteries are available and have been specifically designed to evaluate the work potential of the handicapped and disadvantaged. They are standardized systems of work evaluation, consisting of work samples of varying degrees of complexity and representative of a considerable range of occupational areas. They are quite expensive, however, making them impractical for smaller diagnostic centers or programs.

Among commercial work sample batteries are the TOWER (Testing, Orientation, and Work Evaluation in Rehabilitation) system; the JEVS (Jewish Employment and Vocational Service) system; and the Singer/Graflex system. The selection of one of these systems will likely be based on the relationship of the work samples offered to the training programs of the local district, which in turn are based on the community's need for workers.

The TOWER system, for example, stresses the use of a series of work sample tasks in 14 broad occupational areas that represent job opportunities in the New York and metropolitan areas. (TOWER was developed in 1957 by the ICD Rehabilitation and Research Center of New York City, a comprehensive rehabilitation center which began in 1917.) The basic tools, materials, and apparatus of each occupation are essential parts of the system. During the work evaluation process, the student's work habits, work tolerance, work attitudes, motivation, and production speed are ascertained. Qualitative and quantitative standards by which students are assessed are based upon the performance of nonhandicapped workers in industry. The performance of the handicapped student is rated on the basis of superior, above average, average, below average, and inferior.

The TOWER system consists of work samples in the following occupational areas: clerical, drafting, drawing, electronics assembly, jewelry manufacturing, leathergoods, lettering, machine shop, mail clerk, optical mechanics, pantograph engraving, sewing machine operating, welding, and workshop assembly.

In 1976 ICD completed a five-year research, development, and field testing program that resulted in a new vocational evaluation system called Micro-TOWER. It is one of the few systems to employ *group* vocational evaluation. Micro-TOWER evaluations take one week as compared with three to five weeks for other individualized systems. Field testing included the successful application of Micro-TOWER to prison populations, the mentally retarded and emotionally disturbed, and in public school special education programs as well as at rehabilitation centers.

The JEVS system utilizes written and verbal instructions, demonstrations, and models which participants follow in performing the work samples. The samples focus on worker traits (finger dexterity, color discrimination, eye-hand coordination, etc.) to determine skills related to many jobs.

Singer-Graflex is an audiovisual work sample system consisting of filmstrips and cassette tapes, which allow for a greater degree of self-administration. The system consists of work samples in the following occupational areas: basic tools, bench assembly, cooking and baking, drafting, electrical wiring, engine servicing, health services, masonry, needle trades, office and sales, plumbing and pipe-fitting, refrigeration, heating and air conditioning, sheet and metal work, and soldering and welding.

All commercial systems offer certain advantages and disadvantages. Potential purchasers will have to examine each system in terms of their particular needs. They should also make an effort to obtain the opinions and experience of facilities using the systems prior to making a final decision.

Behavioral Observations

Another essential component of vocational assessment is the observation of critical work behaviors. Behaviors are observable, countable, and repeatable actions of the student. They are "observed" by seeing and/or hearing them, and they are "countable" when they can be recorded accurately and reliably by an observer. They are "repeatable" in that they must be able to occur more than once.

Work behaviors make a significant difference in whether or not a student will be employed. They relate directly to success in adult occupations, ranging from competitive employment to employment in a sheltered workshop. Appropriate work behaviors are critical for the handicapped—inappropriate behavior rather than inability to do the job is a major reason for their loss of employment.

The critical observation of behavior within an educational setting is an indicator of the student's work characteristics and reveals some of the dynamics of his or her personality within a work setting. Such observation should not be limited to the relatively brief and formal vocational assessment process. It should occur in prevocational laboratories in the vocational classroom, and in community work stations as well.

Observed work behaviors should constitute or reflect:

1. ability to analyze and reason
2. attention span and work tolerance
3. cleaning up of work area
4. cooperation
5. dependability
6. enthusiasm
7. flexibility or willingness to try new tasks
8. grooming
9. initiation of own tasks
10. maturity in relation to group
11. neatness
12. perseverance
13. punctuality
14. reaction to frustration and stress
15. returning from breaks without being reminded
16. following safety instructions
17. seeking help when necessary
18. need for supervision
19. thoroughness
20. following verbal instructions
21. work attitude
22. work improvement with experience
23. work speed
24. following written instructions
25. emotional stability
26. self-confidence and self-concept (Szoke and Vest, 1975)

Although some of the items above are not behaviors in

and of themselves (for example, self-confidence and self-concept), these can be determined only by the observation of behaviors that indicate their presence. For example, "willingly trying new tasks" is a behavior that may indicate self-confidence.

Summary

At the completion of the formal vocational assessment period, the vocational evaluator or the individual who performs this role should prepare an individual report on each student. The person who prepares the report and the amount of time and effort available for its preparation will vary from school to school. Figure 4-2 provides a comprehensive sample report prepared by the vocational evaluator of a mobile vocational evaluation unit.

Figure 4-2
INDIVIDUAL VOCATIONAL
ASSESSMENT REPORT*
MOBILE UNIT
FOR VOCATIONAL EVALUATION

NAME: Evaluation Period: 4/5/76
BIRTHDATE: Through: 4/12/76
SCHOOL:

BACKGROUND INFORMATION

At the present time, she resides with her father, mother, brother, and one sister. Her father is employed as a truck driver and her mother is a school bus driver. Both siblings are currently in school. Neither of her parents completed their high school education. No other financial resources are available to the family, and the father is the primary source of support. She states there are no significant home problems.

Concerning her medical background, the records indicate that she has a history of scoliosis, or a curvature of the

---

*Adapted from Szoke and Vest, 1975, pages 236-240.

Figure 4-2 (continued)

spine as it is commonly known. She has a gym excuse and indicated that she cannot engage in bending, lifting, and other heavy activities. She said that she can stand or sit for long periods of time without difficulty. However, no orthopedic information has been received regarding her condition at this time. Contact with the Board of Education of _____ County Public School indicates this youngster is not known to them. She also stated that she needs glasses. She has had an eye examination recently and will receive her glasses as soon as possible. She had a back operation at _____ Hospital approximately nine years ago, but she does not recall the exact date. She is currently under the care of Dr. _____, orthopedist. She states that she wears a brace on her back. It would be helpful to obtain further medical information from Dr. _____ to determine the exact restrictions relative to competitive employment. Completion of a DVR orthopedic form would be of value to the DVR counselor.

She indicated that she has been employed as a counter girl at a Rexall Drug Store. She left several weeks ago and does not know if she will return. The reasons for her termination are not clear at the present time.

She attended _____ Elementary School through the sixth grade and then went to _____ and _____ Junior High Schools. She is currently attending the _____ Senior High School, Special Education Class.

She has no stated vocational goals at this time and her special interests are swimming, sewing, and tennis. On her vocational tryout sheet, she stated she was interested in the adding machine, cash register, cosmetology, office filing, and nurse's aide work samples.

In a simulated job interview, she presented herself well. She was responsive, interested, and answered questions in complete statements. She does need to look more directly at the interviewer and relax more.

STANDARDIZED TESTS

I. On the Picture Interest Inventory, a non-verbal measure of individual interests, her most significant scores

Figure 4-2 (continued)

at the higher level, i.e., at the 70th percentile or greater, were in the interpersonal, business, esthetic, and computational areas. Her most significant scores at the lower level, i.e., at the 30th percentile or lower, were in the mechanical, scientific, and natural occupations. Her time perspective score indicates she would not be interested in a long-term training program in which she would have to forego immediate rewards for future gain.

II. On the Purdue Pegboard, a measure of manipulative dexterity, this student demonstrated an above average aptitude in this area.

III. Testing on the Crawford Small Parts Dexterity Test, a measure of fine eye-hand coordination, shows this student possesses superior aptitude in using small tools and in working in situations requiring well-coordinated, fine eye-hand movements.

IV. On the Revised Beta Examination, a non-verbal measure of intelligence, she is currently functioning in the below-average range of intelligence (80-89), according to this particular test classification.

WORK SAMPLE RESULTS

Basic Skills. She can satisfactorily perform basic addition and subtraction tasks but experienced problems when multiplying and dividing. She can handle the fundamental concepts of change making and can count satisfactorily. However, she could not complete a job application satisfactorily. She knows most of her basic colors including shades but cannot measure with a standard ruler. On a lettering task which measures her ability to organize, plan, copy, and use simple tools, she was given a below-average rating. She can tell time well.

Work Samples. On a standardized TOWER System adding machine evaluation, she received an average rating for quality of performance and an above average score for production speed. This evaluation measures the student's ability to pay close attention to detail, to work with and make entries of small and precisely formed figures within

Figure 4-2 (continued)

limited and specified spaces, to handle multiple digit numbers, and to operate a standard adding machine.

A job tryout on the cash register evaluation in which she had to operate a standard cash register, compute the cost of a food order with the aid of a price splitting chart and a standard sales tax chart, discriminate between taxable and non-taxable items, and make correct change indicates she performed in an unsatisfactory manner in terms of accuracy. She obtained an average rating for work speed. No improvement was noted on a retrial.

An assessment of alphabetical, chronological, and code filing evaluations in which she had to file a total of 900 3 X 5 index cards resulted in an above average rating on alphabetical filing, an average score on the chronological task, and an average score on the code sample. Her score for work speed was average on the code sample. Her score for work speed was average on all three types. This sample measures visual acuity, eye-hand coordination, functional reading, accuracy and tolerance for detailed work.

An important part of the clerical evaluation is the sales book work sample which is part of the TOWER System. This evaluation measures the student's ability to make out multiple copy sales slips. It assesses her capacity to select information pertinent to the task at hand, to work with detailed information, to record that information neatly and accurately, and to compute correctly the amount of sales tax and, finally, the sum total of the bill. She received a below average rating on the first trial. However, on the retrial, she was able to improve her score to average.

A tryout on the departmental and zip code mail sorting evaluations resulted in superior scores with above average scores for production speed.

She tried the duplicator work sample in which she had to operate an Astro-Dial 500 duplicator and make multiple copies. She obtained an above average rating.

Concerning the typing evaluation which is designed to determine a person's potential to learn touch-typing, eye-hand coordination, and dexterity, she was given an average rating. She shows potential for further training in

Figure 4-2 (continued)
this area. Her coordination was excellent as was her rhythm.

Due to her interest, she was given an opportunity to work on the cosmetology work sample. In the first place, she was instructed to select and produce a particular hair style following a printed diagram accurately. Her score was above average. She was then asked to create her own individual hair style. She was also given an above average rating for the final product.

On a standardized TOWER System wire sorting evaluation which measures aptitude in recognizing and identifying colors as they are used in the marking of circuits in the electronics industry, she obtained a superior rating. She worked with solid and two-color wires. She then explored a TOWER System electronics assembly task in which she had to run a small cable harness of ten solid color wires following a diagram. She obtained a superior rating on this also. On a soldering task in which she had to solder 24 wires to terminal plugs, she obtained an average rating.

An exploration of work samples relating to the sewing area indicate that she possesses average eye-hand-foot coordination and that she is capable of being trained further on an industrial type machine. One has to satisfactorily make a hem, pillow case, an apron, and use scissors properly in order to be recommended for this occupation.

BEHAVIORAL OBSERVATIONS

Vocational Strengths. She demonstrated excellent work habits during this session. She was very competent, highly cooperative, dependable, and was very flexible. She would try new tasks and was willing to explore new areas. She followed verbal instructions well. Her frustration and work tolerance levels were above average. She worked independently and needed almost no supervision. She initiated her own work and would ask for additional duties. She persevered and the quality of her work was at least average and, in many areas, above average. She asked questions if she encountered difficulty and she was able to reason well. Her work attitude was above average. She gets along well

Figure 4-2 (continued)

with others and was able to relate to her peer group and to authority figures.

Vocational Weaknesses. She does tend to rush and was overly concerned about doing the task as quickly as she could rather than being concerned with accuracy. She needs to learn to pace herself and this should improve through further training. She also needs to learn how to organize her work better and she will need a great deal of structure and direction.

SUMMARY AND RECOMMENDATIONS

A review of all pertinent psychometric data, behavioral observations, work characteristics, and work sample results indicate that she is capable of competitive employment in a routine capacity in the lower-level positions in clerical, service, and assembly and packing positions. She demonstrated an average aptitude for both areas and is mainly interested in working with others. However, a final decision regarding any placement should not be made until further clarification is obtained regarding her physical limitations.

The following is recommended for her:

1. Orthopedic evaluation.
2. Vocational counseling to help her crystallize her vocational goals. Occupational information would be of value.
3. In-school work experiences in the nurse's office, library, or cafeteria.
4. Community centered work experiences in her senior year. An earlier placement could be considered if one is available at an earlier date.
5. Remediation for vocabulary, multiplication and division skills, completing a job application, spelling, measuring, and organizing and planning her work. Training in office practices and typing would be helpful.
6. Individualized vocational training via visual demonstration techniques in an appropriate area. Training at her _____ Vocational-Technical Center can be considered for her.

Figure 4-2 (continued)

The following occupations can be considered for her at an entry level after graduation from high school:

Clerical—file clerk, duplicator machine operator, copy typist, stock clerk, coding clerk, mail clerk, library assistant, information clerk, office helper, collator operator, mailer (print. & pub.), keypunch operator (if her speed can be increased to 40 words per minute)

Bench Work—TV tube tester, lamp wirer, speaker mounter, printed circuit assembler, solderer, power sewing machine operator, sewer

Service—Various food service placements such as fry cook, kitchen helper, etc., nurse's aide (selective placement), shampooer, wig stylist

_____, Vocational Evaluator

The results of the assessment should be discussed with the student, his or her parents, and the program staff, and potential career goals should be developed. Together with the assessment process itself, this discussion should allow the student to understand him- or herself better in terms of aptitudes, abilities, and interests related to potential career goals. If the assessment indicates a need for support services (for example, medical, psychological, social and/or personal, and work adjustment training), this should be discussed with the appropriate school and community personnel.

DEVELOPING THE INDIVIDUAL EDUCATION PROGRAM

Mainstreaming is a student-centered movement. It is based upon identifying the individual student's special needs and adapting the school environment to overcome student handicaps. It assumes that the educational system is responsible for meeting the *individual* needs of *all* students.

Central to federal legislation that supports mainstreaming is the requirement of *individual education programs* (IEPs). This means a written statement is to be developed for each handicapped student by qualified personnel at the local educational agency. According to the Education for All Handicapped Children Act of 1975 (PL 94-142), such a statement must include:

1. a statement of the present educational performance of the student;

2. a statement of annual goals and short-term instructional objectives;

3. a statement of services to be provided and the extent to which the student will be educated in regular educational programs;

4. the date when needed services will begin and the anticipated duration of such services;

5. objective criteria for evaluating the student's achievement of instructional objectives; and

6. assurance of evaluation at least once a year.

Because legislation requiring the development of individual education programs is so new, it presents more questions than answers. Local education agencies will have primary responsibility for carrying out the law and, of course, the local schools will have alternative interpretations of how to implement its provisions. The questions and issues that educators face at the local level must also be faced at the state level, because the state must ensure that the local agencies meet their mandate and it must also administer state-developed programs. Thus, states and local agencies will need guidance and assistance in determining the content of individual education programs and in developing and implementing them.

The Content of IEPs and a Sample IEP Format

In keeping with the federal guidelines of PL 94-142, states are now developing regulations regarding the content of individual educational programs for the handicapped. California, for example, requires that local agencies develop programs that include at least the following six elements:

1. the individual's present level of educational performance;

2. goals and periodic objectives;

3. specific educational services to be provided;

4. the extent to which the individual will participate in regular education programs;

5. the projected date(s) for initiation and anticipated duration of special education services; and

6. appropriate objective criteria, evaluation procedures, and schedules for determining, on at least an annual basis, the degree of achievement of the instructional objectives (California State Department of Education, 1977).

When the individual assessment is completed and a need for special education services is determined, a written IEP is prepared. The California Child Service Demonstration Center System (CCSDCS) provides a format for writing the IEP (see Figure 4-3).

Figure 4-3

INDIVIDUAL EDUCATION PROGRAM (IEP)
(California State Department of Education, 1977)

California Child Service
Demonstration Center System
Directions for Completing IEP

When is IEP Written:

1. The IEP is written upon the determination that there is a need for special education services.

2. Sections I-VI of the IEP are completed before the student is enrolled. Section VII, the Short Term Objectives/ Individual Instruction Plan, is developed by the personnel responsible for implementing the IEP. These written short term objectives shall become a part of the Individual Program.

3. See next page for explanation of the seven sections of the IEP.

Figure 4-3 (continued)

Who Writes IEP:
A. Initial Placement
   1. Parent
   2. Administrator (or designee)
   3. Teacher(s)
   4. A & T Committee (if required by Ed Code)
   5. Individual who performed assessment
   6. Child (when appropriate)
B. Students Currently Served
   1. Parent
   2. Administrator (or designee)
   3. Teacher
   4. Child (when appropriate)

SEVEN MAJOR PARTS OF THE INDIVIDUAL EDUCA-TION PROGRAM (IEP)

I.   STUDENT IDENTIFICATION
     Student name and ID number
     Parent name
     Language of home and how determined
     Birthdate, chronological age, and grade
II. ASSESSMENT INFORMATION
     Present levels of performance
III. PROGRAM INFORMATION
     Program enrolled in, date and duration
     Rationale for placement
     Extent of regular class placement
     Additional Support Services, date and duration
     Type of PE Program
     Types of Prevocational and Vocational Programs
IV. IMPLEMENTATION INFORMATION
     Learning Style
     Learning Situation
     Behavior Strengths
     Talents and Hobbies
     Special Instructional Media and Materials
     Personnel Responsible for Implementation

Figure 4-3 (continued)

V.   MEETING INFORMATION
      Meeting Date
      Interpreter Required
      Signatures of Those Present
VI.   LONG RANGE GOALS AND PERIODIC
      OBJECTIVES
VII. SHORT TERM OBJECTIVES

I.   STUDENT IDENTIFICATION

Name_____ Sex M___ F___ I.D.#_____
                     Chron.
Birthdate_____ Age _____ Grade_____ Date of Entry into Kdgn_____

School _____ Teacher _____

Parents _____

Address _____ Phone_____

District of Residence _____

Primary Language of:
Home_____ Pupil_____ How Determined_____

II. ASSESSMENT INFORMATION

     Indicate Present Levels of Student Performance if Applicable---

     Based on: Developmental Summary_____ Speech and Language Report_____
                Psycho-educational Reports_____ Physician's Report (as needed)_____

Academic Achievement: _____

_____

_____

Communication Development: _____

_____

_____

Social Adaptation: _____

_____

_____

Prevocational and Vocational: _____

_____

_____

Psychomotor: _____

_____

_____

Self-Help Skills: _____

_____   _____

Figure 4-3 (continued)

PROGRAM INFORMATION

Special Education
Program_____ Date of Enrollment_____

Projected Duration_____ Special Teacher_____

Rationale for Placement_____
(least restrictive concept)
_____
_____

Services to be Provided to Reg. Teacher_____

P.E. Program_____ Prevocational_____

Vocational_____

Additional Support Services_____
(Specify Date of Initiation and Duration
and Personnel Responsible)_____
_____

IV. IMPLEMENTATION INFORMATION

Learning Styles: Effective Reinforcers:

Rate_____   _____
Modality_____   _____

Learning Situation: Special Instructional Media and
Time_____ _____   Materials:_____
Interaction_____   _____
Place, Materials, etc._____   _____
                                    _____
Student Interests, Talents, etc.:
_____   Personnel Responsible for Implementation
_____   of IEP:_____
                                    _____
Behavior Strengths: _____
_____
_____

V. MEETING INFORMATION

IEP Meeting Date_____
Interpreter Required: Yes____ No____   (Specialist/Teacher Signature)

_____   _____
(Parent Signature)   (Pupil Signature)
Attended Meeting: [ ] [ ]
                   Yes   No   _____
                                      (Other: position_____)

_____   _____
(Administrator Signature)   (Other: position_____)

Figure 4-3 (continued)

VI. PRIORITIZED LONG RANGE GOALS AND PERIODIC OBJECTIVES

Student Name _____

LONG RANGE GOAL _____ Periodic Objective(s) _____ (Specify time, observable behavior, evaluation conditions, and criteria.) _____ _____ _____ Person Responsible _____ Date Established _____	Monitoring of Goals and Objectives Date: _____ _____ Achieved _____ Reviewed _____ Revision Recommended
LONG RANGE GOAL _____ Periodic Objective(s) _____ (Specify time, observable behavior, evaluation conditions, and criteria.) _____ _____ _____ Person Responsible _____ Date Established _____	Monitoring of Goals and Objectives Date: _____ _____ Achieved _____ Reviewed _____ Revision Recommended
LONG RANGE GOAL _____ Periodic Objective(s) _____ (Specify time, observable behavior, evaluation conditions, and criteria.) _____ _____ _____ Person Responsible _____ Date Established _____	Monitoring of Goals and Objectives Date: _____ _____ Achieved _____ Reviewed _____ Revision Recommended

VII. SHORT TERM OBJECTIVES

INDIVIDUAL INSTRUCTIONAL PLAN (SHORT TERM OBJECTIVES)

To be completed by personnel responsible for implementation.

DISTRICT/SCHOOL _____ STUDENT'S NAME _____ C.A. _____ DATE _____

LONG RANGE GOAL _____

PERIODIC OBJECTIVE _____

LEARNING STYLE _____ BEHAVIORAL STRENGTHS _____

SHORT TERM OBJECTIVES	INTERVENTION ACTIVITIES AND MATERIALS	MONITORING OF OBJECTIVES
		Person or persons responsible for implementation: _____ _____ Reviewed Date: _____ _____ Achieved Date: _____ _____ Revision recommended _____ _____

Development of IEPs: A Process Model

The content of individual programs will be shaped by those who develop them. Determining who will participate in this task is the major question. PL 94-142 states that *the program should be developed in a meeting involving a representative of the local education agency, the teacher, the parents or guardians, and, when appropriate, the student.* Recent experiences with individual programs, however, suggest that a wider range of professional personnel might be desirable. As with the individual assessment process described in the previous section, a multidisciplinary team approach will most likely be a necessity for educational planning as well.

The role of teachers is critical in the development of individual programs—teachers are the ones who must use them and, therefore, should play a major role in planning. On the other hand, while teacher participation is vital, the feasibility of participation may be complicated by collective bargaining agreements and other school regulations.

While involving a large number of professionals in the design of an individual program may be beneficial for the student, increasing the size of the planning team will also increase the cost and the possibility of disagreement. In addition, while the legislation is designed to encourage parent participation, an increase in the number of professionals may result in a decrease in the number of active parents.

The Office of Special Education of the California State Department of Education has developed a process model for use by local education agencies in developing IEPs. Figure 4-4 summarizes the development process. A detailed process model is included as Appendix C.

The Role of the Vocational Educator

In planning individual programs for the handicapped, the vocational educator should be part of a cooperative, multidisciplinary team, serving either as an immediate member of that team or as a resource person providing input

Figure 4-4
PROPOSED EDUCATION PROGEAM (IEP)
DEVELOPMENT PROCESS
(California State Department of Education, 1977)

Figure 4-4

PROPOSED
INDIVIDUALIZED EDUCATION PROGRAM (IEP) DEVELOPMENT PROCESS

(California State Department of Education, 1977)

LEA PROPOSES TO INITIATE LEA-WIDE, SCHOOL-WIDE, OR CLASS GROUP SCREENING PROCEDURES

LEA-WIDE PARENT NOTIFICATION OF RIGHTS INCLUDING DUE PROCESS PROCEDURES AT BEGINNING OF SCHOOL YEAR

IMPLEMENTATION OF SCREENING PROCEDURES RESULTING IN IDENTIFICATION OF INDIVIDUALS WITH POSSIBLE EXCEPTIONAL NEEDS

NOTICE TO PARENTS OF IDENTIFIED INDIVIDUAL AND CONSULTATION POSSIBLY RESULTING IN REFERRAL

WRITTEN REFERRAL OF INDIVIDUAL WITH POSSIBLE EXCEPTIONAL NEEDS FOR FURTHER ASSESSMENT

SCHOOL STAFF OBTAINS PARENTS' WRITTEN, INFORMED CONSENT FOR ASSESSMENT AND INFORMS PARENTS OF RIGHTS AND DUE PROCESS PROCEDURES — A

ASSESSMENT IS CONDUCTED IN COMPLIANCE WITH MANDATED PROCEDURES

IEP IS DEVELOPED WITH PARENT PARTICIPATION

PARENT CONSENTS, IN WRITING, TO THE IEP INCLUDING THE EDUCATIONAL PLACEMENT OF THE INDIVIDUAL

WITHIN 35 SCHOOL DAYS

INDIVIDUAL'S IEP IS IMPLEMENTED

PARENT IS NOTIFIED OF ANY PROPOSED CHANGE IN THE IEP AND MAY "BEFORE" PARTICIPATE IN THE DECISION

PARENT IS INCLUDED IN REVIEW OF THE INDIVIDUAL'S PROGRESS AT LEAST ANNUALLY

PARENT IS NOTIFIED OF ANY PROPOSED CHANGE IN THE IEP AND PARTICIPATES IN THE DECISION

OPTIONS

CONTINUE IN CURRENT PROGRAM

CHANGE IN CURRENT PROGRAM — A

to that team. A cooperative, multidisciplinary approach is required under PL 94-142 in all areas of providing for the handicapped in mainstream programs—in identification and location of students, in screening, assessment, placement, instructional planning, instruction, and in evaluation. Although the law does not indicate that the vocational educator has any responsibility in the preparation of the IEP, it would be most beneficial to involve him or her, especially if the student has any vocational component in his or her program.

Vocational educators and special educators are already showing signs of developing cooperative relationships. This trend, which began originally between vocational rehabilitation and special education, seems finally to be a part of many public school and university efforts involving vocational programs for individuals with mild and moderate developmental disabilities. Vocational and special educators have begun to increase the communication between the two disciplines and to establish priorities and goals out of which some programs have begun to emerge. With the exception of programs for the deaf, the overwhelming majority of the work that has been done as a cooperative effort has been limited to service to individuals with mild handicapping conditions. Although more students are now receiving better service, expectancies for the vocational capabilities of individuals emerging from such programs have remained not much different than they were prior to cooperative programs being established. At present, then, there is a firm base from which to build programs giving individuals with mild, moderate, and severe handicapping conditions a better chance in the world of work than they ever had before (Gold, 1976).

138   *Mainstreaming Guidebook*

CHAPTER REFERENCES

Birch, Warren. "Work Sample Testing for Adults with Special Needs: A Behavioral Approach to Career Planning." *American Vocational Journal.* March 1976, pp. 36-38.

Brolin, Donn E. *Vocational Preparation of Retarded Citizens.* Columbus, Ohio: Charles E. Merrill, 1976.

California Department of Education, Office of Special Education. *The Individualized Education Program: A Developmental Process.* Sacramento: California State Department of Education, October 1977.

Gold, Marc W. "Meeting the Needs of the Handicapped." *The Sequel: Newsletter for Teacher Educators—Special Needs Vocational Programming.* Urbana, Illinois: Bureau of Educational Research, College of Education, University of Illinois, 1976.

Patterson, C. H. *An Introduction to Counseling in the School.* New York: Harper & Row Publications, Inc., 1971.

Phelps, L. Allen. *Instructional Development for Special Needs Learners: An Inservice Resource Guide.* Urbana, Illinois: Department of Vocational and Technical Education, University of Illinois at Urbana-Champaign, 1976.

Szoke, Claire O., and Vest, Sharon. *To Serve Those Who Are Handicapped: Procedures and Format to Implement a Model Career Education Program for the Handicapped.* Rev. ed. Champaign and Springfield, Illinois: Technical Education Research Centers/Midwest and Springfield Public Schools, 1975.

5

Modifying the Curriculum

INTRODUCTION

Modifying a curriculum for the handicapped is a challenging and rewarding task—it is not the overly complicated and seemingly impossible job that those who have not tried it sometimes think it is. The complications arise in overcoming the barriers preceding modification, for example, overcoming the reluctance to change programs, to employ trained handicapped persons, to deal with fear of the unknown.

Curriculum modification may include course content, instructional materials, physical and environmental changes, and modified teaching techniques. Whatever the specific modifications, they should be based on the needs of individual students, and these needs will vary greatly even among students with the same disability.

First of all, modification requires assessment of individual needs. These needs are determined through the vocational assessment process. This process provides the foundation for individual goal formulation and development of the individual education program. The IEP, in turn, indicates how the curriculum needs to be modified for the handicapped student in a regular classroom.

One general rule of curriculum modification for the handicapped is to modify only to the extent necessary. Modification should be made only to the extent that it permits the student to engage in a meaningful and productive learning experience. Whenever possible, regular tools, equipment, and materials should be used so as not to "coddle" handicapped students. Care must be taken to minimize the attitude that special considerations are always necessary for the handicapped. Also, if training modifications are minimal, the student is better able to fit into an everyday work environment.

One of the most important considerations in curriculum modification is providing for a flexible learning environment—one that takes into account that all students, including the handicapped, work at different rates; that allows students to use different materials and learning methods at the same time; that has different subspaces for reading, lab work, discussion, listening, or viewing self-instructional media; and that is attractive and stimulating for all students.

THREE EXAMPLES OF CURRICULUM MODIFICATION

The following three examples illustrate how readily curriculum modification can be accomplished for handicapped students in a regular vocational program, given a flexible learning environment. In one case, no modification was necessary—only the provision of support services that allowed the handicapped student to function in the regular classroom.

Curriculum Modification for a Deaf Student: San Mateo [California] County Regional Occupational Program

The San Mateo County Regional Occupational Program (ROP) is composed of 15 separate programs and approximately 40 sections located throughout the county. The ROP serves the entire county population and includes six school districts. Enrollment is approximately 1,500 to 2,000 students annually. The prime purpose of the ROP curriculum is to keep up with changes in job trends and to assure that updated training will make students employable. Therefore, the curriculum is not fixed, and this flexibility is one of its greatest strengths. Based on a specific job description, a list of typical tasks or skills is developed. An advisory committee from each occupational area reviews the tasks for relevance. When the tasks are approved by the advisory committee, the instructor identifies the theory essential to performing each task and organizes a course of instruction to prepare students for employment. The program utilizes individualized instruction with a flexible time frame, which permits each student to work toward designated goals at his or her own pace. Some instructional presentations are made on a group basis, and at times instruction is repeated for smaller groups of students.

Assessment

A deaf woman contacted the ROP to take the evaluation for entrance into the Data Entry course. The same evaluation was given to her as was given to other students. She scored well in the typing test and relatively well in the clerical, reasoning, and manual dexterity tests. The woman was nervous during testing and was also concerned about the positioning of some of the keys on the data entry machine, although she had some experience in working with keypunch machines.

It was agreed that the woman would enter the class and that adjustments would be made as the class progressed. An ROP counselor contacted the state Department of Vocational Rehabilitation (DVR) counselor and learned that DVR was willing to provide a tutor to help the student in translation and in sign language.

Curriculum Modification

Prior to class, the instructor prepared a diagram of the numeric part of the keyboard for the student to study at home. During class, the instructor discovered that the student read lips very well and usually had very little trouble using the workbook. After a few weeks, the student became familiar with the keyboard and no longer needed the special diagram.

During lectures and demonstrations the instructor attempted to direct her comments toward the deaf student, but often the student did not understand what had been said and needed clarification. Thereafter, the instructor met individually with the student, and the student asked questions. At times the student could not state the questions clearly because of a speech impairment, so she wrote notes to the teacher to overcome this problem. In addition, the student found it useful to read the instructor's lecture notes and the notes of other students in the class, which they willingly provided for her to read in class or to take home.

The course curriculum was an objective-based, task-oriented curriculum, and it was not altered for the deaf student. The only modifications in the course were the special diagrams and the lecture and demonstration notes made available by the instructor and other students. Within the first week, it was discovered that the services of the special tutor from DVR were not necessary. The student was able to reach her goals faster than had been anticipated by the counselor and instructor. This was due to her high level of motivation and ability to grasp concepts and skills very quickly and to the minor adjustments in the curriculum and mode of presentation to meet her individual needs.

Summary

With a small amount of modification, a curriculum was adapted to meet the needs of an individual deaf student. In this case, the student was motivated, had prior clerical skills, and grasped ideas and skills quickly. Other deaf students in this course, however, have not been as successful (even with a tutor or translator) partially because of lack of motivation and difficulty in getting to class every day. It appears that a student's will and determination, in addition to manual dexterity and general intelligence, are the deciding factors of success.

Academic Support Services for a Mildly Mentally Retarded Student: Waukesha [Wisconsin] County Technical Institute

Waukesha County Technical Institute (WCTI) is 1 of 16 post-secondary, vocational-technical, adult education districts in Wisconsin. WCTI serves Waukesha County primarily and small sections of three surrounding counties, with a total of 13 independent high school districts. The main thrust of vocational education is for high school graduates or adults 18 years and older. The district has an open admission policy; therefore, handicapped students are enrolled in all vocational programs. WCTI provides individualized instruction, allowing the student to progress at his or her own rate.

Academic support instructors provide three kinds of services for special needs students at WCTI:

1. Diagnostic assessment of the student's present level of academic functioning as it relates to his or her present or future academic or vocational goals

2. Preparation of prescriptive guidelines for the regular classroom instructor to better meet the needs of the student

3. Individualized instruction for students in need of additional instruction beyond the regular classroom and beyond what the regular classroom instructor is able to provide

Assessment

A mildly mentally retarded student, already enrolled in a Math for Auto Mechanics course, was referred to a support instructor by his regular classroom instructor. The support instructor interviewed the student and administered the necessary testing. The test results were discussed with the student, his school counselor, and the regular classroom instructor. Given the capabilities of the student, it was decided that he would continue in the course and also meet with the support instructor for additional instruction three sessions per week, on a one-to-one basis. Scheduling was arranged so as not to interfere with the regular classroom schedule.

Academic Support

Prior to receiving the services of the academic support instructor, the student had completed only 4 units of instruction in his vocational program, during an 18-week period. In a period of 7-1/2 weeks, with support services, the student passed 5 additional units, with an 89% accuracy level. All grades met the competency requirements of the course and the regular classroom instructor, thus allowing the student to continue successfully in the vocational program.

The standards set for the student were the same competencies expected of all other students in the class. The student was expected to complete the same tasks as other students and to attain a final grade of passing. Instruction was designed to minimize experiencing failure in working toward the required competencies. The student was not singled out from other students by grades, course content, or setting.

Summary

With the provision of supportive services, a handicapped student was able to continue successfully toward the completion of his vocational goal. The specialized services of the support instructor reached beyond the expertise of the regular classroom instructor. Support services are especially important for handicapped students in order to maintain or support their emotional, social, and material needs at a level that will assure their success in an instructional program.

Curriculum Modification for a Mildly Mentally Retarded Student: San Jose [California] Regional Vocational Center

The San Jose Regional Vocational Center (RVC) is one of six area vocational schools in California. It serves six school districts, has a capacity for 2,000 students, and offers 25 instructional programs. Its offerings are primarily two-year programs for 11th and 12th grades; there are some one-year offerings for 12th grade only. The RVC also has an adult program in which evening classes are offered for working people who want to upgrade their skills.

Individualization of all programs is a major goal of the RVC administration. Because the center operates on an open entry/open exit basis, instructors have been asked to develop individualized materials for variable schedules. Inherent in the concept of individualization also is the provision for the varying needs and abilities of students, including the handicapped. In order to enhance the likelihood of a successful experience for the handicapped student, center policy calls for the identification of jobs in the community at which the student can be placed once the program is completed, the planning of a curriculum appropriate for the strengths and weaknesses of the individual student, provision of necessary support for the teacher, and counseling with parents to assure that the goals for the student are understood and agreed upon.

Assessment

A mildly mentally retarded student wished to enroll in the Food Services Program. To accommodate the student, Food Services staff and a counselor at the center reviewed the records of the student and met with the student's parents to discuss appropriate goals, given the capabilities of the student. Food Services staff then selected from a master list those competencies that would qualify the student to work as a Preparation Cook. After reviewing records and talking with the student and her parents, staff was satisfied that the student's chances of having a successful experience in the program were good. The student and her parents agreed with the goal, and the student was enrolled in the regular program.

Curriculum Modification

The vice principal for instruction encouraged faculty members to compile a master list of competencies needed in Food Services (he has done so for all occupational areas in which training is offered). The competencies were then grouped into those needed for entry into jobs in the community; each student in a class must acquire the competencies needed for entry into the job for which he or she is preparing. One result of this procedure is that each student in a given class works only in those competencies appropriate to his or her vocational goal—some competencies are common to many job goals, some are unique to a single job goal. This feature readily accommodates the handicapped with the nonhandicapped; students in a single class typically engage in a wide variety of activities, and one student is not singled out as unusual if he or she is working on something different from what others are working on.

The standards set for the student on the competencies selected for her were the same as for any other student. The instructor was careful to arrange instruction to maximize the likelihood that she would experience success in working toward those competencies. For example, when giving demonstrations the instructor proceeded at a pace appropriate to the retarded student's rate of learning. The instructor felt this was not only worthwhile in helping the retarded student grasp the steps involved but also advantageous for the other students, allowing them time to think more carefully about what was going on than they might have if the demonstration were conducted more rapidly. Following this procedure did not require that the retarded student be singled out in any way and did not disrupt instruction of the other students.

Another technique the instructor followed was to assign students to work in teams. He always used this approach when a difficult activity was undertaken. By pairing the handicapped student with a nonhandicapped student, the likelihood of success was increased, and the retarded student was able to learn from the performance of the other student while experiencing success in having helped to produce a satisfactory product. This had the additional benefit of helping the handicapped and nonhandicapped students to learn to work together and to understand one another.

Summary

Task analysis in an individualized setting was the

approach to curriculum modification used by RVC staff. Such analysis can be useful in identifying jobs that place task demands that are within the reach of persons with a particular handicap; it also provides a model whereby students can be integrated in the regular classroom. (The increasing specialization of work is an advantage in using this approach, as a person needs to be proficient in fewer types of activities. This makes it easier to identify jobs for which a person's attributes make him or her a suitable candidate—this is especially important for the handicapped as the inability to perform one or two types of activities need not eliminate him or her as a candidate for work, as often occurred in the past.)

If time is not available to conduct careful task analyses, the instructor can rely on his or her own professional judgment to identify tasks that are within the student's capabilities. Similarly, some districts may be able to provide help from special educators or the state vocational rehabilitation unit about how best to make use of the student's capabilities.

Task analysis is a valuable approach as long as it focuses on the capabilities of the handicapped person and the tasks that a person with those capabilities can perform. Focusing on tasks that handicapped people cannot do would be a misuse of this approach, which could serve to exclude handicapped students rather than open opportunities. The emphasis should be on the question, "How can this student's capabilities be used to acquire vocational skills?" not on "What does this person's handicap prevent?"

MODIFYING THE CURRICULUM: SELECTING INSTRUCTIONAL TECHNIQUES

Selecting teaching techniques to use with the handicapped in the regular classroom is one of the most important areas of curriculum modification. Such techniques provide the basis for communication between the teacher and the student. Because these techniques need not be limited to the classroom and because many apply to all individuals who come into contact with the handicapped (not just the teacher), they are viewed here broadly as methods of communication. In the section that follows, basic techniques are provided for each of the major handicapped groups.

Techniques to Use with the Hearing Impaired

The hearing impaired student has some degree of hearing loss—anywhere from slight to profound, depending on the individual. Because of the varying degrees of hearing loss, the varying ages of onset, and the types of hearing loss, the individual's hearing impairment is unique. The vocational educator should become familiar with the nature of the individual's impairment and use the techniques that follow in consideration of the specific student. Some of the techniques may seem simple and obvious and not necessarily different from the ways of communicating with nonhandicapped students, but they are very important and should not be overlooked.

1. To help the hearing impaired student lipread better:

   a. Always face the student when speaking. Even a slight turn of the head can obscure his or her vision, making lipreading more difficult. Avoid holding your hands or books where they will hide your face.

   b. Articulate clearly and with normal speed, enunciating each word but without exaggerating or overpronouncing. Exaggeration and overemphasis distort lip movements, making lipreading more difficult. Try to enunciate each word but without force or tension. Short sentences are easier to understand than long sentences.

   c. Speak in a natural tone of voice. Increasing the volume of your voice won't necessarily help the student.

   d. Stand still when talking and keep within close range of the student.

   e. Rephrase sentences if the student doesn't seem to understand; you may be using words he or she is not familiar with, or a particular combination of lip movements may be very difficult to lipread.

f. Avoid standing with your back to a window or other light source. Looking at someone in front of a light source practically blinds a hearing impaired person. Lipreading is difficult, if not impossible, because the speaker's face is left in shadow. Light should come from in front of the speaker and shine on him or her.

g. Let your expressions and motions indicate emphasis and feeling. Make the most of body language—the hearing impaired are very responsive to it.

2. Be sure that the student is paying attention when you assign him or her a task. The student may not hear the usual call to attention and may need a tap on the shoulder, a wave, or some other signal.

3. Try to maintain eye contact with the student. Hearing impaired people, like most people, prefer the feeling of direct communication. Eye contact establishes this feeling. Even in the presence of an interpreter, try to communicate directly with the student. The student can then turn to the interpreter as the need arises.

4. Write on the board without speaking; then turn back to the class and speak. Similarly, turn when pointing out parts or demonstrating.

5. Use many visual aids and written materials. Vision is a hearing impaired student's primary means of receiving information. If large, complex visual displays (for example, of an engine or of the process of cell division) are used, build them up in successive overlays rather than presenting the whole and identifying the parts.

6. Provide outlines and vocabulary lists for any complicated topic being discussed. New vocabulary or complex topics are difficult, if not impossible, to lipread.

7. Seat the student advantageously when he or she is participating in a group. The student should be able to see the lips of all the group members.

8. Provide the student with a brief outline or script printouts to follow a lecture, movie, or filmstrip. Provide these in advance or accompanied with a special lighting arrangement.

9. When presenting vital information, don't leave out the hearing impaired student. Write out any changes in class and meeting times, special assignments, or additional instructions. Allow extra time when pointing out the location of materials or referring to manuals or texts; the student must have time to look and then return his or her attention for further instruction.

10. Repeat questions or statements from the back of the room. Hearing impaired students are cut off from whatever happens that is not in their visual field.

11. When providing instruction, consider the things all good instructors should do:

    a. Provide an introduction to each lesson, describing the content to be covered and how the lesson will unfold; provide a separate introduction to each step in the lesson.

    b. Be as concrete as possible in discussions and explanations, and include activities for the students to carry out as often as possible.

    c. Present information in small chunks, allowing students time to assimilate the information. Frequent pauses are necessary for assimilation.

    d. Pause frequently to allow notes to be taken. Hearing impaired students cannot take notes while you are talking—they have to be watching.

    e. A question-and-answer format is useful; it keeps students involved and lets you know if the message is getting through.

12. When an interpreter is present, consider the following:

    a. Stand close to the interpreter to minimize the amount of shifting back and forth the hearing impaired student has to do.

b. Pause frequently to allow the interpreter to translate; this is especially important when the discussion involves visual information. For example, in pointing out the parts of a motor, give a brief portion of the lesson, pause, allow the translator to sign the information, pointing to key portions of the display or diagram as the translator goes along. (The translator should pause to give the instructor time to point.) If hearing students are in the class, you can repeat the material as the translator signs.

c. You should know something about signing, and the interpreter should be knowledgeable in the subject matter. At the very least, you should get together with the translator before class and discuss the lesson. (English and signing are different languages. The problems that arise in translating between any two languages arise in signing something that is spoken in English. For example, the word "call" has at least three signs, depending on its use—"call" as in "to call out," "call" as in "to call on the telephone," and "call" as in "to call attention to." Thus, you should inform the translator of the sense of terms that will be used when this is not clear from the context. Likewise, you should be aware of cases in which the translation of a single word may require several signs.)

d. Determine with the interpreter whether he or she is to try to preserve feeling and intonation in the translation or to give a "cold" translation.

Techniques to Use with the Visually Impaired

The visually impaired student has some degree of visual loss—from various degrees of residual vision to complete loss of sight. Because of the varying degrees of visual loss, the varying ages of onset, and the various causes of visual impairment, the individual's impairment is unique. Again, the vocational educator should become familiar with the nature of the individual's impairment and use the techniques that follow in consideration of the specific student. Generally, the instructional approach will not need to be changed. The visually impaired student has various methods to compensate for reduced vision. A student may choose to read braille materials, large type materials, or listen to a recorded book or lecture. He or she may choose to write by using a braille writer or metal slate or may tape record information. Regardless, keep in mind these common sense guidelines when communicating with the visually impaired:

1. Do not raise your voice. The blind are not hearing impaired.

2. Speak directly to the blind person, not to a third party.

3. When talking to a blind person, use the words you normally use. Do not try to avoid words like "look" and "see," which are part of everyone's vocabulary, including the blind person's.

4. If discussing a form or passing out materials, describe these to the visually impaired.

5. When teaching or explaining something to a blind person, be consistent in your directions since he or she cannot watch what you are doing. Explain fully and, whenever possible, let the sense of touch substitute for vision.

6. Say what you are doing when you demonstrate. Check your terms to avoid abstractness (for example, "This fastens on there").

7. Make clear how similar parts or processes can be distinguished by touch or sound.

8. Make sure that you *say* everything you write on the blackboard.

9. Encourage sighted classmates to be helpful but not to do the student's work.

10. Seat the visually impaired student in a position where he or she can hear you clearly and has adequate lighting.

11. Be sure to provide the student with an opportunity for adequate exploration of the classroom or work area and any tools of equipment. Often blind students will wish to get a general impression of an area or object, followed by detailed explanations of specific portions of the area or object. Keep the students informed of *any* changes in arrangements of furniture or equipment.

Techniques to Use with the Physically Disabled

The physically disabled student has some degree of physical or health impairment that restricts the kinds of things he or she can do and the places he or she can go. The range of physical disabilities is great: it includes orthopedic impairments (for example, traumatic conditions—paraplegia, quadriplegia—and amputations); neurologic impairments (for example, cerebral palsy, epilepsy); and other health impairments (for example, diabetes, nephrosis, osteomylitis). These impairments vary in degree of handicap, length of time the individual has had the condition, and the stability of the condition. Because of these great variations, the vocational educator must be informed about a student's particular physical condition. Physically disabled individuals differ sharply in physical and health status and, accordingly, in their capacity to engage in particular vocational programs. As individuals they have quite different motivations for affection and recognition, for self-realization, and for security. They also have different levels of intellectual ability. Finally, they have different levels of frustration tolerance and different ways of reacting to frustrating circumstances.

Typically, relatively little modification of instructional techniques will be necessary for the physically disabled. (One of the primary causes of concern to such students is the *physical barriers*—for example, access to controls—in the school; these barriers are surmountable, and ways of overcoming them are discussed in other chapters.) Do keep in mind, however, the following general guidelines when providing instruction for the physically disabled:

1. Develop a positive attitude toward the student. Be **prepared to maintain** a positive reinforcement style when confronted with problems. Closely observe the personal and vocational progress of the student.

2. Be sure the presentation methods allow the student to see and hear what is being demonstrated.

3. Be sure the student has access to personal assistance, perhaps through a buddy system, when he or she needs it to accomplish some intermediate level task.

4. Emphasize individualization to the extent possible.

Techniques to Use with the Mentally Retarded

The mentally retarded student has less-than-normal intellectual capacity. The degree of retardation can range from mild to profound. Typically, the mildly retarded student is the one likely to be in the regular classroom. With proper education and training, the mildly retarded are capable of becoming self-sufficient citizens. The retarded student, just as anyone else, has a unique work personality. He or she has distinct patterns of interests and abilities that are not necessarily similar to that of other retarded persons.

The mildly retarded student can be trained in essentially the same manner as nonhandicapped students. Training will generally take longer, but a lot is known about how mentally retarded persons learn. Interest and motivation are critical factors. Try to involve the student in class activity from the beginning. Be sure he or she understands what is happening and becomes familiar with the work area, tools, and other students. In the very beginning, provide tasks that are simple and failproof. If the student has an expectancy to fail, which is common among the mildly retarded, initial success will start him or her off in a more positive direction. Encouragement and positive reinforcement are essential at all stages of training but are particularly important in the beginning.

Instruction for the mildly retarded should be:

1. Organized. Look over your instructional plan. Steps of instructions should be logical and clearly follow each other. Later instruction should be based on materials already learned.

2. Specific. The student needs to know exactly what she or he must do. She or he may not be able to see obvious connections unless they are pointed out.

3. Visual. Whenever possible, demonstrate what must be done. Use films, slides, drawings, and *simple* charts and diagrams.

4. Spaced in small steps. Instruction should be presented in small increments with time for practice.

5. Repeated and checked. Instruction should be repeated at spaced intervals. Check often to see if the student can *demonstrate* that she or he understands.

6. Overtaught. Allow time for the student to practice each skill even after he or she appears to have mastered it. Check periodically to see if the student remembers important operations, and encourage him or her to practice them.

7. Reinforced. Praise the student for work accomplished, no matter how small the task. Make it clear that new assignments are the result of satisfactory performance. "You've done a good job of soldering these wires. How would you like to begin soldering resistors to terminals?" (Smith, 1977)

Also, a few basic techniques for communicating with the mentally retarded are:

1. Talk with the student on a person-to-person level, as you would with anyone else. Only try to be more specific, more precise, and crystal clear. Don't "talk down" to the student as though she or he were a small child.

2. Speak in concrete terms, not abstractions. If, for example, you want the student to put a tool away, show exactly where "away" is.

3. Demonstrate what you want the student to do; don't just tell him or her.

4. Ask a question now and then to be sure the student is keeping up with you.

5. Take your time, don't rush, and be sure the student understands.

MODIFYING THE CURRICULUM: SELECTING INSTRUCTIONAL MATERIALS

Selecting instructional materials for the handicapped is another important area of curriculum modification. According to a recent survey by the Educational Products Information Exchange (EPIE), however, adequate instructional resources to support effective individual education programs for each handicapped student are not yet widely available at the local level. "Teachers structure 95% of their classroom experiences with some form of instructional materials, but only 1 to 2% of school budgets are allocated for these materials" (National Center on Educational Media and Materials for the Handicapped, 1977).

Standard Criteria for the Selection and Evaluation of Instructional Materials for the Handicapped

Most instruction is accompanied by the use of some type of instructional materials. Educators have historically been faced with the problem of how to select the appropriate materials for a specific student or group of students. Over the years, different rationales and systems have been developed to assist the educator in the selection and evaluation of instructional materials. Many educators, not having access to well-developed systems for selecting and evaluating instructional materials, devised their own selection and evaluation processes at the classroom or building level. While it is helpful to have multiple systems to choose from so that specific student needs can be met in different instructional settings, the question has been asked throughout the educational community: "What criteria do you use for the selection and evaluation of instructional materials?"

The question of appropriate criteria was addressed by the former Special Education Instructional Materials Centers and Regional Media Centers Program (SEIMC/RMC Program) sponsored by the Bureau of Education for the Handicapped (BEH) from 1966 to 1974. The work of establishing a listing of criteria statements was continued by the Area Learning Resource Center, Specialized Office, and the National Center on Educational Media and Materials for the Handicapped Program (ALRC/SO/ NCEMMH Program) also sponsored by BEH. The following Standard Criteria for the Selection and Evaluation of Instructional Materials is the result of the efforts of both programs. The criteria were developed for application at two levels: teacher, for assistance in selecting and evaluating materials for individual learners; and national, for assistance in selecting and evaluating materials for groups of learners. (The two sets of criteria have been synthesized here; although the criteria still represent a very comprehensive materials assessment, they can be adapted and streamlined to meet local needs.)

The criteria statements are not intended to be an exhaustive listing but rather the basic considerations essential to the appropriate selection and evaluation of instructional materials. Use of the criteria may identify other types of statements or questions that may be used to identify an appropriate instructional material for use with an individual learner. Potential users of the criteria are urged to investigate other instructional materials selection and evaluation criteria and/or systems and to be aware of local or state requirements, if any, for the selection and evaluation of instructional materials.

Standard Criteria for the Selection and Evaluation
of Instructional Material

(Prepared by the ALRC/SO/NCEMMH Program)

1. IDENTIFICATION OF NEEDS

The outcome of Stage I will be identification of the availability and adequacy of sources of need information prior to any selection of suitable instructional materials.

A. Sources

_____1. The National Needs Assessment sponsored by the Bureau of Education for the Handicapped

____2. Consumers who are currently working with handicapped children

____3. Analysis of curriculums and instructional priorities at
        learner level

____4. Analysis of learner characteristics

____5. Availability of appropriate materials for curricular areas

____6. Availability of effective materials for learners

II. INITIAL SELECTION

*The outcome of Stage II will be the identification of alternate
pieces of instructional material which, on first screening, appear
compatible with learner requirements and which will be considered for
further review. Identificaiton of alternate materials for examination
will facilitate final selection decisions on a comparative basis.*

A. Search

   *(The items listed below encourage the user to investigate various
   potential materials information sources and to consider essential
   points when gathering information about materials.)*

Yes No NA

___ ___ ___   1. Have you identified resources for materials which
                    have potential use with the handicapped?

___ ___ ___   2. Have materials been identified which may be appro-
                    priate for the learner characteristics of the
                    handicapped?

___ ___ ___   3. Have materials been identified which may be appro-
                    priate for the curricular needs of the handicapped?

B. Screen

   *(Under optimal conditions, a written product abstract or review
   will provide information pertaining to all of the items listed
   below, so that actual inspection of the product is not necessary.
   In the absence of thorough and accurate material descriptions,
   however, scrutiny of the material itself will be required.)*

Yes No NA

___ ___ ___   1. Is it a learner-use material?

___ ___ ___   2. Is it an instructor-use material?

___ ___ ___   3. Are all components of the material available?

___ ___ ___   4. Does the material have potential for use with the
                    handicapped?

___ ___ ___   5. Is the material designed for use by the handicapped?

___ ___ ___   6. Does the material appear to be easily usable by the
                    handicapped?

___ ___ ___   7. Is the format of the material appropriate for the
                    target handicapped audience?

___ ___ ___   8. Is the material of acceptable technical quality?

___ ___ ___   9. Does the material have instructional objectives?

___ ___ ___ 10. Does the material appear to meet the curricular
                    needs of the handicapped target population?

___ ___ ___ 11. How does the cost of the material affect the accessi-
                    bility to the material?

___ ___ ___ 12. Does the material appear to present any physical
                    danger to the target handicapped audience?

III. REVIEW

*The outcome of Stage III will be an in-depth analysis of an instructional
material in order to match (section D) the material for use with a
specific student based on Section A, Learner Characteristics, section B,
Teacher Requirements, and section C, Materials Characteristics. Implementation of this stage necessitates actual examination of the instructional material.*

A. Learner Characteristics

*(The following outline is intended to serve as a guideline to the
selector of instructional materials in identifying the characteristics and educational requirements of the specific learner for
whom material is being sought.)*

1. What are the possible modes of input?

    ___ auditory   ___ tactile

    ___ visual   ___ kinesthetic

2. What are the preferred modes of input?

    ___ auditory   ___ kinesthetic

    ___ visual   ___ multisensory

    ___ tactile

3. What are the possible modes of response?

    ___ verbal   ___ written   ___ gesture

4. ___ What is the learner's instructional level?

5. ___ What is the learner's interest level?

6. ___ What is the learner's reading level?

7. ___ What is the learner's interest areas?

8. What are the learner's interest/motivation requirements?

    a. ___ use of a game-type format

    b. ___ use of humor

    c. ___ use of a variety of stimuli

    d. ___ use of suspense

    e. ___ use of novelty

    f. ___ use of an interaction system of immediate feedback

g. ____ use of cartoon format

h. ____ use of puppets

i. ____ use of characters

9. ____ What are the learner's entry-level skills?

10. ____ What are the learner's reinforcement requirements?

B. Teacher Requirements

*(The following outline is intended to serve as a guideline to the
selector of instructional materials in identifying the requirements
to allow a teacher/instructor to use the material effectively.)*

1. ____ Are a teacher's manual and/or instructions provided?

2. If a teacher's manual and/or instructions are provided, does
   it include:

   a. ____ philosophy and rationale

   b. ____ statement of objectives

   c. ____ statement of instructional and interest levels

   d. ____ statement of reading level

   e. ____ statement of prerequisite skills

   f. ____ listing of material/program elements

   g. ____ listing of required materials and equipment

   h. ____ suggestions for teacher/instructor use

   i. ____ suggestions for student/learner use

   j. ____ suggestions for instructional alternatives

   k. ____ suggestions for evaluation

   l. ____ suggestions for additional resources

3. Instructor time requirements:

   a. ____ training

   b. ____ preparation

   c. ____ use

   d. ____ clean-up

4. What is the degree of instructional staff involvement?

Full-time	Part-time	None	
_____	_____	_____	a. teacher
_____	_____	_____	b. aide
_____	_____	_____	c. parent
_____	_____	_____	d. peer

5. Is the material practical?

Yes	No	NA	
___	___	___	a. maneuverability
___	___	___	b. ease of storage
___	___	___	c. number of parts
___	___	___	d. identification of parts
___	___	___	e. size of parts
___	___	___	f. storage/organization of parts
___	___	___	g. durability of product and packaging
___	___	___	h. replaceability of consumable and nonconsumable parts
___	___	___	i. use of specialized equipment

6. Is the total cost reasonable?

Yes	No	NA	
___	___	___	a. inservice training
___	___	___	b. initial cost
___	___	___	c. per use cost (replacement of consumables)
___	___	___	d. required supplementary materials costs
___	___	___	e. replacement cost (replacement of nonconsumables)

7. ___ ___ ___ Is the material appropriate for the curriculum?

8. ___ ___ ___ Has this material been field tested?

9. ___ ___ ___ If so, has it been found to be effective?

C. Materials Characteristics

(The following outline is intended to serve as a guideline to the selector of instructional materials in identifying specific characteristics a material requires to allow for communication with a learner.)

1. Technical quality

    a. Quality of auditory presentation:

	Acceptable	Unacceptable
(1) clarity (easily understood, recording quality good)	___	___
(2) amplification	___	___
(3) voice level	___	___
(4) dialect/accent	___	___
(5) voice speed	___	___
(6) voice quality	___	___
(7) sequence	___	___
(8) quality of narration (reader style)	___	___

    (9) music/sound/voice mixing   ____   ____

b. Quality of visual presentation:

    (1) sharpness   ____   ____

    (2) color   ____   ____

    (3) distracting elements   ____   ____

    (4) complexity   ____   ____

    (5) size relationships   ____   ____

                                          Acceptable Unacceptable

    (6) sequence   ____   ____

    (7) subjective angle (learner point of view)   ____   ____

    (8) objective angle (observer point of view)   ____   ____

    (9) composition (visual format, visual arrangement)   ____   ____

  (10) figure-ground definition   ____   ____

c. Quality of print and graphic presentation:

    (1) legibility (style and size)   ____   ____

    (2) captioning (location and pacing)   ____   ____

    (3) clarity of print (contrast)   ____   ____

    (4) accuracy   ____   ____

d. Quality of tactile presentation:

    (1) braille (clear and easily discriminable)   ____   ____

    (2) tactile drawings (clear and easily discriminable)   ____   ____

    (3) texture (clear and easily discriminable)   ____   ____

    (4) composition (physical format, physical arrangement)   ____   ____

    (5) manipulables (discriminable, dimension, shape, mass)   ____   ____

2. Instructional quality

Yes   No   NA

____   ____   ____ a. Does the selection of subject matter facts adequately represent the content area?

____   ____   ____ b. Is the content presented in the material accurate?

Yes   No   <u>NA</u>

___   ___   ___   c. Is the content logically sequenced?

___   ___   ___   d. Is the content organized for ease of study?

___   ___   ___   e. Are various points of view, including treatment of minorities, handicapped, ideologies, personal and social values, sex roles, etc., objectively represented?

___   ___   ___   f. Are the objectives of the material clearly stated?

___   ___   ___   g. Is the content of the material consistent with the objectives?

___   ___   ___   h. Are the prerequisite skills for use of the materials stated?

___   ___   ___   i. Are essential subskills required included in the instructional sequence?

___   ___   ___   j. Is the reading level of the material stated?

___   ___   ___   k. Is the vocabulary systematically introduced?

___   ___   ___   l. Is the vocabulary consistent with the stated reading level?

___   ___   ___   m. Is the instructional level stated?

___   ___   ___   n. Is the interest level stated?

___   ___   ___   o. Is the material self-pacing?

___   ___   ___   p. Does the material provide for frequent reinforcement of major concepts?

___   ___   ___   q. Does the material summarize and review major points?

___   ___   ___   r. Does the material provide frequent opportunities for active student involvement and response?

___   ___   ___   s. Does the material provide for evaluation of user performance?

___   ___   ___   t. Does the material provide criterion-referenced assessment?

___   ___   ___   u. Are all of the supplementary materials needed for instruction included in the materials package?

D. Matching Material to Learner

(The following questions require a synthesis of information gained from Stage III, Review. The synthesis is essential before proceeding to Stage IV, Decision.)

Yes   No   <u>NA</u>

___   ___   ___   1. Are stated objectives and scope of the material compatible with learner's need?

___   ___   ___   2. Are prerequisite student skills/abilities needed to work comfortably and successfully with the material specified and compatible with the learner's characteristics?

___ ___ ___ 3. Are the skills and abilities needed by the instructor to work effectively with the material specified and compatible with the instructor's expertise?

___ ___ ___ 4. Are levels of interest, abstraction, vocabulary, and sentence structure compatible with characteristics of the learner?

___ ___ ___ 5. Is the degree of required teacher involvement (constant interaction, supportive or monitoring role, largely student directed, variable) compatible with teacher resources and learner characteristics?

___ ___ ___ 6. Does the material incorporate motivational devices to sustain student interest which are appropriate to the learner's characteristics?

___ ___ ___ 7. Are input and output modalities (visual, auditory, motor, tactile) compatible with learner characteristics?

___ ___ ___ 8. Is the demonstration of task mastery (e.g., written test, performance test, oral test) compatible with or adaptable to intended learner's characteristics?

___ ___ ___ 9. Is the format of the material (e.g., game, book, filmstrip, etc.) compatible with the learner's mental and physical abilities?

___ ___ ___ 10. Is the durability and safety of the material adequate for the learner?

___ ___ ___ 11. Is information provided indicating (successful) field testing of the material with students similar in learning characteristics and interests to those of the learner?

IV. DECISIONS

The outcome of Stage IV will be a final determination of material suitability for use in a specific learning situation. Individualization of the decision making, based on items of priority concern, is implicit in this process.

After the review process, it was found that the material was:

Yes   No   NA

___ ___ ___ needed by the learner

___ ___ ___ usable with the learner

___ ___ ___ usable by the instructor

___ ___ ___ effective

Decision to:

A. Use

B. Adapt

C. Field Test

can be made by identifying from the review data responsiveness of the material to learner need, usability with the learner, usability by the instructor, and effectiveness.

Directions: For each criterion met, place a "+" in the appropriate box. For each criterion not met, place a "-" in the appropriate box. If no information is available, place an "NI" in the appropriate box.

Needed	Usable with Learner	Usable by Teacher	Effective

Match your review summary with the decision matrix below:

D. Recommendations

N	UL	UT	E	Recommend for:
+	+	+	+	U = Use/make available for use/information dissemination
+	+	+	-	A = Adapt
+	+	+	NI	U/FT = Use/Field Test
+	+	-	+	R/A/D = Reject/Adapt/Develop
+	+	-	-	R/A/D = Reject/Adapt/Develop
+	-	-	-	R/A/D = Reject/Adapt/Develop
+	-	+	-	R/A/D = Reject/Adapt/Develop
+	-	+	+	R/A/D = Reject/Adapt/Develop
+	-	+	NI	R/A/D = Reject/Adapt/Develop
-	+	+	+	R = Reject/not acceptable
-	-	+	+	R = Reject/not acceptable
-	-	-	+	R = Reject/not acceptable
-	-	-	-	R = Reject/not acceptable
-	-	-	NI	R = Reject/not acceptable

V. EVALUATION

The outcome of Stage V will be a final judgment, either positive, negative, or inconclusive, as to the usefullness and effectiveness of the material with the learner in a given learning situation.

<u>Yes</u>   <u>No</u>   <u>NA</u>

____ ____ ____ 1. Does this material meet the requirements of the

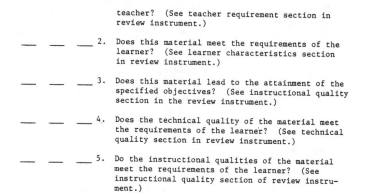

teacher? (See teacher requirement section in review instrument.)

___ ___ ___ 2. Does this material meet the requirements of the learner? (See learner characteristics section in review instrument.)

___ ___ ___ 3. Does this material lead to the attainment of the specified objectives? (See instructional quality section in the review instrument.)

___ ___ ___ 4. Does the technical quality of the material meet the requirements of the learner? (See technical quality section in review instrument.)

___ ___ ___ 5. Do the instructional qualities of the material meet the requirements of the learner? (See instructional quality section of review instrument.)

ENHANCING STAFF SKILLS
THROUGH IN-SERVICE TRAINING

Successful mainstreaming that benefits *both* handicapped and nonhandicapped students in regular vocational programs will require, above all else, competent, well-trained, professional personnel. A Congressional conference report on legislation which in November 1975 became PL 94-142 supports this contention.

If the integration of handicapped children into the classroom is to be accomplished, several important changes must take place in that classroom. A most important element is the teacher who will be responsible for the management of the handicapped children in that classroom. The fact can be well documented that appropriate educational services to handicapped children must be delivered by qualified personnel trained for that specific purpose (U.S. Senate Report, 1975).

The lowered birth rate in recent years and the current economic situation through the country—decreasing job mobility in nearly all fields including education—will mean a low turnover rate of educational staff. Thus, to meet the needs that mainstreaming has created, educators now employed must be retrained. This, of course, calls for an emphasis on in-service training. To illustrate the type of training teachers will need, a model developed by the Wisconsin Vocational Studies Center, University of Wisconsin-Madison, is provided.

University of Wisconsin-Madison: An In-Service Training Model (Tindall and Gugerty, 1976)

One of the services provided by the handicapped project staff at the Wisconsin Vocational Studies Center, University of Wisconsin-Madison, is in-service sessions for teachers. As a component of the in-service sessions, the staff has developed a 12-session course called *Curriculum Modification and Prescriptive Teaching for Handicapped Students.* The staff works through VTAE (Vocational, Technical, and Adult Education) District Administrators and teacher in-service committees to design the course around specific needs of the teachers who will attend the sessions. Staff is prepared to deliver instruction in ten disability areas and seven content areas, depending upon the needs of the prospective class. A survey (see Figure 5-1) is used to determine teacher interest in each of these areas. Teachers interested in participating in the training are then asked to fill out another survey (see Figure 5-2) which asks for specific goals, objectives, and problems they hope to solve by taking the course.

The two surveys provide staff with sufficient information to construct a tailor-made curriculum for teachers enrolled in the course. The surveys provide an indication of the disability and content areas that concern the teachers and an indication of the present level of teacher awareness of the needs of the handicapped. Usually the top four or five disability areas and the top three or four training areas are selected for inclusion in the course. Teachers desiring information in areas not selected for major emphasis are given materials, handouts, and individual help to solve problems they may be having in teaching specific handicapped students. By following this process, staff is able to identify individual class needs as well as set an example of individualization to meet student needs.

Preparing Teachers for Building a Prescription Foundation

At the first class, a model (see Figure 5-3) outlining the development of an "education prescription" is presented to

Figure 5-1
SURVEY ON THE DESIRABILITY OF INSERVICE TRAINING TO WORK WITH SPECIAL NEEDS STUDENTS*

District _____   Job Position _____

Campus _____   Teachers Include

Date _____   Specialty Area _____

In serving Special Needs Students, it is often helpful to have a working knowledge of teaching techniques and program modifications that have been found to be effective with these students. In order to determine your need and desire for inservice training which emphasizes these teaching techniques and program modifications, we ask you to answer the following questions.

1. Do you feel that inservice training in methods to teach and modify programs for people with handicaps is necessary?

   Yes _____   No _____

2. Would you be willing to participate in any such inservice training if it were offered at or near your campus?

   Yes _____   No _____

3. If you answered "Yes" to number two, please review the following topic areas and mark those that you would most like to learn more about.

Training Content Areas \ Disability Areas	Physical Disability	Mental Disability	Hearing Impairment	Visual Impairment	Emotional Disturbance	Learning Disability	Drug/Alcohol Dependency	Speech Disability	Ex-Offenders	Language/ Cultural Disability	Multiple Disabilities
Awareness of Needs, Characteristics, and Capabilities											
Evaluation: Strategy, Techniques, Utilization											
Adaptation of Classroom and Building Facilities											
Modifying Curricula Appropriately											
Specialized Teaching Techniques											
Job Placement Strategies											
Role of Other Agencies in Serving People with Handicaps											

4. What type of inservice format would be best suited to your needs?

   _____ One-Day

   _____ Mini-Course (2-3 sessions offered in the late afternoon or early evening, over a period of time.)

   _____ Multiple-Session (4 or more sessions offered in the late afternoon or early evening over a period of time.)

5. Comments:

_____

*Wisconsin Vocational Studies Center
University of Wisconsin - Madison

FIGURE 5-2
CLASS SURVEY*

1. What specific objectives do you wish to achieve in this course?

2. What are some of the problems which you are currently having in teaching the physically, visually, hearing, EMR, or learning disabled students?

3. Do you have handicapped students in your classes at present?

   Yes _____ No _____ If yes, what are the handicaps?

4. Have you had handicapped students in your class previously?

   Yes _____ No _____ If yes, what are the handicaps?

5. What formal training and/or work experience have you had with handicapped students?

6. Please list the resource persons whom you feel would contribute to the success of the class.

_____

* Wisconsin Vocational Studies Center
University of Wisconsin - Madison

Figure 5-3
BUILDING VOCATIONAL EDUCATION
FOR THE HANDICAPPED*

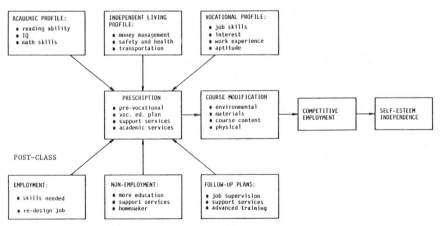

_____

*Showing the approach taken by the
Wisconsin Vocational Studies Center
University of Wisconsin - Madison

initiate the procedure that will lead to a modified course. (As a culminating activity, teachers are required to modify one course for students in at least two disability areas.)

In explaining the model, training session staff stress that teachers must have adequate background information about each student if they are to build an appropriate vocational education program for the individual. The information needed to make an appropriate individual educational plan is divided into two categories:

1. those things necessary to know before the class starts or early in the class

2. those things necessary to consider after the class ends.

Vocational educators need to be aware of areas in the student's background that may provide information of value in developing a plan. Some knowledge of the student's *academic profile* is important, especially reading ability, math skills, and learning styles. A review of the student's *independent living profile* provides information about his or her ability to get along with peers, money management ability, safety and health situations, the need for transportation, and other aspects of independent living. The student's *vocational profile* gives clues to his or her job skills, work experience, interests, and aptitudes.

Vocational educators must also look ahead with the student to the postclass environment. What *employment skills* will be needed? Will the student need a special job or a redesigned job? In thinking of *follow-up plans,* will job supervision, supportive services, or advanced training be required? If the study may be headed toward a *non-employment status,* what is the next step? More education or some supportive service?

Why is all this background information necessary and where can it be obtained? All such information may not be necessary; however, an attempt should be made to obtain enough about the student to make a realistic prescription. Sources of information include the student, school counselors, rehabilitation counselors, and parents.

As an educational plan for the student is developed, help which the student needs outside the vocational classroom must be considered. Prevocational, supportive, and academic services may be necessary to supplement the plan. The plan should include the tasks that are to be learned and the method for teaching the tasks or competencies. It should also identify any necessary course modifications, which may involve course content, materials, physical and environmental changes, and modified teaching techniques.

Plans calling for individualized instruction, materials development, and physical modification in the classroom may not be completed during one semester or school year. But this does not mean that handicapped students must remain outside the regular classroom until the ultimate modifications are completed. Handicapped students are usually able to succeed in the regular classroom with modifications that are made before or during the early stages of the class.

The ultimate goals of building vocational education for the handicapped are competitive employment, independence, and self-esteem.

Preparing Teachers for Work with Students Having Specific Disabilities

After the first class session in which the model outlining the development of an educational prescription is presented, the remaining class sessions are devoted to preparing teachers to work with students having specific disabilities. The format of these sessions consists of four phases, regardless of the specific disability under consideration:

1. *Awareness Phase:* creating the experience of being a handicapped person in a classroom geared to nonhandicapped learners

2. *Reassurance Phase:* soliciting input from the class concerning their success experiences with handicapped learners

3. *Problem Definition Phase:* spelling out the learning characteristics often associated with a student hav-

ing a specific disability, and examining those aspects of the teaching process for which modification should be considered

4. *Problem Resolution Phase:* presenting strategies designed to compensate for or overcome the problems raised.

The following discussion will use mental retardation as the specific disability to illustrate how the four phases are conducted by the staff.

The ultimate goal of the prescriptive programming approach to the education and training of retarded students is threefold:

1. to assist the student's efforts to develop a broader behavior repertoire and more complex behaviors

2. to help the student develop control over him- or herself

3. to aid the student in his or her efforts to achieve functional control over academic, employment, and social environments.

A key determinant of the extent to which a retarded student will achieve these goals is the *degree of success* that the individual experiences in the vocational training environment. The student's chances of success in this environment are enhanced or hindered by the efforts of the *teachers* whom this student encounters. Hence, the in-service training for teachers is directed at increasing the likelihood that the student will experience positive and productive education and training.

During the first phase of the in-service process, the *Awareness Phase*, the experience of being retarded in a mainstream educational setting is provided by asking the in-service trainees to solve a problem in abstract reasoning:

Given: 1. *12 billiard balls, 11 of which are of equal weight, and 1 of which is odd (heavier or lighter than the rest)*

2. *a balance scale*

Problem: Using only 3 weighings on the balance scale, determine

1. which of the balls is the odd one, and

2. whether that ball is heavier or lighter than the others.

After teachers work on that problem for about ten minutes, a problem in precise communication is given along with reassurances that even if they were unable to solve the reasoning problem, they should find the communication problem easier to do:

Direction: Paraphrase the following sentence in a clear, concise, and accurate manner.

Given the circumstances whereby an individual is favorably disposed toward engaging in industrious travail designed to endue a substance which could prevent the desiccation of an equestrian solid-hooofed herbivorous mammal, the potential recipient of such egregious education may be predisposed to traverse the expected outcome.

After allowing an additional ten minutes to work on the problem, the trainer asks if anyone solved either problem. In the likely event that no one has, the trainer elicits the feelings of the trainees. Such feelings are typically those of inadequacy, frustration, anger, embarrassment, and failure. After exploring these emotions together, the trainer tells the trainees that:

1. they have now experienced a *small* taste of what a retarded person can undergo when classes are presented in ways that are too complicated for him or her to cope with;

2. they would probably have experienced much greater success if they had received more complete instructions and procedural guidance. Examples of more

adequate instructions are then given for each of the problems the teacher attempted to solve.

The *Reassurance Phase* of the in-service training is designed to remind participants that:

1. they have already successfully educated retarded students, although students may not have been so labeled; and

2. they have the teaching skills needed to do so even if they have yet to enroll a retarded learner in their courses.

The trainer solicits from teachers examples of successful classroom experiences with retarded students and reviews the skills in which they are currently proficient.

The *Problem Definition Phase* includes both a description of the learning characteristics frequently manifested by retarded students and a review of matters that should be considered when modifying a course for a retarded student. Such matters include:

1. Assessment and Evaluation Results
   a. Existence
   b. Availability
   c. Utilization

2. Employment Goals
   a. Skill levels
   b. Stress factors
   c. Supervisory considerations

3. Physical Plant Modifications (classroom, lab, etc.)

4. Course Content
   a. Quantity
   b. Areas covered
   c. Reading level
   d. Math level (when applicable)

5. Identification, Selection, and Sequencing of Skills and Concepts to be Taught and Rate of Presentation

6. Textbooks, Workbooks, Manuals, and Other Written Materials

7. Teaching Materials and Aids for Teacher Use

8. Learning Materials and Aids for Student Use

9. Teaching Methods

    a. For use with the entire class

    b. For use with the handicapped student on an individual basis

10. Testing of the Student for Mastery of the Course Material

    a. Content

    b. Methods

    c. Success criteria

11. Grading

    a. Types

    b. Criteria

12. Emotional Climate of the Classroom

    a. Feelings of nonhandicapped students

    b. Feelings of handicapped students

    c. Feelings of the instructor

13. Supportive Services

    a. In-house

    b. Outside agencies

14. Administrative Policy

15. Employer Contact and Job Placement

The *Problem Resolution Phase* is presented in several learning modes:

1. A hands-on experience, which might include classroom practice in the determination of instructional objectives, task analyses, sequencing exercises, construction of instructional materials, development of a list of survival vocabulary for the trainees' courses, and the analysis and appropriate modification of texts and manuals

2. A field trip to other classes or rehabilitation facilities in which retarded persons are receiving skill training. Where possible, the trainees are paired with others teaching a similar or comparable skill, e.g., auto mechanics with small engines.

3. Classroom presentation, which might include audio-visuals, visuals, handouts, and resource people (both handicapped and nonhandicapped). For example, a series of visuals is used by the trainer in presenting problems frequently experienced by the retarded learner in a classroom situation and strategies designed to overcome these problems. Such problems include shaky self-confidence, deficient short-term memory, deficient long-term memory, difficulty in attacking problems, slowness in responding to assignments, difficulty in making associations and generalizations, deficient skills of observation. The visuals serve as the framework for the presentation in which the trainer elaborates on both the problems likely to be encountered and the possible solutions for them. The rate of presentation and depth of elaboration is tailored to the needs and desires of the particular group of trainees.

CHAPTER REFERENCES

National Center on Educational Media and Materials for the Handicapped. "The Individualized Educational Program and NCEMMH." *Apropos*, Winter 1977, pp. 1-2.

Tindall, Lloyd W., and Gugerty, John J. "Curriculum Modification and Prescriptive Teaching for Handicapped Students." A paper presented to the New and Related Services Division-Special Needs Section of the 1976 American Vocational Association Convention, Houston, Texas, December 5, 1976.

U.S. Senate Report No. 94-168. *Education for All Handicapped Children Act,* June 2, 1975, p. 33.

6

Eliminating Equipment and Work Environment Barriers

INTRODUCTION

As used in this chapter, "equipment" means tools, machines, and other implements used to perform tasks in the lab or shop *and* instructional implements such as tape recorders, slide projectors and other devices used by students to support learning. "Work environment" is shorthand for other items such as instructional manuals, diagrams, visual or auditory signals, storage containers, and equipment dollies present in the work environment that the student must use, perceive, or comprehend, as the case may be, to perform successfully.

Pieces of equipment and work environments, like buildings, place demands on those using them. To get the job done, a person may have to manipulate objects, adjust settings, take readings and recognize their significance, exchange information with coworkers, and perform a host of other activities that require certain minimal levels of strength, dexterity, sight, hearing, speech, or intellectual ability—most of these are equipment or work environment related demands.

Sometimes a demand is unavoidable because it is part

179

and parcel of the job. For example, a machinist must be able to adjust equipment to meet specifications, and a cook must be able to select the ingredients and combine them in the correct proportions. At other times, demands are more dependent upon the design of particular pieces of equipment than upon the requirements of the job. For example, the machinist may or may not need excellent eyesight to make proper adjustments, depending on the design of the controls, meters and gauges. Likewise, the cook may or may not have to be strong to gather needed ingredients, depending on the size and location of the containers in which they are kept. Thus, some demands arise because of necessary job tasks— make adjustments, take readings, measure, and the like; other demands arise not because of job tasks, but because of the particular piece of equipment or environment used to perform the task—read tiny gauge, lift item from high shelf, reach poorly placed control, and so on. Good designs eliminate unnecessary demands as much as possible. Poor designs multiply unnecessary demands and can interfere with the performance even of very competent persons; such designs have caused almost everyone annoyance, frustration or rage at one time or another.

A barrier results when demands made by equipment or the work environment are very difficult to meet. This is true for nonhandicapped people as well as for the handicapped. Whether or not a particular demand leads to a barrier depends, of course, to a large extent on the innate characteristics and learned capabilities of the individual trying to meet the demand. For example, a short person may face a barrier if supplies are on high shelves, while a tall person will not. Skilled workers know many "tricks of the trade" to meet demands that might present barriers to beginners. Most teachers recognize awkward or difficult tasks in their shops or laboratories and devise ways to overcome whatever problems such tasks present and pass this knowledge on to their students. Handicapped students, like others, will face barriers in learning to operate equipment properly or to function smoothly in the work environment. Sometimes a handicapped student will face barriers in situations where the non-handicapped do not. Often the strategies that are best to help handicapped students overcome barriers differ from those that work best with the nonhandicapped. Vocational educators, working in cooperation with other professionals, can overcome or minimize the importance of many barriers facing the handicapped even as problems confronting nonhandicapped students can be overcome. The purpose of this chapter is to help you to identify barriers that the handicapped student may face because of equipment or work environment designs and to arrive at strategies for overcoming these barriers. Specifically, the chapter will:

- Familiarize you with some of the equipment and work environment barriers faced by handicapped people

- Provide key questions to ask when you assess equipment or work environments to determine if they present barriers to handicapped students

- Suggest strategies you can use to avoid or eliminate barriers and give examples of how the strategies can be applied. These examples come from a wide variety of vocational fields. It will be up to you and your associates to adapt them to fit particular situations that arise in serving individual students.

- Suggest sources to which you can turn for further information.

DEMANDS THAT GIVE RISE TO BARRIERS AND SOME STRATEGIES TO OVERCOME THEM

Equipment and work environments may present barriers to handicapped students because of demands in four main areas. These areas and some sample demands are:

1. *Physical Demands*—grasping, pushing, pulling, or twisting controls which, because of their location or shape, are hard to manipulate; performing operations that require the coordinated movement of both hands

or that demand finger dexterity and steadiness of hand; and lifting or moving heavy or bulky objects.

2. *Visual Demands*—reading operational instructions, blueprints, or diagrams; using standard meters, gauges, and other measuring devices or indicators; distinguishing among color-coded wires or other items intended to be identified by sight; positioning and aligning tools or materials; and guiding materials through equipment such as power saws and sewing machines.

3. *Auditory and Speech Demands*—exchanging information with instructors or fellow students; listening to determine if equipment is functioning properly; and detecting warning buzzers, timer bells, and other auditory signals.

4. *Intellectual Demands*—understanding instructions; comprehending the significance of readings; remembering a sequence of operations; and making measurements and computations.

Clearly, the handicapping condition helps to determine whether any given demand will cause problems beyond those it presents to the nonhandicapped student. Physical demands are most apt to present problems for those with orthopedic or neuromuscular impairments; visual demands affect the blind and visually impaired most significantly; the deaf and hearing impaired are most affected by auditory demands; and intellectual demands present the greatest problems for the retarded.

Still, your primary concern in assessing whether and in what ways unusual difficulties may arise should be with the capabilities and limitations of the individuals with whom you are dealing. One blind student may be able to memorize long sequences of steps readily while another may not. Therefore, the number of "memory aids," such as recorded instructions needed by the former will be less than needed by the latter. This chapter is intended to alert you to problems that may come up and to give you practical suggestions about what to do if they should arise. Your own observations and judgment as to individual capabilities, coupled with the suggestions of other professionals, should help you to decide what modifications, if any, need to be made for a particular student.

An Overview of Strategies

There are three general strategies that you can use to overcome equipment or work environment barriers. The specific strategies suggested in the balance of this chapter exemplify one or more of the following:

1. *Select a standard piece of equipment that does not lead to the problem in the first place.* This is often the most desirable solution because the handicapped student is not set apart by using a special device. Moreover, the equipment is immediately suitable for use by other students during other class periods and after the handicapped student completes the course. This strategy does have drawbacks if the equipment is very uncommon in commercial use *and* students would have difficulty in transferring their skills to more common equipment. The selection of drafting tables without crosspieces to avoid impeding the approach of the wheelchair user, as discussed in the last chapter, is one example of this strategy. Another is the use of gas ranges, as opposed to electric, because the blind can tell when they are on by the sound of the flame.

2. *Provide the student with an aid that makes it possible to use the piece of equipment or to function in the work environment.* In this case, no alteration of equipment or of the work environment is made; rather, the student is provided with an implement that makes the task easier. This approach is best if no easily usable standard equipment is available or if equipment modifications are costly or complex. Disadvantages occur if aids are expensive, difficult to obtain, or cannot be kept by the student at the end of training. A powered prosthesis to allow an upper

limb amputee to use a trigger activated power drill is one example of such an aid. Another is a stand magnifier that a mildly visually impaired student can use to read wiring diagrams.

3. *Modify an existing piece of equipment to make it usable by a handicapped student.* This strategy is required when aids are not available or when stock equipment that is usable is extremely expensive and unlikely to be used by local employers. A major advantage is that touring employers can see for themselves the practicality of making equipment modifications. This strategy is disadvantageous if modifications are terribly complicated, very expensive or can only be done in a way that makes it more difficult for a nonhandicapped student to learn to use the equipment in the usual fashion. Examples of this strategy are the installation of guides to allow blind students to use power saws and the repositioning of sewing machine treadles to allow operation by the knee instead of the foot by those in wheelchairs.

Because of the diversity of vocational fields and the variability among students, situations will inevitably arise that do not really fit any of the questions and strategies given in later portions of this chapter. When that happens, you and other members of the assessment team can take a step back from the problem and ask yourselves which of the three general strategies seem to hold the most promise, and to work out a specific strategy on that basis.

ASSESSING EQUIPMENT AND WORK ENVIRONMENT BARRIERS

In assessing equipment and work environments, three basic questions arise: What barriers are present for a particular student? What options exist for overcoming the barrier? Which option is the best in terms of cost and preparation of the particular student for employment?

Note the emphasis on the *particular student* in these questions. Chapter 3 gave recommendations for doorway and ramp designs, for example, that are *generally* useful to the orthopedically impaired. In following the recommendations, you did not have to be overly concerned about which wheelchair user was trying to enter the building. Similarly, overhanging and protruding objects should be cleared from hallways for the benefit of the blind person—any blind person. In this chapter we are dealing with more custom modifications and it is important that you consult with special educators, rehabilitation personnel or similar specialists in making your plans to be sure that you have selected the best approach for a given student. (For example, some partially sighted students will be able to see printed materials better if high intensity lamps are installed above the work surface. For others, this will only increase the glare and make matters worse.) The suggestions in this chapter should help you to overcome a great many barriers; interdisciplinary cooperation is a key to using them most effectively.

The Assessment Team

The assessment team should include persons of the following types:

1. *Someone (or several people) familiar with problems encountered by persons with the handicap in question, and with ways of overcoming such problems.* This person (or these persons) should be responsible for making sure that all possible sources of difficulty are assessed and that solutions are chosen that take into account the capabilities and limitations of the individual in question. Rehabilitation professionals, special educators and physicians may fill this role. Staff of Goodwill Industries, the Lighthouse for the Blind and similar organizations may be especially helpful as they have had experience in overcoming barriers that arise in offering vocational training to handicapped people.

2. *Faculty or staff members who will be affected by any changes that are made.* This is crucial for three reasons: to ensure the cooperation of appropriate staff so that they do not feel that something is being forced upon them from the

outside; to make sure that all vocationally relevant concerns are taken into account during planning—for example, adjusting a welding torch can be a problem for a deaf student because such adjustments are based on the sound of the flame, but somebody unfamiliar with welding may not know this; and to familiarize faculty members with new or modified equipment or work environments—for example, the teacher may require instruction on how to teach a blind student to use a micrometer with braille markings.

3. *Parents and the student.* Parents and students will be very familiar with problems that the student has in reaching, grasping, seeing, hearing, or comprehending. Thus, they will often be able to provide valuable information as to whether or not a particular situation is likely to cause trouble. Moreover, parents and students may have worked out solutions to common problems, which solutions can be transferred to the vocational setting. An added advantage to involving parents is that they then will have firsthand knowledge of why a task or training program is beyond the capabilities of their children when, in fact, it is.

Conducting the Assessment

The assessment has two goals: to identify barriers that the handicapped student may face in using presently available equipment or in operating in the existing work environment; and to settle upon the best strategy for overcoming such barriers. The strategy selected should allow the student to capitalize on his or her abilities to get the same task done, even if it is done with a special tool, a modified piece of equipment, a piece of standard equipment of a design not previously used, or following some work environment modification.

1. *Identify potential problem areas and suggest tentative solutions.* Hold a meeting as soon as it becomes known that a handicapped student will be enrolled so that careful assessment and planning can take place. Close interdisciplinary cooperation is crucial to making this meeting a success. Vocational staff present can make sure that the

others understand the tasks to be mastered by the student and the way in which equipment is used. Special educators, other professionals who work with the handicapped, parents, and the handicapped student can identify problems that particular tasks or pieces of equipment are likely to present. By pooling their efforts, those at the meeting will be able to develop tentative strategies that make sense from vocational and special education points of view. They will also be able to determine what additional information, if any, is needed about the student, about details of tool or equipment operation, or about the nature of task outcomes.

The next four sections of this chapter provide key questions that you can use to guide your discussion. The questions will help you to cover systematically the major demands that may give rise to barriers. In some cases, a particular question, or a whole section, will not be relevant; in other cases you may have to go into greater detail. Those at the meeting should use their expertise in deciding how far to go in pursuing any of these questions. Possible strategies for overcoming barriers are given following each question. Again, the expertise of those at the meeting is crucial for selecting and applying a particular strategy.

2. *Collect further information.* Gather whatever further information was identified by meeting participants as necessary for determining the best strategy to follow. You may need to gather several kinds of information. Possibilities include a more detailed assessment of demands made by the equipment or the work environment and more detailed information about the capabilities of the student and the practicality of making certain types of equipment modifications.

3. *Take safety into account.* Vocational teachers are properly concerned with the safety of their pupils in labs and shops. To prevent student injuries, equipment should be kept in top condition, safety devices used, and correct safety practices established in the use of materials and operation of equipment.

Properly instructed in an appropriately equipped lab or shop, most handicapped students can probably perform most tasks as safely as the nonhandicapped. However, it behooves the assessment team to review all potentially dangerous situations to assure that the particular handicapped student has the capability to perform safely, to work out a modified instruction program in safety procedures, to provide special guards or guides if needed. The assessment team should also determine if there is some equipment the student should not use or tasks he or she should not perform.

Close cooperation between those most familiar with the student's capabilities and limitations and those who know the dangers inherent in labs and shops is critical. Information must be freely exchanged and nothing left hidden or unspoken. The objective is to provide safe learning experiences for handicapped students, as well as for nonhandicapped students.

4. *Decide on strategies to be used and how to implement them.* Hold a second meeting to decide on the strategies to be used. Again, interdisciplinary cooperation is crucial as the strategies chosen must be adequate to allow the student to overcome barriers and they must be practical to implement in the vocational setting. Allow enough time for ordering equipment and for modifying equipment in the work environment. Also, be sure to provide support for the vocational teacher in learning to use special equipment to instruct handicapped students.

ASSESSING BARRIERS RELATED
TO PHYSICAL DEMANDS

Each physically handicapped student will have unique needs and capabilities. The questions below will help you to identify possible problem areas and to arrive at tentative solutions. Only a few of the *possible* problems will be *actual* problems for any given student. It is up to you and other team members to decide which problems apply for a particular student and to work out a solution. The solutions suggested here are designed to give you some ideas. Since situations vary so greatly among students and from vocational field to vocational field, you will probably have to modify or adapt possible solutions in most cases.

1. Is Normal Hand or Arm Strength or Reach Required?

Every vocational field includes tasks that require the student to grasp and operate controls or to reach, position, and use tools and materials. Any number of orthopedic and neuromuscular conditions may sufficiently impair strength and reach as to make this difficult. Some common problems and solutions pertaining to restricted reach, to weakness, or both are described here.

Work station layout puts tool or supply areas out of reach. Possible solutions:

• Provide a tool that the student can use to gather in items. Useful tools include: surgical forceps for grasping paper, small manuals, and sheets of plastic (Figure 6-1); pliers, too, can give a couple of inches of extra reach; grocer's hooks for reaching light items on high shelves; and croupier sticks for drawing in tools, bolts, electrical components and other items loose on the work surface. Many of these solutions are also helpful to the student who has trouble picking up small objects because of poor finger coordination.

• Reorganize tool and supply areas at the work station without making any physical modifications. Place those objects which, because of size, shape, or weight, are most difficult for the student to reach on shelves or in trays closest to the student.

• Put items into trays that are easy for the student to pull in and push back. This may involve the installation of trays where there were none, or the modification of existing trays to make handles easier to grasp, for example, by replacing small knobs with larger ones.

• Install or relocate shelves and cabinets to place items within reach. This may include storage space for supplies or tools that are not normally stored at work stations, but which it is unreasonably time-consuming for the handicapped student to fetch from central locations.

• Put small items on a lazy Susan that the student can turn to bring objects within reach. (Lazy Susan bearings are inexpensive and can be ordered through most suppliers of shop equipment.)

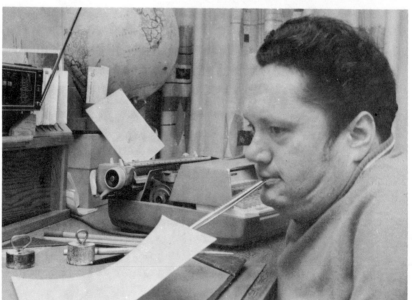

FIGURE 6-1. Man using forceps and mouthstick to position paper and type. Hand-held forceps also extend the reach of many handicapped people. (Courtesy J.R. Wallace.)

Equipment controls are positioned where they are difficult to reach. Possible solutions:

• Consider this problem when ordering new equipment. Favor those radial saws, stoves, and other pieces of equipment with front mounted or otherwise easily reached controls.

• Provide the student with an implement with which to reach controls. The type of implement required varies greatly depending on the type of control. For one person, a simple stick may do to push buttons or to press levers, rings, or handles. (Figure 6-2). For another, a more sophisticated device may be needed to operate the same control (Figure 6-3).

• Extend, reorient, or otherwise modify levers. Figure 6-4 shows a tube slipped over the carriage return lever of a standard typewriter; other possibilities are extending each arm on a four-star handle and reorienting a drill press handle for use by a seated person.

• Mount the equipment so that it can be approached from all sides where controls are present. For example, move a drill stand with side controls from the center of a bench to the corner. Figure 6-5 shows a work table that allows an easy approach from three sides; the end of a narrow workbench would be as good.

Hand tools or hand-held implements require excessive strength to Use. Possible solutions:

• Provide the student with a manually operated tool that supplies more mechanical advantage than is usually necessary. For example, if a student cannot apply enough force using a standard screwdriver, or short spanner wrench, then try an offset, or spiral screwdriver, or a socket set with a long handled wrench. Another example: provide a power lever arm for a stapler.

• Provide a power tool. For example, an electric stapler eliminates the need for downward pressure entirely. Similarly, electric scissors greatly reduce the need for hand strength.

FIGURE 6-2. A simple wooden spoon used to control stove temperature. (Courtesy Sister Kenny Institute.)

FIGURE 6-3. A more sophisticated tool for operating the same stove control. (Courtesy Sister Kenny Institute.)

FIGURE 6-4. Lever extension puts carriage return within easier reach. (Redrawn, courtesy Equipment for the Disabled, Oxford, England.)

FIGURE 6-5. Workbench allowing easy approach from all sides. (Courtesy Brodhead-Garrett Company.)

The student's hands must be held above the work area which is fatiguing for the weak. Possible solutions:

• Purchase or construct a stand to support the student's arms. A padded board or other very simple support is often enough. (Figure 6-6) Mobile supports that pivot and dip in response to the students movements are available for many uses, and special supports can be designed when stock items do not exist—select them in cooperation with a rehabilitation professional. (Figure 6-6)

• Select a tool or utensil, such as a flat-bottomed measuring spoon or an offset screwdriver, that does not require the hand to be held up to use the item.

• Rearrange the work area so that the student does not have to reach over one item to get to another.

• Select equipment with surface mounted controls. For example, stoves with controls on the top are superior to those with controls on the back panel.

FIGURE 6-6. Arm rest to support typist's hands. Also note keyboard template to prevent inadvertent striking of keys by the poorly coordinated. (Courtesy T.E. Fruend.)

2. Is Normal Upper Limb Dexterity or Steadiness Required?

Timers, knobs, buttons, switches, and other controls that must be pushed, pulled, twisted, or squeezed may prove difficult to grasp or manipulate. Also troublesome can be small diameter tools such as mixing spoons, pencils, or probes that require fine finger motions to pick up, and rulers, t-squares, and other implements that have no easily grasped protruding parts. Some common problems and solutions are:

A knob must be twisted, but is difficult to grasp. Possible solutions:

• Attach a lever to the knob that can be pushed with a mouthstick, a prosthesis, or a gross movement of the hand (Figure 6-7).

• Enlarge the knob with a temporary spoked handle that can be operated with a prosthesis or gross movement (Figure 6-8).

• Replace on-off knobs with toggle switches and adjusting knobs with slide adjustment mechanisms. Be sure that toggles and slides are large enough to grasp and pull easily.

A small diameter tool or small part is difficult to grasp. Possible solutions:

• Put rubber tubing around the tool handle to increase the diameter. Alternately wind masking or electrical tape around the tool.

• Construct a holder for the tool.

• Select a standard tool or utensil with a large handle.

• Provide a tool such as a nail-holder or a "grab all tool." The wires at the end of a grab-all tool come together to grasp an object as a plunger on the top is released, in much the same way as extended fingers close around an object. This is especially handy for grasping wires or other small items that are in out-of-the-way places and must be drawn toward the student.

FIGURE 6-7. Levers attached to control knobs allow this man to operate radio equipment. (Courtesy J.R. Wallace.)

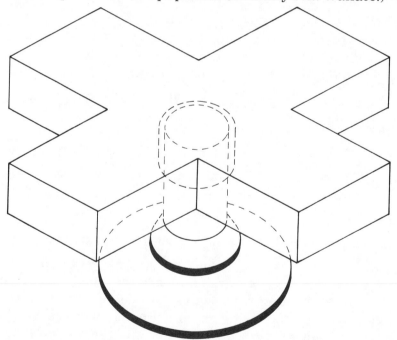

FIGURE 6-8. Spoked handle in place of faucet knob allows easier use with prosthesis. (Redrawn, courtesy Sister Kenny Institute.)

Control buttons are small or close together making it difficult for a poorly coordinated person to strike the desired control. Possible solutions:

• Consider this problem when purchasing new equipment. Many items, such as tape recorders, differ greatly in the location and operating characteristics of controls.

• Build or buy a template to give the student a "path" between closely spaced controls. This is a particularly good strategy when controls operate in response to a light touch. An example is the typewriter template shown in Figure 6-6.

• Install lever extensions over the controls so that less dexterity is needed to activate the controls (Figure 6-9).

A large lever handle or control wheel provides no easily grasped surface for a person with a prosthetic arm, or for someone who cannot grip firmly with the hand. Possible solutions:

• Attach rings, hooks, or straps to the item to be grasped to provide points of purchase. (Figure 6-10)

• Replace a small crank handle with a longer or larger diameter handle that is easier to grasp.

• Add a crosspiece to levers or four-star handles to provide a point of purchase.

A t-square, ruler, or other flat item is difficult to grasp or to push across the work surface. Possible solutions:

• Provide the student with a rubber finger pad, such as are used by bank tellers for counting bills, to give a better grip with finger tips.

• Drill a hole in the object large enough for a finger, mouthstick, or prosthesis tip.

• Attach a handle to the object so that it can be pushed and pulled.

• Select a standard piece of equipment with ridges or other surface features that make it easy to push or pull.

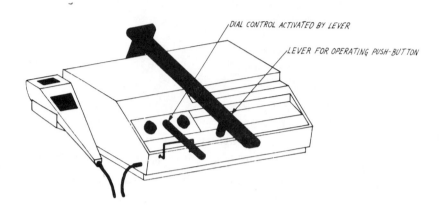

FIGURE 6-9. Lever extensions for operating recording equipment. (Adapted from a photograph, courtesy Kalis-ankar Mallik.)

FIGURE 6-10. A strap allows this oven door to be opened more easily. (Courtesy Sister Kenny Institute.)

A student is unable to hold his/her hand steadily enough. Possible solutions:

• Purchase or make a brace to support the student's hand or arm as described above—shaking is sometimes partially a result of fatigue from keeping the limb extended.

• Work with rehabilitation professions to select an orthosis (Figure 6-11).

• Purchase or make a stand to hold the piece of equipment so that the student must only position the item, not hold it steady—this may be as simple as two boards nailed together to form a vee, or a custom built stand or guide.

• Supply the student with a weighted cuff to cut down on gross tremors for tasks that allow the whole arm to be rested on a smooth surface. Such a cuff can be made by sewing a piece of cloth into a tube and sewing lead weights into the cloth.

A telephone must be used on the job for which the student is training, but the student has trouble lifting the receiver or dialing. Possible solutions:

• Call the telephone company for information about "card dialers" that automatically dial numbers from pre-punched cards, "speaker phones" that allow numbers to be dialed and calls to be received without lifting the receiver, "headset jacks" that connect to standard telephones and allow lightweight headsets to be worn by the user (Figures 6-12 and 6-13).

• Try a pushbutton model as many find it easier to push buttons than to turn dials. Obtain an extension arm to hold the handset near the user's ear.

3. Are Two Hands Required?

Some tasks truly require the use of both hands, but many that are usually done using two hands can be done with one. Similarly, many tasks that do require two hands can be done with less participation by one of the hands than is normally the case. Thus, people with restricted use of one

FIGURE 6-11. Hand orthosis in use by computer programming student. (Courtesy Woodrow Wilson Rehabilitation Center.)

FIGURE 6-12. Automatic "card dialer" calls number given on pre-punched card. (Courtesy A. T. & T. Co.)

FIGURE 6-13. Headset jack eliminates the need to lift the receiver. (Courtesy A.T.&T. Co.)

arm can perform many tasks normally requiring the normal use of two hands. Some common problem situations and ways to overcome them are:

One hand is needed to brace an object while the other hand does the work. Possible solutions:

• Provide a device to hold the tool if a light object that is not possible (or desirable) to clamp down is to be worked. Examples: hold a file in a vise and clamp a sanding block to a workbench for fine finishing; attach a clipboard to a workbench to hold paper for making computations; build a simple stand to hold a tool or utensil (Figures 6-14 and 6-15).

• Provide a device to hold the object being worked on. For example, fasten a "bench hook" to the workbench to provide a backstop, or attach a protruding prong to a cutting board to impale tomatoes, potatoes, and other vegetables while they are being peeled or sliced (figures 6-16 and 6-17).

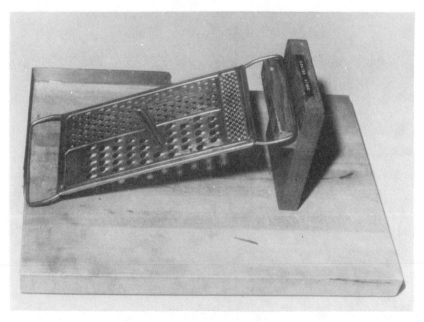

FIGURE 6-14. Simple stand to hold grater for one-handed use. (Courtesy Sister Kenny Institute.)

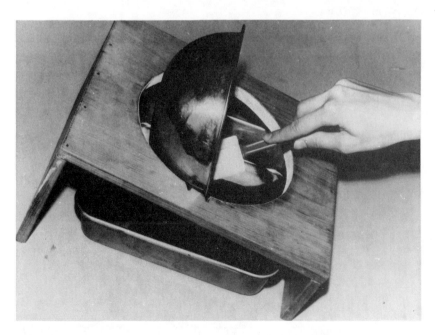

FIGURE 6-15. Stand to steady mixing bowl for stirring and emptying. (Courtesy Sister Kenny Institute.)

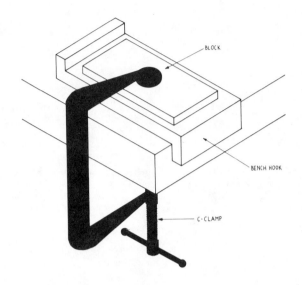

FIGURE 6-16. Bench hook and C-clamp for holding object to be worked on.

FIGURE 6-17. Cutting board with nails to hold potato for peeling. (Courtesy Sister Kenny Institute.)

• Select an auxiliary piece of equipment to allow the device to be held with another part of the body or not to be held at all—for example, attach a telephone rest to a receiver so that the latter can be held against the ear with the shoulder, or an extension arm to hold the receiver (Figure 6-18). Eliminate the need to hold things by providing non-skid work surfaces, such as rubber mats, to keep light objects from "running away" under light pressure. Alternately, apply a non-skid material to the underside of the objects.

• Select a piece of standard equipment that requires only one hand—for example, an automatic center punch, an electric pencil sharpener, a magnetic brad pusher, some models of electric can openers, or tongs.

Machine operation requires two hands. Persons with full use of only one arm or hand may face problems in using many types of table mounted or hand held power tools. Be

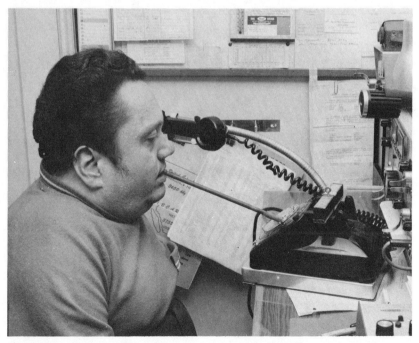

FIGURE 6-18. Extension arm for holding telephone receiver. (Courtesy J.R. Wallace.)

sure to ask yourself whether it is necessary to use both hands, or whether it is merely convenient or usual to do so. Possible solutions:

• Provide clamps to hold stock in cases where they are usually not necessary. For example, one-handers can use drill press clamps to hold stock in position. Similarly, boards can be clamped to the bench for sanding.

• Consider the mechanical efficiency with which pressure may be applied with one hand when selecting hand-held power tools. For example, if the student must apply pressure when operating the tool, then choose a model that allows one-handed pressure on the tool that matches as closely as possible the direction in which the pressure is to be applied from the tool to the stock.

• Select machines that do not require the manipulation of bulky stock when the machine is in operation. For example, radial saws allow wood to be clamped to the table and the blade drawn through the wood by pulling or pushing a single control, whereas two hands are sometimes needed to guide large pieces through table saws. Similarly, a hand-held scroll saw may be used to cut large clamped-down pieces of wood which could not be controlled on the table of a standard scroll saw with a single hand.

4. Must Manuals, Instruction Books, or Diagrams Be Referred to Frequently?

Students who are weak, who have limited reach, or who have serious incoordination of the hands, fingers, or arms may be slowed down in their work if they must make frequent reference to manuals or diagrams because of the physical difficulty of manipulating such items. Possible solutions:

• Post enlarged copies of diagrams or the most frequently referred to pages of manuals near the student's work station (Figure 6-19).

• Take pages out of a loose-leaf manual and post them around the work station.

FIGURE 6-19. Enlarged programming manual posted on the wall makes key sections easily available to this student. (Courtesy Woodrow Wilson Rehabilitation Center.)

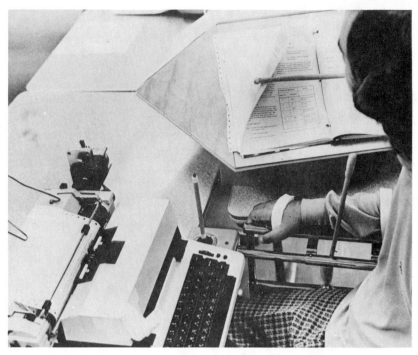

FIGURE 6-20. Programming manual sections mounted on a lazy Susan make information easier to get. (Courtesy Woodrow Wilson Rehabilitation Center.)

• Break large loose-leaf manuals into smaller sections and place these at different points around the work station or on a lazy Susan, so that fewer pages must be turned to go from section to section (Figure 6-20).

• Make slides of key pages so that the student need only activate the slide advance on a projector at the work station to "turn" pages.

These kinds of modifications are particularly important in jobs, such as computer programming using keyboard entry systems, that place minimal physical demands on the worker.

5. Must Foot Controls Be Operated?

People with partial or total limb paralysis find foot controls difficult or impossible to operate. Such controls are often variable speed switches, such as sewing machine treadles, which you can reposition. The student may be able to operate a repositioned switch with the knee, elbow, chin, or head. In addition, you may have to substitute a switch that requires lighter operating pressure or that is shaped to accommodate the member that will operate it.

ASSESSING BARRIERS RELATED TO VISUAL DEMANDS

Barriers to performance for the blind and partially sighted arise primarily in the areas of making measurements, guiding materials through equipment, gaining information that is usually presented in writing or illustrations, and in telling apart items that most students discriminate by sight. The questions below will help you to find ways to overcome problems facing blind or partially sighted students. In using these questions and potential problem solutions, be sure to remember the great variation among individual students. What will work for one will not necessarily work for another. For example, jewelers loupes may help some partially sighted students, but be useless for others. Some blind students can read braille, some cannot. And so on. Therefore, individual assessment and close interdisciplinary cooperation are crucial in assessing and overcoming barriers related to visual demands.

1. Must Measurements Be Made, Dials Set, or Meter Readings Taken?

Students in every vocational program have occasion to set controls, make measurements, or read meters, gauges, and like devices. Such items seldom have markings that are easy to read by touch, or that are large enough to be easily read by the partially sighted. Possible solutions:

• Select digital readout measuring instruments for partially sighted students. Multimeters, clocks, and some other instruments are available. Be sure to consider whether the controls used for adjusting the device (e.g., for multimeter range and function) are usable or can be made so.

• Provide an aid that the partially sighted student can use to read the instrument. Jewelers loupes, hand-held magnifiers, and illuminated and other stand magnifiers (Figure 6-21) are all helpful for some. A "reading slit" made of black cardboard with slit through which the person reads is also sometimes helpful; these can be attached directly to many dial faces.

• Provide enlarged markings. For example, paint heavy lines around the most commonly used levels in measuring cups or graduates. Similarly, you can attach rings or strips with enlarged numerals to the face of the instrument. This works best if only a few positions must be marked. Generally, light lettering on a dark background is easier to read than the reverse.

• Choose standard items that come with markings in high relief or that are otherwise detectable by touch. For example, some timers have high relief markings and standard sewing gauges for marking tucks, pleats and the like. Search through equipment catalogues for items that appear to be suitable. Before making a purchase, particularly an expensive one, be sure to check with a rehabilitation professional or the blind student to make sure that the markings are big enough to be read. This advice also applies to strategies below that involve attaching relief labels. Also bear in mind that a blind person may "read" such markings in a non-traditional way. For example, the markings on a timer may be too small to allow a person to distinguish 5 from 10 by touch, but the student could count the number of large markings to set the time; "the first large mark is 5," "the second large mark is 10;" and so on. Again, you may have to check with the blind person or rehabilitation worker to make sure that this will work in a particular case.

• Provide relief markings. Depending on the instrument, you can provide such markings by scratching indentations at key points, by attaching raised labels, or some similar device. This, of course, is effective only if a relatively few points must be marked. Choose a standard code for scratches; for example, a long scratch for a centimeter and a short scratch for half a centimeter. Make raised labels using a Dymo Tape machine or similar device. Braille Dymo Tape wheels are available as is transparent tape allowing the sighted student to read labels over which the braille labels are mounted. Alternately, if you plan only to use simple codes, a stroke "/" from a standard Dymo Tape wheel can be used for full units, for example, a dot "." for half units. You can mark some metal instruments, such as metal measuring spoons or gap gauges, with indentations in the instrument itself—consult with a rehabilitation professional if you have trouble working out a satisfactory code.

• Choose devices with position controls that can be located or set using touch or hearing. If only a few discrete settings must be made (e.g., multimeter range and function selectors, or washing machine cycle controls), choose models that have clearly audible click stops, and controls that allow the setting to be clearly determined by touch (Figure 6-22). A related strategy is to choose instruments that indicate by sound when a desired setting has been reached. For example, some torque wrenches make a click when a preset

FIGURE 6-21. Stand magnifiers help these students with their work by enlarging and illuminating the work surface. (Courtesy The EDNALITE Corporation.)

pressure has been reached, eliminating the need to read the torque setting as the bolt or sparkplug is being tightened.

• Purchase a measuring instrument specifically designed for the blind. Precision measurements usually cannot be made with improvised equipment, and precision measuring instruments for the blind have been developed for this reason. Among the tools available through the American Foundation for the Blind are: multimeters, carpenter's levels, sphygmomanometers, calipers, rulers, and micrometers. Other precision measuring instruments include: an electronic pressure gauge for use in checking a refrigeration system for gas leaks, and an audio readout dial indicator for use by machinists to determine if a lathe is rotating true, to check the size of completed parts and other tasks. Some of these tools are shown in Figure 6-23, 6-24, and 6-25.

• Provide a light probe with which the blind can make readings or check the operating status of a machine. Light probes emit sounds which vary in pitch as a function of the amount of light falling upon a sensitive element in the tip.

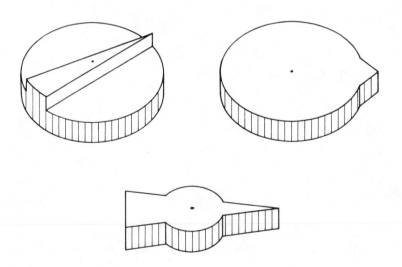

FIGURE 6-22. Control knobs that allow position to be easily determined by touch.

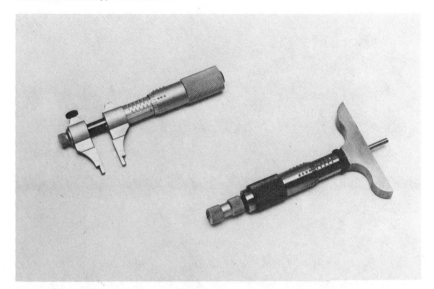

FIGURE 6-23. Micrometers with raised markings. (Courtesy American Foundation for the Blind.)

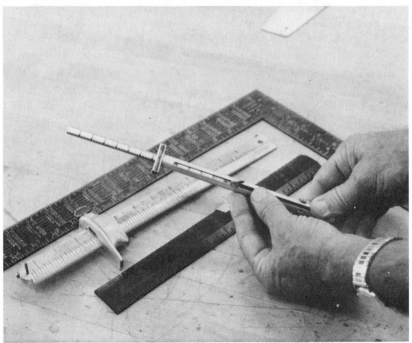

FIGURE 6-24. Measuring instruments with raised markings. (Courtesy R.A. Weisgerber.)

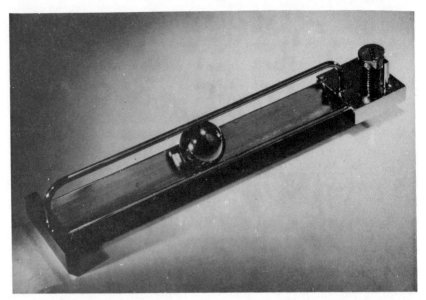

FIGURE 6-25. Carpenter's level. (Courtesy American Foundation for the Blind.)

Most probes operate in one of two ways: either they respond to light supplied by the environment, or they emit a beam to reflect from the surface being examined. An example of the first mode of operation is examination of switchboard lights to see which is active. An example of the second mode is the identification of color coded containers, as different colors reflect different amounts of light. Other uses include the detection of liquid level in transparent measuring cups and the location of needles on meters and gauges.

2. Must Controls or Other Items Be Told Apart By Low Relief Lettering, Color, or Some Other Visual Cues?

Cases in which this is required pose particular problems for beginners. The experienced user, sighted or not, often reaches for controls without looking at them—for example, the expert typist who does not look at the keys, or the machinist who grasps a control crank without looking at it. Thus, some of the solutions suggested below may become less and less necessary as the student gains skill.

• Try light probes, enlarged markings, or relief markings as discussed above according to the capabilities of the student and the demands of the equipment.

• If controls are so close together that the student frequently grasps one when reaching for another, then you can alter the controls so that the student can distinguish them by touch to detect the error and make a correction. This can be done by roughing a control with a file or substituting a knob of a different shape, size, or texture. Remember that it is not necessary to alter each control so that it is distinguishable by touch from every other control; only when controls are so positioned that they might be confused is alteration necessary.

3. Must the Student Operate Tape Recorders, Hand Calculators, or Other Ancillary Devices While Working in the Lab or Shop?

The main problems arise in setting controls properly and in reading the output in the case of calculators. Possible solutions:

• Calculators. For the partially sighted, calculators with large buttons and displays may suffice. For the blind, a variety of special calculators give output in braille (either on paper tape or on a braille cell that gives the answer one symbol at a time) or audibly. The latter type, "talking calculators" have earphone jacks to avoid disturbing others working nearby. Figure 6-26 shows one model.

• Tape Recorders. Special recorders with relief control markings are available (Figure 6-27). You can add Dymo Tape labels to standard recorders or other devices with large controls to achieve a similar effect. Note the simple symbols used on the illustrated recorder. You can employ a similar strategy, using single, easily discriminated symbols, rather than trying to spell out the whole word to identify the control.

4. Must the Student Read Blueprints, Diagrams, Instruction Manuals, or Other Printed Materials to Perform Shop Tasks Properly?

There are few vocational fields in which the student is

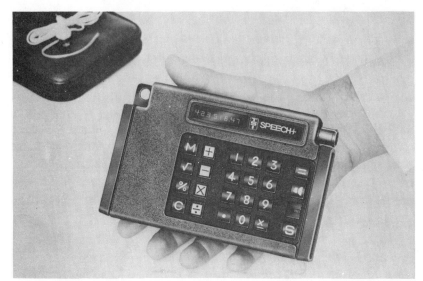

FIGURE 6-26. "Talking" calculator gives results in visual and auditory forms. (Courtesy Telesensory Systems Incorporated.)

FIGURE 6-27. Tape recorder with controls that can be told apart by touch. (Courtesy American Printing House for the Blind.)

not required to do one or more of these things frequently. Possible solutions to problems that arise for the blind and partially sighted are:

• Tape record instructions. This is particularly effective if machine operation, an assembly task, or some other activity involves several steps that must be performed in a sequence that the beginner is likely to forget. Taped instructions can aid the blind person during learning just as printed instructions aid the sighted. You can do short items yourself and ask volunteer groups to do longer items—ask your local rehabilitation agency for the names of such groups.

• Enlarge instructions. Most vocational centers have facilities for making photo enlargements. Such enlargements whether compiled in notebooks, posted at the work station or put on file cards can be used by the partially sighted as tape recorded instructions are by the blind.

• Have materials brailled. Volunteer agencies that make tape usually perform this service also. They may also be able to make raised line drawings and diagrams. The latter is an art form if materials are complex, so a lot of lead time is often required, and you should expect a large number. You or a student helper can do simple diagrams using specially designed sheets available through most organizations for the blind (Figure 6-28).

• Provide the partially sighted student with an aid to make reading of print materials easier. Magnifiers, as discussed earlier, are useful for many. Closed circuit televisions (CCTV) that greatly enlarge documents allow students to read invoices, recipes, diagrams, and other such items; attachments are available that hold a CCTV camera over a typewriter carriage to allow the typist to proof materials before they are removed (Figure 6-29).

• Provide a device that allows the blind to read inkprint. Such devices "convert" inkprint to another modality. For example, the OPTACON (Figure 6-30) senses an inkprint symbol and produces a similar pattern. The user holds a small camera over the letter to be read, where the pattern of dark and light is transmitted to the electronics section

FIGURE 6-28. Simple diagrams can be produced in raised-line versions for use by blind students. (Courtesy American Foundation for the Blind.)

which activates a matrix of small rods beneath a pad on which the user's fingers rests. The instructions cause roads corresponding to the dark area on the page (that is, corresponding to the letter) to protrude for the user to "read."

5. *Is Sight Normally Involved in Positioning, Guiding, or Otherwise Using Hand Tools or Other Hand-held Objects?*

It is difficult to imagine a vocational field in which the answer to this question is "no." Fortunately, a variety of strategies exist for helping an individual to position or guide objects without sight. Some solutions to common problems that arise in this regard are:

• Select a tool or aid that eliminates the need to make fine visual discriminations. For example, self-threading needles allow the blind sewer to perform an otherwise almost impossible task. Similarly, one handed screwdrivers allow the user to align the groove in the screw with the screwdriver blade, secure the screw to the tool, and to

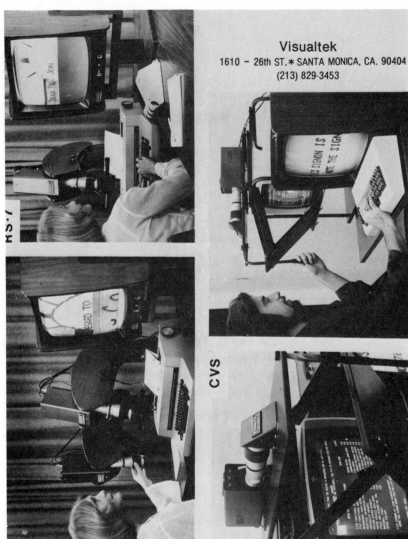

FIGURE 6-29. Closed circuit TV attachments for use in typing and reading a CRT display. (Courtesy VISUALTEK.)

release it once it has been tightened into place; this is much easier than holding the screw with one hand while trying to align place and groove by touch.

• Provide a guide or template to help the student align objects properly. Drill guides can be used by students to drill at 90° angle to the board. A mitre box will help the student

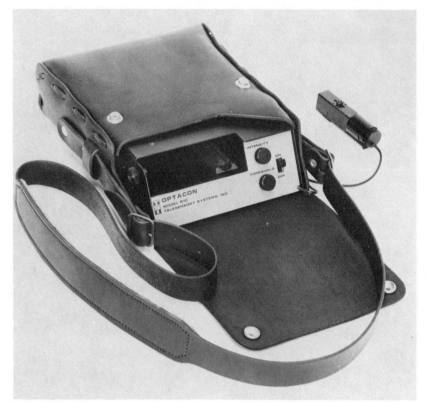

FIGURE 6-30. An OPTACON reading machine. Note the grid on the right-hand side of the aperture through which the message is imparted to the user's finger. (Courtesy Telesensory Systems, Inc.)

to make straight cuts that a sighted student may make unguided. Figure 6-31 shows another method of aligning a handsaw; you can make similar arrangements in many cases where rigid material must be cut. Knives with built-in guides and other cutting guides have been developed that allow the blind to select desired food portions. Figure 6-32 shows how a wood scrap can be used to align a counter-sink perpendicular to a surface. You should be able to improvise similar guides for many tasks that arise in your courses or programs. Figure 6-33 shows a template for check writing. Similar templates for completing other forms are easy to make with an X-acto® knife and a piece of cardboard. You

FIGURE 6-31. Using a carpenter's square to assure a straight cut. (Courtesy R.A. Weisgerber.)

can attach braille labels indicating the information to go in various spaces on the cardboard if the form is complex.

• Select a tool or implement that is easy to align. Many hand tools such as wrenches and spatulas, can easily be used by blind students. Whether or not any specific item in your classes present unusual difficulty is something you will, in general, have to determine in cooperation with others on the assessment team. One factor that you should consider when making equipment purchases, however, is that hand held power tools, such as drills, are much easier to align if handles are perpendicular to the line of force than if the handles are at some other angle.

6. Materials Be Guided Through Power Equipment?

Instructors are justly concerned for the safety of students operating power saws and other dangerous equipment. By and large, blind students can operate such equipment safely when properly instructed and when suitable safety guides are installed. This is an area in which cooperation between vocational and rehabilitation or special

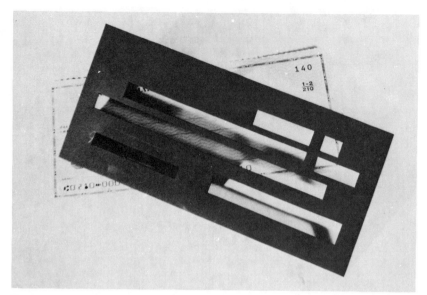

FIGURE 6-32. Check-writing template allows the blind to write on the proper lines. (Courtesy American Foundation for the Blind. Photo by Sally di Martini.)

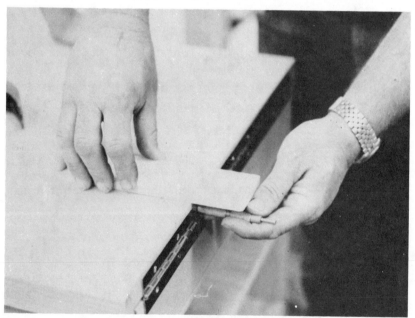

FIGURE 6-33. Using a piece of wood to align a punch. (Courtesy R.A. Weisgerber.)

education staff is critical. Consult with these professionals to identify all potential safety hazards and appropriate guides. Also, have them work with you and the blind student to make sure that the student learns to operate the equipment safely.

ASSESSING BARRIERS RELATED
TO SPEECH AND AUDITORY DEMANDS

Barriers arise either because of listening or speaking demands. Listening demands include attending to what others are saying either in class or on the job, and monitoring equipment for proper functioning or operating status. Speech, of course, is used on almost any job for exchanging information with clients, customers, or fellow workers. As with other handicaps discussed in this chapter, the significance of a particular condition for instruction will depend on the individual student and on the situation in the classroom. For example, a mild hearing loss may be much more handicapping in a class where individual instruction is given against a background of loud machinery than in one where lab or shop equipment does not make much noise. Similarly, a person whose speech is at first difficult to understand will have fewer troubles in a job where he or she speaks with the same people day after day than in one that requires frequent conversation with strangers.

1. Must the Student Hear the Instructor Under Difficult Listening Conditions?

Difficult listening conditions include high level background noise and situations in which the instructor looks at machinery when operating it for demonstration purposes. Possible solutions:

• Provide a translator to sign the instruction. Procedures for working effectively with translators are given in an earlier chapter.

• Make more complete notes on the blackboard or in hand-out materials. Alter instructional style in accord with the suggestions in an earlier chapter as much as possible.

• Obtain an "auditory training system." These systems consist of a small radio receiver with a hearing aid earpiece worn by the student and an FM microphone worn by the teacher. Auditory training systems typically have jacks for phonographs and tape recorders, and can be adjusted to take maximal advantage of the student's residual hearing. Consultation with a hearing specialist is crucial in deciding whether to buy such a device.

2. Must the Student Use the Telephone?

The telephone presents great problems for the deaf and hearing impaired, not only in the obvious sense of being hard to use per se, but also in seeking a job as many occupations require the use of the telephone. Thus, many of the solutions suggested below may be more applicable when you place a student than when teaching the student. Except as noted, the solutions below make use of equipment available through the telephone company.

• Obtain a handset with adjustable volume control (Figure 6-34). Another device, the "bone conductor amplifier" transmits vibrations to the skull just behind the ear whence they are transmitted to the inner ear as the bone vibrates in response to the receiver. This bypasses the middle ear and is very helpful for people with certain types of hearing losses.

• Obtain a device to alert the person to incoming calls. A variety of gongs, loud bells, and devices that produce sounds in the best frequency range for most hearing impaired people are available. So, too, are devices that flash lights when the phone is ringing.

• Obtain a device that eliminates the need for hearing or that makes it easy for a hearing assistant to aid the conversation. The "watchcase receiver"—so called because together with the jack cord, it is about the size of an old fashioned watch and chain—attaches to the telephone. A hearing person listens in using the watchcase receiver and repeats the message, while the deaf person lipreads. A second kind of device transmits typed messages. There are several such devices. Some display the message on television screens, others print using a teletype machine. Figure 6-35

FIGURE 6-34. Handset with adjustable volume control allows this hearing-impaired man to conduct business as usual. (Photo by D.H. Lipe.)

FIGURE 6-35. The Manual Communications Module allows on-the-road deaf employees to communicate with the home office. (Courtesy MICON Industries.)

shows a lightweight portable device that displays 32 characters that move from right to left across the face allowing long messages to be transmitted.

3. Must the Student Monitor or Adjust Equipment Based on Auditory Cues?

Possible solutions:

• Install a loud buzzer or bell or one that makes sounds of a frequency that takes advantage of residual hearing. This will work for warning signals, timers, or sounds that signal the operating status of a machine.

• Install a light for an auditory timer, warning device, timer, or monitor. If monitoring is by pitch or volume a light that varies in intensity as pitch or volume change will serve the same function.

4. Must the Student Use Slide/Tapes or Other Audio-Visual Aids?

Individualized instruction often involves the use of such supports. Some possible solutions to problems that arise in using them are:

• Provide a script for the student to read while using a slide/tape. Since the student will have to look back and forth between the screen or the script, slide advance should be under the control of the student, rather than being automatic.

• Shoot slides explaining what will be shown in the standard set of slides and intersperse them throughout the set of slides.

• Allow the hard-of-hearing student to sit next to the speaker if a film is being shown to the class.

• Supply an "auditory training system" (see Question 1, above) or other individual amplifier and jack.

• Have a translator present to sign for the deaf student.

• If there are several films available, pick the one that is easiest to understand when the sound is off. Test this with someone who, like the student, has not yet mastered what is in the film. Such a film will probably have an unusually large number of labeled diagrams, and other shots of printed lists introducing and summarizing key points.

5. Must the Student Speak to Fellow Students or the Instructor to Carry Out Learning Activities?

Possible solutions:

• Be patient as the student speaks and encourage her or him to speak frequently. Often, speech which is difficult to understand at first will become easier as you get used to it.

• Encourage other students to speak with the speech impaired student frequently, and do not let other students say things for him or her.

• Help the student obtain a device that will help to overcome speech problems. The "artificial larynx" (Figure 6-36), for example, allows a person with a dysfunctional larynx to speak by substituting electronically generated vibrations for natural ones.

ASSESSING BARRIERS RELATED TO INTELLECTUAL DEMANDS

Mildly retarded students find it hard to solve problems or to perform tasks that present little difficulty for others. Most of these problems are not uniquely associated with using equipment and you can seek means to overcome them using the strategies for individualized instruction discussed in an earlier chapter. Breaking tasks into small steps, concrete as opposed to abstract instruction, and other such techniques are as useful in teaching the operation of equipment as in teaching other information. Some common problems and possible solutions as they apply to using equipment are given below. Be sure to train the student carefully in the use of any memory aid or other item.

1. Must the Student Carry Out a Long Sequence of Steps in Using a Piece of Equipment to Complete a Task?

Such sequences are often difficult for mildly retarded

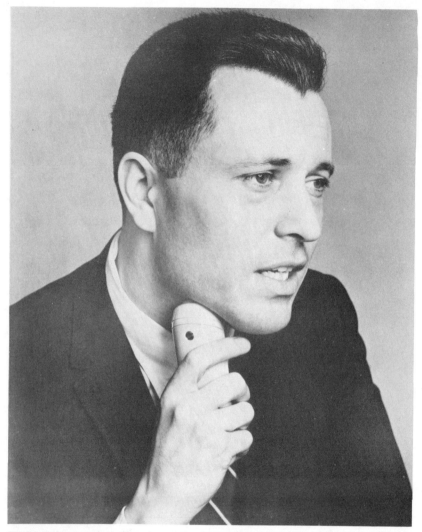

FIGURE 6-36. The artificial larynx shown above allows some speech-impaired workers to converse with their colleagues. (Courtesy A.T. & T. Co.)

students to recall. Moreover, they will sometimes be unable to read standard written instructions. Possible solutions:

• Utilize an aide or advanced student to provide one-to-one instruction as the student masters the task.

• Provide a device to aid memory. The telephone dialing aid

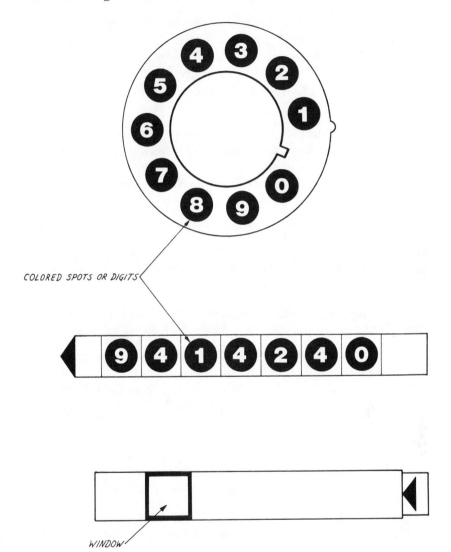

FIGURE 6-37. Dial-a-Phone™ Telephone dialing aid to help the retarded use the telephone. Similar devices could be used to help the retarded remember other sequences of activities. (Dial-a-Phone is patented under Patent No. 3878623. It was developed by Ruth B. Leff, M.S. and may be purchased from Instructo/McGraw-Hill, Paoli, Pennsylvania 19301. Reproduced courtesy of Instructo/McGraw Hill and Ruth B. Leff.)

shown in Figure 6-37 is one such device. The user pushes the slide through the holder and dials the number corresponding to the color that appears in the window. This concept could be adapted to other uses such as by coding the buttons or switches that the student should use to shut down equipment.

• Tape record the sequence of steps so that the student can get access to them without reading or asking someone else.

2. Must the Student Gather Tools and Materials from Around the Lab or Shop?

This can be a confusing additional task. Possible solutions:

• Arrange the room so that the student is near the materials and tools.

• Make up a package of all the items needed for the job so that the student has to fetch only one item.

• Give the student a memory aid to follow when gathering tools and materials. For example, a sketch of what the student should pick up at each color-coded storage area. You can have sketches printed on paper colored to correspond to the storage areas and prepare a packet for the student each day.

3. Must the Student Master Abstract Ideas or Solve Intellectual Problems to Complete Work Tasks?

Counting, measuring, and other operations involving mathematics or other abstract concepts may present problems. Possible solutions:

• Provide an aid that simplifies the problem. For example, if the task is to cut a pie into eight equal pieces, a cutting guide eliminates the need to figure out where to cut. If the student must count out a large number of items—say 20 or 30, provide a container which will be full when the proper number of objects are in it. Alternately, provide a notched board with the same number of holes as the number of objects to be counted; the student can move a marble from notch to notch as items are counted out until the top is reached. (A board with nails would do as well, with the student moving a washer from nail to nail.)

• Eliminate the need to use the concept. For example, color code measuring devices so that the student has only to fill, or cut, or whatever to the blue, or green, or red line. Thus, the student does not need to master concepts such as "half a cup."

RESOURCES

1. National organizations to serve the handicapped (see Appendix B) will be able to supply richly varied information about existing devices, vendors, and the address of local chapters. Some, such as the American Foundation for the Blind and the American Printing House for the Blind, are themselves vendors and supply many tools and other devices for use in the vocational classroom.

   • Local chapters of national organizations and other local groups may be able to supply names of local vendors or service providers. The latter may include translators for the deaf or braille transcribers for the blind.

   • State departments of education and rehabilitation often keep libraries of materials upon which you can draw, supply consultants to assist with instructional problems, and can help defray the cost of aids and other appliances under certain circumstances. These agencies may also be able to refer you to other state and local agencies which can be of assistance to you.

2. Equipment Catalogues and Suppliers

   • Standard office supply catalogue will include items which, by virtue of their design, are especially well suited for use by handicapped people. Take the factors discussed in this chapter into account when selecting new equipment.

232 *Mainstreaming Guidebook*

- Specialized equipment catalogues and listings are produced by a wide variety of groups and organizations. Some very useful items are:

American Foundation for the Blind—*Aids and Appliances for the Blind and Visually Impaired*
A catalogue available from the American Foundation for the Blind contains listings of tools, timers, kitchen utensils and other objects of potential use in vocational programs. Updated annually. Write: American Foundation for the Blind, 15 West 16th St., New York, New York 10011.

Bell Telephone System—*Service for Special Needs*
A listing of telephone equipment available through the Bell System for the deaf, hard-of-hearing, and physically handicapped. Available from any telephone company business office.

Library of Congress—*Aids for Handicapped Readers*
A Library of Congress reference circular describing reading aids for the blind and physically handicapped. Write: Library of Congress, Reference and Information Section, Division for the Blind and Physically Handicapped, Washington, D.C. 20542.

Recommended Aids for the Partially Sighted— Louise L. Sloan, 1966
A listing of magnifiers, enlarged templates, and other items, with suggestions for their use. Available from the National Society for the Prevention of Blindness, Inc., 79 Madison Avenue, New York, New York 10016.

- For the addresses of suppliers of items pictured in this chapter, see the acknowledgment section at the front of this book.

7

Placing Handicapped
Students in Jobs

INTRODUCTION

One proof of the quality of a vocational program is its rate of placement success. To place students has been a legal expectation since the Smith-Hughes Act of 1917, and has been constantly reinforced in subsequent legislation. Vocational programs are required to provide placement services for their graduates, and evaluations take success in placement into account. Thus, the vocational educator has considerable reason within the legal and administrative structures of vocational education to seek a high placement rate.

Even more important, however, is the educator's desire to see students enter and succeed in jobs for which they have trained. This is a critical factor for students, too. It is terribly discouraging to prepare for years for a particular line of work only to find such work unavailable. These concerns are general throughout vocational education; they arise for all students. No wonder then that they arise for the handicapped as well.

Can the handicapped graduate be placed in a position with a good opportunity for job success? If not, the whole

233

training effort may in the end be just a source of frustration, rejection, and disappointment.

This chapter assumes that the answer to this question is a resounding "Yes!" Handicapped students *can* be placed and they *can* succeed. Your program will have trained its handicapped students in the technical skills they need to be considered legitimate job candidates. Thus, the technical basis is there. Moreover, employers who have tried the handicapped generally like them, showing that the merits of handicapped employees are recognized on the job.

Still, some special problems may arise in placing handicapped students. These problems have been overcome by vocational educators, rehabilitation professionals, advocacy groups, and individual handicapped job seekers themselves. The purpose of this chapter is to provide procedures by which your program can effect successful placements of handicapped students.

COMMON PROBLEMS FACED IN PLACING THE HANDICAPPED STUDENT

Job search and placement are problems for all workers and particularly inexperienced ones. The handicapped face all of these problems and more. For discussion we enumerate some of the general challenges faced by all job seekers and then identify and discuss the following four special areas in which problems may arise in placing handicapped students:

1. The student cannot clear entry hurdles—entry requirements often make greater physical or intellectual demands than does the job itself.

2. Employers fear increased employee-related expenses —they may fear insurance rates, accident frequency, or some other expense of doing business will rise.

3. Employers do not see how the handicapped person can get the job done at all, or they fear that accommodation will be terribly expensive—they may fear that environmental adaptations and special tools may be costly or that the handicapped worker cannot get the job done, accommodations or no.

4. Employers fear that other workers will not be able to work well with the handicapped—other employees may have poor attitudes toward working with the handicapped, or may lack communication or other skills needed to function efficiently with handicapped colleagues.

Each of these problems can present substantial barriers to the handicapped student. Each type of problem can be overcome through early planning, effective employer contacts, and timely use of various members of the placement team. The description of each problem area, below, sets the stage for the discussion of steps to take to place handicapped students.

The Student Faces the General Challenges of Job Search

The teaching of job search skills is perhaps the most neglected aspect of preparing people for successful working careers. The problem is that most employers recruit and most job seekers search in very informal but personal ways which tend to exclude "outsiders." Employers want to reduce the risks entailed in taking on a new employee. They want people who are as familiar as possible. At the same time, work groups who have good jobs try to protect them from competition by various forms of labor market segmentation—licensure, requirements for memberships in various associations or unions, academic degrees, merit systems, and so forth. These protect incumbents but at the expense of those who cannot find their way into the employment system. Anyone who would assist in the placement process needs to understand and be able to intervene effectively in this process.

Almost any employer needing to fill a job will first look internally to see if there are those who could be effectively promoted or transferred to fill the spot. If not, the employer will turn next to one of two groups: (a) friends and relatives of the employer or of current employees, or (b) those whose applications are on file. The first will be chosen because they have familiar attributes and the second because they have shown extra initiative. Then there will be a range of jobs for which access is closed to the general applicant by the segmentation devices identified above. Only when all of these sources are exhausted does the employer ordinarily announce to the general public the availability of a job opening. This is normally done by listing the job in the newspaper want ads, at the public employment service, or with a private fee-charging employment agency. But these jobs have already been thoroughly screened by the priority applicants and only the hardest to fill jobs as well as the hardest to place workers are left.

Anyone who would be helpful in the placement process should assist the job seeker to find access at the earliest possible stages of the job search/recruitment process, before the more attractive jobs have been filled.

The Student Cannot Clear Entry Hurdles

This problem can arise either because the student lacks job skills or because entry requirements go beyond what is required to do the job. In the former case, the student has simply been inadequately trained and should be returned to the vocational program to gain the competencies he or she lacks. The latter case poses one of the most frustrating barriers to handicapped job seekers—it is sometimes called the "Greek God Problem" because selection standards are often designed to pick out the brightest and most physically fit whether or not these characteristics are required on the job. Some examples: (1) pre-employment medical examinations weed out those with impaired vision or hearing whether or not visual or hearing impairments stand in the way of doing the job, (2) a test given to all prospective employees requires the test taker to read questions and to indicate answers by filling in small circles even in cases where reading and fine motor coordination are not required on the job. The situation is analogous to that which you would have faced if someone had scratched a line on the wall three inches higher than you can jump and demanded that you leap up and touch it before you were hired for your present job, assuming, of course, that great jumping ability is not needed to get your job done.

A closely related problem arises because many handicapped students lack job-seeking skills. They may not know how to seek out openings, how to write letters of inquiry, or how to present themselves at interviews. This can be overcome by the specific teaching of such skills, and courses in job seeking can be open to nonhandicapped students as well. You should not assume, of course, that handicapped students will all lack such skills or that all nonhandicapped students will possess them. Rather, handicapped students are, as a rule, less likely to have had experience seeking out jobs and you should, therefore, take care that they have a chance to gain job-seeking skills.

Employers Fear Increased Employee-Related Expenses

Fears include: increased insurance rate, more on-the-job accidents, greater absenteeism, or some other employee problems. Generally speaking, these fears are unfounded. Handicapped people typically turn out to be safe, reliable employees. Often, they are superior to the nonhandicapped. Naturally, there will be exceptions, but the employer has no cause for worry beyond that associated with any new hire and probably less. You should be able to supply data to substantiate that the employer is taking no unusual risk as regards such expenses. Such data could apply to the handicapped in general and to the job candidate of interest in particular.

Employers Do Not See How the Handicapped Person Can Get the Job Done, Or They Fear that Expensive Accommodations Will Be Necessary

These are legitimate concerns. They are very similar to those you will have already faced in training the student. With special tools or properly laid out work stations, handicapped students can accomplish many tasks that may, on the face of it, seem impossible, or at least improbable. You will be in a good position to show potential employers how handicapped students can accomplish various job tasks and to arrange opportunities for employers to observe handicapped students perform in the classroom.

In addition, you should be able to help employers determine what modifications they will have to make in their buildings and the most economical ways for carrying out the modifications. In many communities, there are resources, such as rehabilitation agencies, upon which the employer can draw for technical or financial assistance in assimilating the handicapped worker; you should become familiar with such resources and put the employer in touch with potentially helpful individuals or agencies.

Employers Fear that Other Workers Will Not Be Able to Work Well With the Handicapped

Although often unfounded, this fear will sometimes be correct, at least at first. There are at least two aspects of this problem: (a) in an attitudinal sense, some employees may feel that it reflects poorly upon themselves if a handicapped person can do the same job that they do or for some other reason they dislike having handicapped co workers; and (b) in an informational sense, co workers may not know how to communicate with a deaf, blind, or retarded person. The co worker may not know how to help a blind person become familiar with his or her surroundings or when a blind person should be offered help or when such help is unnecessary. They may not know when an orthopedically handicapped person truly needs assistance in handling objects or in getting about or when such help is intrusive and annoying. You can help overcome such problems by providing workshops for co workers or by arranging for someone to be present for the initial employment period to smooth the transition to work.

FINDING JOBS FOR HANDICAPPED GRADUATES

The preceding section described some problems that you may encounter in placing handicapped students. The balance of the chapter discusses steps you can take to avoid, minimize, or overcome such problems.

The Placement Team

The following types of people can make valuable contributions to the placement effort. Possible roles for each are suggested below. Exactly what a given individual will do is, of course, a function of the person and the community in which placement is to take place.

1. *Vocational school staff familiar with the student to be placed.* These staff, generally teachers, aides, and counselors will know the capabilities and limitations of the student and will be well situated to help determine if employer needs and student capabilities are compatible. This is a role that such staff can play in the placement of any student, but it is particularly important in placing the handicapped student; they will be able to answer technical questions about student skills, lessen fears about the ability of the student to get on with nonhandicapped coworkers, and give practical advice based on their experience about physical accommodations, communication, or other matters that may seem to present problems.

2. *Vocational school placement staff.* Placement staff, of course, are aware of openings in various occupations and may also know which employers are most willing to hire handicapped students and which plants or offices present the fewest physical barriers to the handicapped employee. As the primary contact between the employer and the school, they will have the bulk of the responsibility for alerting employers to the qualifications of handicapped students, arranging employer meetings with the student or his/her teachers and otherwise take steps to overcome reluctance that employers might feel about hiring the handicapped. Placement staff also serve as a valuable interface between employers and agencies or interest groups who provide special services to achieve physical accommodations or to smooth the transition of the handicapped employee to work. In some cases, school placement staff may provide such

services directly. Follow-up and trouble shooting to assure that the graduate and employer are both satisfied also usually falls within the domain of the placement staff.

3. *Employers and labor organizations.* Employers and labor organizations are usually represented on advisory committees, and many vocational programs maintain extensive contacts with them through work/study programs, on-the-job training programs and coordination of training efforts with apprenticeship committee requirements. If involved early, employers and labor can be very effective in removing barriers to handicapped job applicants: they can examine entry requirements for unintentional discrimination against the handicapped; they can help to include handicapped students in work/study programs; they can employ or accept handicapped graduates; and they can encourage others to do so too. Perhaps most importantly, early involvement will demonstrate to employers and labor that handicapped people *can* get the job done and that frequently without great cost or inconvenience. Thus, many concerns related to job performance can be eliminated or greatly reduced as employers and unions observe successful performance in the vocational program.

4. *The handicapped student.* A placement is more likely to be successful if it is in accord with the student's interests and aspirations. Therefore, the handicapped student should be as involved in working with placement personnel as would any student. In addition, the handicapped student, by demonstrating his or her expertise to visiting employers or at the employer's place of business can help to overcome many of the concerns that an employer might feel.

5. *Rehabilitation agencies, school special education departments, advocacy groups, and other organizations with a special concern for the handicapped.* Such groups include publicly financed rehabilitation services and local chapters or affiliates of such organizations as the American Foundation for the Blind, the American Occupational Therapy Association, the National Association for Retarded Citizens, the Council for Exceptional Children, the National Easter Seal Society, and the Council on Education of the Deaf. Such

groups can often provide suggestions about integrating handicapped people in the work setting, and some of them may provide direct services in job placement. Identifying agencies and the services they provide is a task that must be undertaken locally. The last section of this chapter gives suggestions for locating groups and agencies that may be helpful in placing handicapped students.

The Basic Steps

Every occupation functions in a labor market of differing characteristics. Analyze those in which you hope to place the handicapped student. Is there strong demand for people in the occupation so that the employer will be seeking new employees? Is there slack demand of numerous capable and nonhandicapped people available? What are the normal hiring patterns? Is there a union or other employee organization which has control or influence in the hiring process? Are licenses or academic credentials required? What kinds of examinations are required? What recruitment procedures do the employers use? What have proven to be the most effective job search techniques for that occupation? Minimize your students' frustrations by guiding them along the most promising path.

Once you have identified promising job opportunities, the five steps outlined below will help you to achieve successful placements. The steps are important in the placement of any student but are particularly crucial in placing the handicapped. The steps clearly overlap and many of the activities that you undertake in accomplishing one step will go a long way toward achieving others. The rest of the chapter provides practical suggestions and examples for each step.

1. *Gear training programs for placement.* Your concern for placement properly begins when the student is accepted into the program. This concern may lead you to include instruction in job-seeking skills, use of public transportation, and interpersonal skills needed on the job as well as instruction in skills and knowledge needed to perform job

tasks. You may find it best to work out a cooperative agreement with special education or general education staff for teaching skills that are not usually part of the vocational curriculum. Whatever the details of such arrangements, the important point is that students should emerge with competencies adequate for them to succeed in job hunting and on the job.

2. *Make effective employer contacts.* When handicapped students enroll in your program, you should begin to alert employers to their upcoming availability and to convince them of the practicality of employing handicapped people. This can take the form of newsletters, talks before business groups, tours of the school to see handicapped students at work, inclusion of handicapped students in work/study programs, or some other methods. The goal is to get employers thinking in terms of hiring handicapped graduates so that the idea will be firmly planted well before the actual interviewing and hiring process begins for a particular job candidate.

3. *Deal with employer concerns.* The employer wants an effective employee whom it is profitable to have on the payroll. When you present a candidate for employment, you must be able to deal effectively with concerns raised by the employer that relate to the desirability of having this particular handicapped person on the payroll. Very likely, the employer will have many of the fears discussed earlier in this chapter. You should be able to answer questions specifically related to possible increases in employee-related expenses, to demonstrate—or arrange to have the handicapped student demonstrate—how the candidate can perform difficult-appearing tasks, and to outline steps to take to assure the smooth transition to work. Specific information showing how a concern can be overcome or why the employer does not need to be concerned over a particular issue is crucial to success in this step.

4. *Smooth the transition to work.* In this step you will help the employer solve whatever problems arise as the handicapped student enters the work force. This may include, among other things, assistance in equipment or

facilities modification, communication training sessions for supervisors and coworkers, or arranging for someone from the school to be present for a period of time to help the graduate learn the job. You may either perform these services directly or put the employer in contact with an agency or individual in the community who can perform them, depending on the strategy that promises to be most effective in a particular set of circumstances.

5. *Conduct placement follow-ups.* Inevitably some placements will not go smoothly. Generally speaking, you can overcome placement difficulties if you catch the problem in time and work with the employer and your former student to eliminate the source of the trouble. This will not only give the placement a greater chance of succeeding, but it will also enhance your program's reputation in the business community, as other prospective employers will know that they can expect help if a placement begins to go sour. Satisfaction with your services will make it easier to place handicapped students in the future.

GEARING TRAINING PROGRAMS
FOR PLACEMENT

Concern for placement should begin when the student first considers enrolling. At that time the counselor works with the student, the student's parents, and other vocational staff to select a training program. The primary goal in program planning is the same for both the handicapped and the nonhandicapped—to map out a course of study consistent with the student's interests and abilities that will prepare the student for success in an entry-level job.

Preparing handicapped students sometimes requires special steps in two areas: (1) teaching specific job skills and (2) teaching ancillary skills needed to secure and hold a job. The teaching of specific job skills was discussed in detail in previous chapters. Therefore, we will now concentrate on skills of the latter type.

Often, handicapped people fail to obtain or hold jobs not because they lack the required *job* skills, but because they are ineffective job seekers, do not know how to conduct themselves on the job, or fail in some other way to do the things expected of work force members. If your program graduates fall short in these areas, then your skill training efforts, no matter how excellent, will have been for naught.

We will discuss two particularly important skills: job seeking and appropriate on-the-job behavior. As these are skill areas in which the necessary depth of treatment may be well beyond that appropriate in a vocational program, they provide excellent opportunities for coordinated efforts between vocational educators and special and general educators. As with all skill training, instruction must be based on individual student needs. Whether, how much, and what kind of training is needed will vary substantially from student to student. Many times handicapped students will outshine nonhandicapped peers.

Job-Seeking Skills

Does the student know how to locate job openings; how to complete an application; how to prepare a resume; and how to behave during an interview? Placement staff of the Nassau County (New York) BOCES whose mainstreaming program was discussed in the "Enhancing Staff Skills" chapter recommend the following as a minimum in each area:

- How and where to look for work. This involves the common and routine activities, such as reading the want ads, registering with public and private employment agencies, and applying to as many employers as possible. But this is only a beginning. The chance of locating a job is enhanced considerably through use of friends, relatives, neighbors, and acquaintances who often have specific, inside information which is so essential in job finding.

- How to complete an application blank and/or resume. Since it is standard practice for employers to screen applicants by requiring them to complete an application blank or submit a resume, it is imperative that applicants learn to do this accurately and effectively. Much of the information required on an application form and resume is fairly standard.

- How to act effectively in an interview. The employment interview is usually the final, and often the most important, part of the application process. Applicants must be totally prepared for this step or all their other job search efforts, no matter how intense, could prove futile.

- The job applicant should know what the company does, the kind of jobs they have, and what kind of people they hire.

- The job applicant should be neat and clean and wear clothes appropriate to the type of work being sought. The applicant should be enthusiastic about the company and be specific about his skills in relation to the job. In explaining skills and abilities, the applicant should emphasize strengths and assets in a positive manner.

- The applicant should present as much positive information as possible during the initial portion of the interview. Hiring decisions are often made during the first few minutes of the interview. Information which might be considered unfavorable should be held to a minimum and be supplemented with a positive statement about abilities and interests.

- The applicant's answers to questions about disability, job history, institutionalization, etc. should be brief and stated in a way that relieves the employer's concern. When problem areas arise in the interview, the applicant should present all the information to the interviewer at once and in a positive way. This leads to a better impression than the situation where the interviewer has to ferret out negative information on a piecemeal basis.

In addition, the applicant should know what documents to bring to the interview. This may include a birth certificate, social security card, driver's license, transcript, and sample products. The placement counselor, when and where necessary, should make an introductory call or visit to the prospective employer. Also, when and where necessary, the placement counselor should accompany the special needs student to the interview.

Helping Students Gain the Needed Skills

Specific instruction in perusing want ads, completing job applications, and preparing resumes provide excellent vehicles for gaining academic skills, particularly for the mentally retarded. These undertakings require reading, decision making (for example, as to whether or not a question is applicable or whether a job is appropriate), following instructions, and asking questions when a decision is too difficult to make or written material is hard to understand. You can suggest these activities to academic or special education teachers as practical exercises that are likely to interest the student.

Other handicapped students are typically less experienced in job seeking than their nonhandicapped peers as the former are less likely to have sought parttime or summer jobs. Many formats are suitable to help students gain these skills, including mini-courses, workshops, individual sessions with vocational counselors or rehabilitation personnel, or the inclusion of a section on job seeking in the regular curriculum. The choice of which to use should depend on the needs and capabilities of the students. The last would be particularly useful as nonhandicapped students would also benefit and the handicapped would not be singled out.

Interview practice is most effective if conducted as a series of role-playing sessions. At first someone whom the handicapped person knows can play the role of the interviewer, but the goal should be an off-campus session in which the student is interviewed by a stranger. (If this is not possible, the interview can be conducted by a staff member whom the student does not know in a part of the campus that the student does not frequent. Better still would be inviting employers to conduct practice interviews on campus. This not only gives students realistic practice, but allows employers to meet students whom they might hire.) The goal is to make the practice sessions approximate an actual interview as closely as possible. In addition, students should assume increasing responsibility for collecting information prior to the interview, deciding how to dress, and determining what to take to the interview. The number of sessions will vary considerably as a function of student experience, the handicapping condition of the student, and the complexity of preparation required before the interview.

Appropriate On-the-Job Behavior

Does the student have appropriate work habits and social skills? All jobs require appropriate behavior in at least some of the following areas: interaction with supervisors, coworkers, subordinates, and customers; dependability; maintenance of suitable standards in appearance and grooming; and the ability to interact pleasantly and courteously with other workers in social situations. The graduate who enjoys these skills is in a far better position to hold a job and to advance than is one who does not. Some commonly needed skills in each area are shown in Figure 7-1, which can double as a checklist for use in evaluating students at entry into the program and again before placement. Vocational courses and work/study programs typically teach appropriate on-the-job behavior as part of the regular curriculum, and instruction that suffices for nonhandicapped students will frequently be adequate to instruct the handicapped as well. Still, handicapped students will often have had less opportunity for gaining first-hand experience in working and socializing with others than will their nonhandicapped peers and may, therefore, lag behind the typical nonhandicapped student. Such deficits can be overcome through appropriately structured learning experiences.

Helping students acquire appropriate on-the-job behavior

The key factor is to provide realistic settings in which students can learn what is expected of them and practice

	Student Status				Needed for Job Entry?			Needed for Advancement		
	Excellent	Satisfactory	Poor	No Chance to Observe	Greatly	Moderately	Slightly	Greatly	Moderately	Slightly

I. Work Habits

  A. Relationship to Supervisor

- Follow instructions
- Accept correction gracefully
- Alter behavior in accord with correction
- Maintain appropriate balance between asking for help and working independently
- Suggest ideas or procedures to supervisor

  B. Relationship to Subordinates

- Give clear instructions
- Coordinates activities of others
- Correct the work of others tactfully
- Maintain appropriate balance between letting others work out problems and offering help
- Be open to suggestions from subordinates

  C. Participation in Group Efforts

- Participate in group decision making
- Advocate a point of view appropriately and effectively
- Adjust pace for smooth group functioning
- Switch tasks to pick up slack
- Ask for help only when appropriate-- avoid overdependence
- Offer help only when appropriate-- avoid intrusiveness
- Avoid unnecessary chatter or other distracting behaviors

  D. Relationship to Customers

- Put customers at ease regarding handicap
- Overcome communication problems
- Determine customer needs and respond appropriately
- Behave courteously
- Refrain from unnecessary touching, irrelevant chatter, and other annoying behaviors

  E. Dependability

- Punctuality
- Sign tools in and out
- Maintain equipment and work area
- Complete tasks on schedule
- Maintain consistent quality

II. Social Skills

  A. Appearance/Grooming

- Maintain suitable level of hygiene
- Dress appropriately for work
- Dress appropriately for social functions

  B. Conviviality/Courtesy

- Initiate discussions on suitable topics
- Respond appropriately to others
- Keep on topic
- Speak at appropriate volume
- Refrain from interrupting
- Express opinions in an agreeable way
- Maintain eye contact as appropriate
- Wait turn
- Request desired items
- Use "please," "thank you," etc. as appropriate

FIGURE 7-1. On-the-Job Behavior

behaving accordingly. The following example shows how one teacher implements his approach.

Example: The El Paso [Texas] Vocational Educable Handicapped (VEH) Program.* Owen Hill instructs General Mechanical Repair courses that include cerebral palsied, speech impaired, and mentally retarded students, as well as students with poor motor coordination resulting from disabilities other than cerebral palsy. Students learn small engine repair, small electrical appliance repair, and evaporative cooler repair. The procedures he uses can also be applied in the mainstream course.

In designing his course, Hill's first objective was ". . . to assist the student in developing a work pattern that will carry over into his work as a wage earner and also in his home life by duplicating working conditions and methods in the shop that he will meet in industrial employment and also at home." Included among the specific objectives, in addition to those directly related to technical expertise, are the following:

- To instill in the student the importance of being a capable employee and having a good work record.

- To assist the student in developing a work pattern that will carry over in his work as a wage earner and also in his home life.

- To impress on the student the importance of punctuality, perseverance, reliability, and honesty both on the job and in their association with others.

- To show the student the importance of socialization by allowing him to work with students who have different backgrounds, variable emotional problems, and who come from other ethnic groups.

- To develop good habits of personal grooming and health.

---

*A cooperative undertaking of the Texas Education Agency, the State Vocational Rehabilitation Commission and the El Paso Public Schools, Technical Education Center.

Thus, the objectives of this program focus deliberately upon work habits and social skills needed for job success.

How does Hill help students reach these objectives? "In order to prepare the VEH student for industrial employment," he says, "you must duplicate shop conditions as near as possible to those found in industry and develop curriculum to teach procedures that may be used in the industrial shop." At the same time, he suggests that instructors develop curricula and instructional techniques in a way that leads each student to successful task completion in order to build feelings of competence and confidence needed for job success. Among the steps taken by Hill to put these principles into practice are the following:

- Work in cooperation with an advisory committee to make sure that the program keeps up with changes in the job market and to overcome instructional problems.

- Pair fast and slow learners. This will help the slower learners to achieve success and will provide practice in working cooperatively with people of differing abilities.

- Have students make shop rules and put them into effect. This helps students to learn what makes for a good work pattern and gives them practice in seeing to it that good habits are maintained.

- Give students the opportunity to exercise responsibility. Students can serve as shop supervisors, safety officers, fire marshals, tool keepers, and so on.

- Set a good model for supervision. Be fair. Treat all students equally. Organize tasks to take advantage of student background, interest, and experience. Acknowledge your own fallibility and correct yourself if you make a mistake.

- Arrange field trips to local businesses. Since a classroom can rarely duplicate exactly a place of employment, trips to actual worksites will help students gain a feel for the realities of the working world.

These features of good instruction are already present in many mainstream vocational programs. They are particularly important for handicapped students who may have had less opportunity than others to experience success, develop confidence, take responsibility, engage in group efforts with people whose abilities and limitations differ from their own, and who may be less well informed about what is expected on the job.

A vocational teacher can undertake the steps described above, or similar steps, in the mainstream program. Sometimes the student will lack skills important for getting along on the job, but which the vocational teacher cannot reasonably be expected to teach. For example, a blind student who must meet the public may never before have had to select clothes with well coordinated patterns and colors. Or, a retarded student may never have learned to shave properly by himself. In such cases, cooperative arrangements with special educators, rehabilitation professionals, counselors, or other professionals can often supply the necessary training. If best use is to be made of outside professionals, the vocational teacher should work closely with them to determine which skills are the most important for each student in terms of job placement and advancement.

Example: Cooperative Arrangements at the Blue Hills Regional Technical School, Canton, Massachusetts. Blue Hills is one of 25 regional technical schools in Massachusetts. It serves 1,130 students in the high school program with additional students in post-secondary and evening courses. Learning disabled, behaviorally disordered, mentally retarded, speech impaired, deaf, and orthopedically handicapped students make up approximately 10% of the student body at Blue Hills. Dr. Ronald Linari, Administrator of Special Services, stresses that including special needs students in vocational/technical education can only be successful if special and vocational educators work together to set mutually agreeable goals for special needs students through the development of individual educational plans. This cooperation then continues in service and vocational training provisions.

Deaf students, for example, are given specific instruction in academic areas by resource teachers. A counselor with sign language skills provides direct personal/social and school adjustment services, and a speech therapist is available for those who need that specialist's services. Additionally, training in nontechnical skills that may be needed on the job is provided by appropriate specialists, allowing vocational teachers to concentrate on those skills they are best able to teach.

MAKING EFFECTIVE EMPLOYER CONTACTS

Employer contacts should begin well before you present a particular handicapped student as a job candidate. The purpose of these contacts is to begin to overcome the four main placement problems discussed earlier. That is, you will want to show employers that the handicapped can be capable employees and that your program trains handicapped students in the skills needed for job success.

This step and those that follow to a large extent emphasize the *education of the employer*. This is as it should be—a successful placement often depends as much upon the employer and nonhandicapped coworkers as upon the handicapped worker. Vocational educators need to acquire special skills to be successful with the handicapped; there is no reason to suppose that employers and coworkers do not need to gain them too.

Specific Goals of Employer Contacts

Your main goal at this stage is not to get the employer to hire any particular individual. Rather, your purpose is to prime the employer to do so when the times comes. Specifically, you should seek to:

- Demonstrate to the employer that many of the jobs in his or her plant or office can be performed by handicapped persons.

- Suggest that the employer give handicapped workers a chance to prove themselves by one of several procedures, such as work/study programs, which imply no long-term commitment.

- Inform the employer of special programs or other resources that enhance the practicality of hiring handicapped workers.

- Make the employer sensitive to entry hurdles that stand in the way of the handicapped, and offer to help the employer develop screening procedures more closely tied to actual job requirements.

- Let the employer know about services that you can provide to smooth the transition to work, for example, by giving supervisors instruction in communicating with hearing impaired people.

Of course, if you have a qualified candidate available, you should discuss the possibility of a placement with any employers showing an interest at this stage.

Methods for Making Employer Contacts

Three main methods are available: one-to-one personal contacts; personal contacts with groups of employers; and mail or media contacts. Each has its place, although the first is ultimately the most important. Your program probably uses some or all of these approaches already in placing nonhandicapped students, and placement activities for the handicapped can build upon established relationships with employers.

One-to-one employer contacts

Although the details vary, the following steps are used by most successful placement personnel. They should, of course, be tailored for the particular employer whom you are contacting.

Step 1: Plan employer contacts carefully. Become familiar with the products or services in which the firm deals and the skills needed to produce and deliver these goods and services—this will show the employer that you are well informed and will allow you to zero in on those jobs for which students are trained by the programs you represent. Identify other employers in similar businesses who have handicapped employees. This will allow you to refer employers for appraisal of the handicapped worker. Find out who in the company has the power to influence hiring decisions and attempt to make contact with that person. This will allow you to focus your efforts where they will do the most good; be sure to include unions or other employee groups that can influence hiring decisions. Find out about entrance requirements and hiring practices. This will allow you to determine if any entry hurdles exist that pose particular difficulties for the handicapped. Try to anticipate employer concerns—you can handle such questions more effectively if you are ready for them.

Step 2: Conduct an effective employer interview. Approach things from the employer's point of view—the employer wants a dependable employee who can help the organization operate effectively; make sure your presentation is cast in those terms. Speak the employer's language—do not use educational or psychological jargon. Treat employer concerns about the feasibility of employing the handicapped as serious matters. Be businesslike and practical in describing how such concerns can be overcome. This will show the employer that you take his or her business seriously and can be relied upon to suggest realistic solutions to genuine problems. Provide the employer with options for finding out more about how the handicapped would fit into the company or how they would perform. Options might include work/study placements, community work stations (as described in the section, Smoothing the Transition to Work, below), and job analyses that you would conduct. This allows the employer to gain experience with handicapped workers without making a firm commitment to hire. Discuss entry requirements in an effort to identify further those that present a barrier to the handicapped. Help the employer analyze the realism and necessity of the requirements imposed. Explain how entry requirements not related to job performance can stand in the way of the handicapped. Show how reworking requirements in terms of skills actually required on the job will be to the employer's advantage in making wise hiring decisions, whether or not the job candidate is handicapped. Tell the employer about special programs or services available to help smooth the transition to work; this may include special services you can provide, reimbursement for the first few weeks' wages from an advocacy group, or some other benefit. Make arrangements for some further step, such as job analysis or interviews with work/study candidates. This will keep the contact warm by giving you a legitimate reason for follow-up contacts. Leave something with the employer, such as a brochure describing the program and successful handicapped graduates; at the least, leave your card.

Step 3: Make use of the interview results. Follow up with a thank you letter or phone call, whether the interview ended on a promising note or not. The employer will appreciate your courtesy and may call if possibilities arise for including the handicapped. Schedule the next step; this may include job analyses, detailed reviews of entry requirements relative to actual job demands, tours of the vocational school to see handicapped students at work, arrangements for work/study placements, or some other follow-up that seems appropriate. Think back over the interview to determine which approaches worked best and which worked least well. Discuss these approaches with others so that you can improve them.

Contacts with groups of employers

Employers have the same questions and concerns whether you encounter them in one-to-one or group situations. Therefore, the steps for making group contacts closely parallel those for making one-to-one contacts. As with one-to-one contacts, your presentation should be tailored to the audience.

Step 1: Plan your presentation carefully. Know what kinds of jobs employers present have available—this will help you to focus on programs at your school that prepare students in areas of interest to those present. If any of the employers present have handicapped workers on their payrolls, be sure to highlight this fact. This will allow others to turn to people they know for candid opinions about hiring the handicapped.

Use information gained in previous one-to-one contacts to identify probable questions, objections, or doubts in the minds of employers. This will help you prepare a presentation that shows employers that you are sensitive to their concerns. Identify a few common job entry hurdles that present difficulty for the handicapped, but which are not related to job performance. This will allow you to show how selection procedures can be improved.

Step 2: Make an effective presentation. Pick out four or five key points most appropriate for your audience—do not try to cover every aspect of hiring the handicapped. Approach each point from the employer's point of view and use the employer's language. Provide practical examples for each point you make; use examples in your community if at all possible. This will show employers that you are speaking in realistic terms about things that can be accomplished locally. Give the audience something to look at; this could be slides, overheads, or brochures. A picture showing something being done is more impressive than all the talk in the world about how it could be done. Prime employers for the next step by giving them literature, programs, and services that can benefit them and by asking them to complete a checklist of areas in which they anticipate openings, whether or not they would be willing to have handicapped students participate in work/study programs, major questions left unanswered by your presentation, and other pertinent information. This will help you to decide where to place your major follow-up efforts, and the best approach for each follow-up.

Step 3: Make use of the presentation results. Schedule the next step with those employers who express a willingness to consider handicapped students; this may be a personal interview or one of the follow-up steps discussed above. Send a thank you to the group and to the organizer. Provide answers to questions not addressed in your presentation. This will show the employers who asked them that you are serious in responding to their concerns.

Mail and media contacts

Mail contacts are most effective when they focus

explicitly on one or two main points that can be of immediate use to the employer. For example, Figure 7-2 shows sample listings from "JOB READY HANDICAPPED" put out jointly by several Santa Clara, California agencies serving the handicapped. Note how these listings concisely describe the capabilities and experience of the individual job candidate, suggesting to the employer the potential value of the person as an employee. There is no mention of the handicapping conditions of the individuals in question and there is no appeal to charity or benevolence. The point of the listings is that well-prepared candidates are available for jobs that the employer may need done.

Another example is the brochure shown in Figure 7-3 which describes the On-the-Job Training Project of the National Association for Retarded Citizens. In introducing the program, this brochure emphasizes the value to the employer of hiring the retarded in general, and the benefits of participating in this program in particular. Again, the appeal is not to largess, but to the employer's need for reliable, effective employees.

Media contacts should be catchy and interesting and should be designed to get across one or two main points. The President's Committee on Employment of the Handicapped has prepared a booklet, "Publicity Hints," to show how to prepare newspaper articles attractive to editors. The same features make them interesting to readers. Try to incorporate these features in your news releases:

- *Photographs that tell the story.* Next to a live demonstration nothing is so convincing that a person can do something as a picture of the person doing it.

- *Stories about well known people or organizations.* The famous are naturally interesting. A recent article "Blind Financier-Trader Manages Multimillions for General Motors" which appeared in many papers around the country was sure to catch attention. Not only is GM always news, but such a corporation is not about to risk its "multimillions" with anyone but the best person available. Your stories can feature locally well known firms or people to equally good effect.

THE USEABLE SKILLS IDENTIFIED IN THE MINI-RESUMES BELOW ARE AVAILABLE TO YOU NOW. IN ADDITION TO HAVING SKILLS, THE JOB-READINESS OF EACH PERSON ON THE LIST IS ATTESTED TO BY THE INDIVIDUAL IDENTIFIED BY NAME AT THE END OF EACH RESUME. PLEASE CALL THESE INDIVIDUALS. THEY REPRESENT THE MAJOR SANTA CLARA COUNTY AGENCIES SERVING THE HANDICAPPED. THEY WILL PROVIDE YOU WITH INFORMATION ABOUT THE PERSONS LISTED AND ABOUT THE SERVICES THEY ARE PREPARED TO RENDER YOU AND THESE JOB SEEKERS BEFORE AND AFTER EMPLOYMENT. DON'T LET THE WORD "HANDICAPPED" DETER YOU. EXAMINE THE LIST TODAY. CALL TODAY.

PROFESSIONAL

J.C. - 0344 Administrative Assistant. B.S. degree, June 1975. Interest in purchasing, sales and personnel. Four years experience in marketing, seven years in electronics in equipment repair supervision and financial planning.
Contact:

R.W.B. - 0157 Senior Electronics Engineer. Twenty-three years experience; also Design Specialist, Instrument Research Engineer and Project Manager.
Contact:

SALES/CLERICAL

J.C. - 228: 1976. Int. ability a. Types 40 WPM.
Contact:

L.R.L. - 0814 Key Punch Operator. Approximately 9 months experience and training (3 months course). 10,000 plus strokes. Knows verifying.
Contact:

J.P. - 6988 General Office. Completed Business and Office Occupations course; 10 key by touch, types 55 WPM and 6 years broad clerical experience.
Contact:

INDUSTRIAL

J.R. - 546C. ting machin. operation.
Contact:

D.F. - 1436 Computer Programmer. Trained in computer programming and operation. Certification from Condie College, 1976.
Contact:

J.L.H. - 6735 Box Stapler. Trained and experienced working on stapler machine assembling.
Contact:

J.M. - 7483 Assembler. Trained in mechanical assembly, small parts assembly, collating, packaging, wiring; uses small hand tools.
Contact:

S.L. - 7501 Medical Lab Assistant. Recent training Bryman School, special interest in lab routines, five years experience in medical lab.
Contact:

FIGURE 7-2. "Job-Ready Handicapped" shows what people can do. Note that handicapping conditions are nowhere listed.

Strong points that most mentally retarded men and women show on the job

- They want to make good. They will work particularly hard to make good.

- They want to stay on the job. They're not anxious to job-hop. They're happy to learn the job and remain with it.

- Their attendance record is usually better than average.

- They are willing workers and will stay at routine tasks.

- Mentally retarded people are not mentally ill or mentally deranged. They are just slower intellectually.

- The mentally retarded worker constitutes a relatively untapped manpower resource. It is estimated that there are approximately 3 million mentally retarded persons of working age who are capable of full-time employment in the United States today.

- Hiring mentally retarded people not only benefits an employer but also enhances the retarded person's sense of dignity and personal worth and makes him a productive, tax paying member of society.

The plan for action

The On-The-Job Training Project, funded by the U.S. Department of Labor and administered by the National Association for Retarded Citizens (NARC), encourages business to provide job opportunities for mentally retarded persons. NARC assists a business in pointing out occupational areas where retarded workers can alleviate manpower shortages. In addition, NARC will reimburse an employer ½ of the entry wage for the first 4 critical weeks of employment and ¼ of the entry wage for the second 4 weeks of employment.

1 The NARC Project and an employer enter into an agreement whereby the employer agrees to hire a mentally retarded person at the same rate of pay he would hire a non-retarded employee. For providing a retarded person with an on-the-job training opportunity, the NARC Project agrees to reimburse the employer the specified portion of the training costs, as indicated.

2 All potential trainees are screened and certified to be work-ready prior to referral to the employer. Certification of being work-ready means the retarded individual can adequately perform in a normal work environment and has had some job training. The NARC Project works closely with the employer and the potential trainee in evaluating the requirements of the work situation and the trainee's needs and abilities.

3 The employer has absolute right of selection. Trainees selected are considered regular employees from the start. The employer also has absolute right to trainee termination.

4 AFL-CIO and other labor unions have indicated their interest in this program and have expressed their desire to assist in its implementation where possible.

66 *...employers still have trouble finding anyone who will design to take a position considered boring or menial.... Some restaurateurs are hiring the mentally retarded because they are the only people willing to try and even take some pride in mopping floors and washing dishes.* 99
TIME Magazine
"America the Inefficient"

66 *The AFL-CIO is committed to the principle that everyone should have full opportunity to achieve his maximum personal development and fulfillment. Unions participate in the establishment of training programs and other community service facilities to enable the worker who is mentally retarded to take his place as a wage earner and a positive factor in our economy and society.* 99
George Meany
President, AFL-CIO

66 *"We have found that hiring the mentally retarded can be sound personnel practice. Carefully selected and thoroughly trained, such workers have earned our respect by their performance–eager, loyal, dependable. We recommend their employment to all who are interested in reducing the steadily rising personnel turnover in that kind of work."* 99
Louis C. Lustenburger,
Past President,
W. T. Grant Company

FIGURE 7-3. On-the-job training program brochure.

- *Descriptions of unusual ways to get the job done.* Clever solutions and innovative approaches always command attention. Could a blind person be an audio engineer, a job that requires reading dials and gauges, and making proper settings? Yes. How? Most people will read a few paragraphs to find out. Highlight how your graduates can accomplish tasks that seem surprising at first glance.

- *Stories showing what a chance has meant to someone.* Stories showing how people blossom when given a break carry a lot of human interest; for example, in almost every community there are retarded people who have excelled and won high praise from previously skeptical supervisors. Prepare articles about some of your graduates who have proven their worth on the job. Use quotations from former students and their supervisors for added interest.

Special Topic: Job Analysis

The purpose of a job analysis is to find out what a worker must do on the job and to discover what is expected of the worker for job entry. Figure 7-4 shows a sample form for use in job analysis developed for work/study programs serving the educable mentally retarded, but with broader applicability. Notice that this is closely related to the "Job Demands and Physical Capacities Appraisal" form presented in Chapter 4. The main difference is that this form is designed for use in a particular workplace with its own unique demands whereas the earlier form was for use in generally identifying requirements for a given type of job. This is important because entry requirements will vary from employer to employer even though each is hiring an automobile mechanic, for example. Similarly, working conditions will vary as a function of the physical plant and other activities going on in the plant—some clerical personnel work in hot, noisy offices, others in quiet, air conditioned ones.

The form shown in Figure 7-4 is a prototype. You can adapt it to meet the needs of your program or specific

JOB ANALYSIS REPORT [a]

JOB REQUIREMENTS

PHYSICAL DEMANDS

A. How much strength is required?

	Hands	Arms	Legs	Back
Great	___	___	___	___
Some	___	___	___	___
Little	___	___	___	___
None	___	___	___	___

B. PHYSICAL ACTIVITIES

___ walking	___ sitting	___ working fast
___ running	___ standing	___ handling
___ jumping	___ kneeling	___ feeling
___ pulling	___ crawling	___ fingering
___ pushing	___ throwing	___ talking
___ turning	___ climbing	___ hearing
___ lifting	___ crouching	___ seeing color
___ carrying	___ balancing	___ perceiving depth
___ stooping		

C. WORKING CONDITIONS

Location: ___ inside ___ outside
Temperature: ___ hot ___ cold ___ humid ___ dry
Mobility: ___ cramped ___ moving objects ___ high places
Work with: ___ others ___ around others ___ alone
Hazards: ___ mechanical ___ wet ___ noisy ___ ventilation ___ exposure to burns ___ lighting ___ radiant energy

II. PERSONAL AND ACADEMIC INFORMATION

Handle money? ___ yes ___ no

Memory required? ___ much ___ little ___ none

Arithmetic required? ___ add ___ subtract ___ multiply ___ divide ___ fractions ___ measurement ___ sales slips ___ other

Reading required? ___ much ___ little ___ none ___ addresses ___ sales orders ___ patterns ___ directions ___ bulletins ___ letters

Writing required? ___ none ___ listing ___ sales orders ___ production records ___ information to be read by others

Employee meet the public? ___ no ___ seen by public ___ talks to public ___ works with public all the time

Kind of speaking required: ___ little ___ giving messages ___ asking for materials or tools ___ giving directions

JOB TITLE _____

LOCATION _____

Kind of job ___ clerical ___ service
___ sales ___ self-employed
___ agriculture
___ factory

Job level ___ skilled
___ semiskilled
___ unskilled

Experience ___ required
___ not required

PREEMPLOYMENT INFORMATION

Test given ___ employment test ___

Licenses required? ___ yes ___ no
Driver's license ___ other ___

Health certificate ___

Written application ___ yes ___ no

Belong to a union? ___ yes ___ no

How are employees found?
___ employment service ___ help-wanted ad ___ labor unions ___ people come in ___ referral by friends

How much education is required?
___ no formal education ___ little formal education ___ elementary school ___ some high school ___ high school diploma

How are employees paid? ___ by the hour ___ on the basis of piecework ___ weekly ___ monthly

How much on-the-job training is given? ___ less than 6 weeks ___ 6 weeks to 6 months ___ Can the school help in the training?

How much supervision is the employee given? ___ none ___ some ___ little ___ much

Adjustment to change required? ___ none ___ some ___ little ___ frequent

Pressure on the job? ___ none ___ some ___ little ___ great

---

[a] From *Work Study Handbook for Educable Mentally Retarded Minors Enrolled in High School Programs in California Public Schools* by L. Wayne Campbell, Medford Todd and Everett V. O'Rourke, 1971.

FIGURE 7-4

employers by adding or deleting sections, or by expanding the information collected. For example, you might wish to provide space to indicate whether each item under "B. Physical Activities" is required "frequently," "occasionally," "seldom," or "never." You may wish to know exactly how heavy a standard supply container is, or you may wish to include a brief prose description of what the person does in a way that shows exactly what it is the person has to see, feel, hear, comprehend, pick up, push, pull, lift, or whatever. The following description, for example, describes a street-washing job one of the authors used to hold:

> Read meter at beginning and ending of the day; record readings on form and compute amount of water used. Open fire hydrant using long-handled wrench; attach hose to hydrant and operate valve to fill truck. Select sprayers to be used in street-washing operations; activate sprayers and adjust pressure to assure that debris is washed to curb. Plan most efficient street sequence for washing assigned route.

Making job analyses

Analyze what actually goes on at the site. Sources of information include: observations of employees at work; discussions of job activities with workers and supervisors; reviews of published job entry standards; and interviews with personnel department members to determine the rigor with which entry standards are applied and how disabilities are taken into account in their application, if at all. Be sure to cover every point on your form to your own satisfaction, even if only to note that certain items are not relevant. Equally important, be alert to other features, such as architectural or equipment-related barriers that might present problems for some students.

Undertake job analyses as soon as possible after making initial employer contacts. This will get the employer actively involved in finding out where and how handicapped students can fit in and will show, in many cases, that only very minor modifications would need to be made in work stations, physical plant, or procedures. The latter will probably be a surprise to many employers, and will surely be a great relief, surprising or not. In cases where substantial procedural changes, special aids or architectural modifications would be needed, you can discuss with the employer how these things can be obtained or accomplished in a practical way. A thorough job analysis shows that you are serious about helping the employer find realistic solutions to problems that arise, not just landing a job for a handicapped student in your program.

DEALING WITH EMPLOYER CONCERNS

Facts to dispel misconceptions and practical solutions to legitimate concerns are the keys to success. These, coupled with a straightforward, honest, businesslike approach will allow you to overcome most employer concerns.

Major Employment Concerns

Employer concerns will arise in four main areas. Not surprisingly, these closely parallel the areas in which problems commonly arise in placing handicapped students.

- Employee related expenses will rise. Common fears are: very expensive equipment or facilities modifications will be needed for the orthopedically impaired and costly aids will be needed for the blind, the partially sighted, or the hearing impaired.

- Handicapped employees will not do a satisfactory job. Common fears are: speed will decrease, errors will increase, the efficiency of others will be impaired because the handicapped will have to ask for help too frequently, and the blind and orthopedically impaired will not be able to use equipment properly, or retarded will be unable to use good judgment or properly care for expensive tools and equipment.

- Handicapped employees will not be able to work well with others or will put excessive burdens on them. Common fears are: communication problems with the hearing or speech impaired will present extreme difficulties, the retarded will not understand simple corrections or changes in work activities, the blind will need someone to lead them around, customers and clients will be ill-at-ease around the handicapped for one reason or another, and handicapped employees will lack one or another social skill to get along with nonhandicapped coworkers.

Concern: Employee Related Expenses Will Rise and Other Hassles Will Increase

Such concerns are usually unfounded. Table 7-1 shows data provided by the President's Committee on Employment of the Handicapped. As shown here, handicapped workers are typically at least as safe and reliable as other employees. Similarly, handicapped workers are at least as stable on the job as the nonhandicapped. For example, the duPont study mentioned in Table 7-1 found that 93% of the handicapped workers were average or better in terms of job stability when rated against duPont workers as a whole (Wolfe, 1973-74). A survey of 100 large corporations by the U.S. Office of Vocational Rehabilitation found that 83% of the respondents had lower turnover rates for the handicapped than for the nonhandicapped, while only 1% reported higher turnover rates. In sum, handicapped workers are, if anything, less likely than others to lead to increased costs by arriving late, being absent, or quitting.

Perhaps the most common concern you will have to deal with is fear of rising insurance costs, a topic closely related to safety. Fears of increased group insurance rates are generally unfounded. Rates are almost always based on two factors: the type of business and past accident records of the company. Neither of these concerns employee handicaps. Thus, a new handicapped employee will cause rates to go up only if that employee has more accidents than the nonhandicapped, leading to increased expenses for the insurance. Since handicapped employees do not typically have more accidents, they will not cause rate increases. The

HOW HANDICAPPED WORKERS DO ON THE JOB[a]

Source	Job Performance	Attendance	Safety	Insurance Costs
Bendix Corporation Report on 6,500 impaired workers	Good	Good	Good to excellent	No special insurance problems
Bureau of Labor Statistics A survey comparing 11,000 impaired workers with 18,000 unimpaired workers	Slightly better than unimpaired	Fair Days absent rate: impaired 3.8 unimpaired 3.4	Better Major injury rate: impaired 8.9 unimpaired 9.5	Fear of higher costs largely unfounded
E. I. du Pont de Nemours & Co. A study of 1,000 handicapped workers	Average or better 81 percent of impaired rated average or better	Average or better 86 percent of impaired rated average or better	Better 98 percent of impaired rated average or better	No increase in compensation costs. No injuries reported.
National Industrial Conference Board A survey of 242 firms	Good	Good	Good	No increase in compensation costs.
A pilot study of employment practices A survey of 111 very large companies.	Good 93.5 percent of impaired rated average or better	Good 91.5 percent of impaired rated average or better	Average or better Accidents: 90.4 percent of impaired rated average or better Lost time: 86.2 percent rated average or better	
U. S. Chamber of Commerce. National Association of Manufacturers A study of 279 firms	Good	Better than unimpaired	Better work habits than unimpaired	Just under 90 percent of employers reported no effect on costs.

Source: President's Committee on Employment of the Handicapped

[a] From "Application for Employment: To American Industry from the Physically Handicapped" by The President's Committee on Employment of the Handicapped.

TABLE 7-1

employer can verify this method for computing rates by making a quick call to his carrier.

In addition, the employer may have questions about the effect of hiring handicapped people on workmen's compensation rates. The method for computing such rates varies from state to state and you should become familiar with locally applicable procedures. To take one example, California's procedures for determining premiums do not allow higher rates if handicapped people are employed, nor do New York's.

Moreover, "second-injury laws" have been enacted in almost every state to encourage the hiring of the handicapped by protecting the employer against exceptional expenses should the handicapped worker become injured on the job. To take California as an example again, Section 4750 of the Labor Code states:

> . . . an employee who is suffering from a previous permanent disability or physical impairment and sustains permanent injury thereafter shall not receive from the employer compensation for the later injury in excess of the compensation allowed for such injury when considered by itself and not in conjunction with or in relation to the previous disability or impairment.
> The employer shall not be liable for compensation to such an employee for the combined disability, but only for that portion due to later injury as though no prior disability or impairment had existed.

To see the full importance of this law, consider a deaf employee blinded on the job who argues that being blinded is a more serious injury when one is deaf than when one can hear and that compensation should, therefore, be greater than that normally given for blindness. Whatever the merit of this argument, the employer is absolved of any responsibility to compensate the employee beyond the level normally associated with being blinded. If additional benefits are justified, they are paid by the State of California at no further expense to the employer.

It is a good idea to become familiar with applicable laws and regulations in your state so that you can accurately advise employers of the effects, if any, on workmen's compensation of hiring the handicapped. You may also discover additional protections and safeguards for the employer.

Specific points related to individual students

Provide the employer with the attendance and safety record that the student has compiled in the vocational program. If the student has performed satisfactorily during training, there is every reason to suppose that job performance will be satisfactory, too. If the student has had any accidents, be sure to explain the circumstances, the severity, and subsequent steps taken to minimize the likelihood of a recurrence. Also, be sure to put any accidents in perspective—if practically all neophyte mechanics skin their knuckles a few times when the wrench slips off the nut, then it is no surprise if a deaf student suffers this mishap a time or two as well.

If attendance was spotty at first, perhaps because the student had initial trouble in adjusting to the mainstream classroom, say so, but indicate what steps were taken to overcome this, and indicate how the student has performed for the past three months, six months, and year. This will show if the student is adaptable to new situations and is currently performing as well as the nonhandicapped.

Whatever the specific concern of the employer, present accurate information about how well the student performs, how this performance compares to that of other students, and how much the student has improved. This information is very likely to be impressive to the employer. If the employer is still skeptical, particularly about safety, suggest a visit to the school to watch the student perform.

Concern: Accommodation Will Be Unreasonably Expensive or Complex

Accommodation is often much less difficult than people expect. This is shown in the experience of Sears, Roebuck & Co. Here are portions of a letter from Paul Scher, Sears' Rehabilitation Services Specialist to the National Center for a Barrier Free Environment:

In the process of carrying out a survey of handicapped people at Sears, we asked our units to indicate when unusual accommodations had to be made. Here are examples of accommodations:

Six cassette tape recorders for six blind maintenance agreement telephone salespeople, $300.

Lowering desk, widening door, installing grab bars in lavatory for two-dozen catalogue order-takers in wheelchairs, $800.

Lowering work tables and installing grab bars in lavatories for two-dozen service technicians in wheelchairs, $300 to $600 (estimates).

Rental of IBM Typewriter with shield for clerk with cerebral palsy, standard rental charge.

Telephones with amplifiers for hard-of-hearing employees, $18 per installation plus 65 cents a month for rental.

Optacon for blind rehabilitation specialist, including training in its use, $3,800.

We are contemplating the possibility of installing $12,000 worth of equipment in our computer department to allow six to eight blind programmers to function.

It is our position that professional handicapped applicants, especially those trained by departments of vocational rehabilitation, should bring their own special equipment on the job.

All new Sears units incorporate barrier-free features—virtually zero cost for handicapped employees.

In short, almost all accommodations for handicapped people require minimal expense, easily absorbed by a company of our size. It has been our experience that in most instances the employment of people with handicaps requires no accommodation and no unusual expense.

(Reprinted from REPORT, May/June 1976, by permission of the National Center for a Barrier-Free Environment.)

Similarly, the duPont survey found that minimal adjustments were required for most disabled employees. A recent study of over 30 corporate facilities found that the minimum modifications necessary to assure accessibility could be made for less than 1¢ per square foot (William Cochran Associates, 1977).

A related point emphasized by Mainstream, Inc., which you can impress on employers is that a building can be made accessible even if not all possible modifications have been made. You will be able to illustrate this from your own experience; for example, it is very unlikely that every desirable architectural feature discussed earlier in this book will have been incorporated in your vocational facility by the time you start training handicapped students. You may never incorporate many of them, yet serve a wide variety of handicapped students. The important thing is to help the employer determine the most economical way to make whatever alterations are needed to allow a handicapped person to get to the work area and get the job done.

Moreover, it is not always necessary to make elaborate modifications. For example, putting blocks under desks for those in wheelchairs or affixing braille labels to storage bins are easily accomplished tasks, and the effort is more than repaid when they lead to the hiring of a dependable employee. Your experience in serving handicapped students in the vocational program will be directly applicable in helping employers to determine the most economical modifications to make in equipment or in the workplace.

Specific points related to individual students

What exactly must I do to accommodate young Jones? That is the question the employer will ask and which you should be in a position to answer. Workplace or equipment adaptations that you have made for students in your programs will probably be very similar to those that will be needed on the job. Invite the employer and the person who will be the immediate supervisor of the student to visit the vocational facility to view these modifications. Then examine the work area at the future place of employment to determine how similar modifications can be accomplished there, if necessary. Also, check for any additional accommodations that must be made at the employer's site. For example, controls on equipment at the vocational center may have raised indicators so that settings could be determined by touch without modification, while those at the employer's site do not.

Although employers' worst fears about the expense of accommodation are often unfounded, there will be cases in which costly barrier removal or expensive aids may be needed to accommodate a given individual in the workplace. In such cases, provide the employer with the names of vendors and suppliers and explore possibilities for defraying expenses in whole or in part. Departments of Rehabilitation are often able to purchase aids for the handicapped for use on the job or to underwrite some portion of the costs. Some tax relief is available for employers who remove barriers under Section 2122 of the Tax Reform Act of 1976. Under the Act, up to $25,000 can be deducted per taxable year for modifications made to increase accessibility. State and local Department of Rehabilitation personnel with whom you have established effective contacts should be able to keep you apprised of the latest developments in these areas. They may also be able to work directly with you and the employer to develop a workable plan at the least cost to the employer.

Concern: Handicapped Employees Will Not Do A Satisfactory Job

Properly trained handicapped employees usually perform at least as well as their nonhandicapped colleagues. Table 7-1 shows uniformly favorable job performance ratings in six large-scale surveys. There are many success stories, but we will discuss only one in detail: PRIDE Electronics in San Diego, California. The following excerpts from the article, "Electronics Plant Offers New Job Opportunities," which appeared in the *San Diego Union* shows how this small company benefited from hiring the handicapped.

One word tells the story of a new and unusual electronics plant on Clairmont Mesa.

PRIDE is the work and the name of the electronics plant.

A group leader, Connie Walker, 20, married to a builder and wearing two hidden aids to her deafness, found no one to hire her previously except her parents. Now she mounts amplifiers so others with normal ears can hear better.

"The Deaf Supportive Services told me there was an electronics job here and if I got hired, okay," she said. "I did and I like the work."

Ron Barrett, formerly an aide to Councilman Leon Williams and a radio amateur (ham) for 20 years, thought it would "be exciting to work in my hobby" and decided to hire the handicapped. He is president of Pride Industries . . .

"The handicapped are the most ignored and valuable resource in industry today," Barrett said. "Any of the light industries that do not take advantage of that fact are making poor decisions. The handicapped are highly motivated, most deserving, eager to do a good job and take pride in their work."

"I saw 100 employers and was unemployed for a year and a half," said John McGeehee, 23, who was left with twisted legs by polio. "I did some janitor work and washed dishes but people said I was an insurance risk. Ron (Barrett) got my name through the state rehabilitation office and called me. I'm assembling things I do not even know the uses of, but doing it right, I hope."

An Ngoc Ly, 41, the quality control technician, will see to that. A former electronics technician who became a lieutenant colonel in the South Vietnam Air Force, he lost his right forearm in a crash.

The supervisor, Jean Hollingsworth, never had any work in management, entered the firm in its "cottage days" after going to a rehabilitation school.

"We sent her some circuitry boards to work on at home and she did so well she is now supervisor," Barrett said.

He said a neighboring employer, Cutter Laboratories, told him about the Regional Employment Training Consortium and how it channels local funds from the U.S. Department of Labor to help pay to train the unemployed and underemployed.

"We got a grant, which helped, so we could do a lot more training," Barrett said. "Some of these people never saw a soldering iron until a few months ago. The supervisor had been unemployed for three years. More than half the workers have been on some welfare or relief program."

"Employers would not hire them because of insurance fears and it is incomprehensible," Barrett said. "They are more careful and less of a risk, by insurance statistics, than anyone else. They have found something special and have it going among all of them—and that is understanding. They even understand me."

Barrett said he credits the enthusiasm of his workers for success of the plant and "will match them against any production line." He said some have become so interested in radio since starting work that he has arranged for a code class so they can become radio operators. He said the firm is experimenting with a code buzzer system that the deaf can read by touch for radio communication between two operators without hearing.

"We may even start a whole new company making electronic items for the handicapped," Barrett said.

(Reprinted from the SAN DIEGO UNION, August 19, 1975, by permission.)

Handicapped employees at PRIDE work in all phases of the business, from production assembly to production supervisor, as discussed in the article. In addition, management responsibilities are assumed by handicapped employees; the buyer, for example, is blind.

An important point to make about PRIDE is that it is *not* a sheltered workshop, but a small business making its way in a very competitive market. PRIDE pays its workers slightly *more* than is typical for similar work in the San

Diego area; PRIDE can do so because of savings resulting from a very low warranty return rate. Barrett credits this low return rate to the care taken by his employees.

Specific points related to individual students

Two things that can help you to overcome this concern for individual students: information about performance in the vocational program and employer observations of the student at work.

In providing the former, focus on skills the student has that will benefit the employer. Use descriptions of skills that are directly relevant to the employment situation; do not just emphasize that the student is a fine, eager person who is a whiz at this or that. Functional descriptions of competencies gained are as useful to the employer considering a job candidate as to the vocational educator evaluating progress in class. For example, describe the kinds of refrigeration systems the student has learned to repair and the speed with which he or she can affect these repairs. Try to anticipate which tasks are most likely to arouse the employer's scepticism about the student's ability to perform. For example, an employer might wonder how a blind student can align a handsaw. Be ready to demonstrate how the handicapped student does seemingly very difficult tasks, or take along photographs of the student doing them.

Give the employer a chance to see the student in action. Invite the employer to the vocational school to see the student demonstrate those skills that would be required on the job. Be sure to include skills about which the employer has the greatest doubts. This way, the employer can see the handicapped student working independently, the retarded student operating equipment safely and carefully, the blind student getting about the shop, and the deaf student exchanging simple information with other students by note or gesture.

Work/study placements are also effective. They allow the employer to observe how the student performs in the actual work situation. The last, of course, is to allow the employer to see how the student gets along with coworkers, the next area of concern.

In all of your contacts with the employer, be frank about the student's weaknesses as well as strengths. Emphasize the latter, of course, but do not feel compelled to represent every handicapped student as an unrelenting paragon. A realistic appraisal is much better in the long run as the realistically apprised employer will know what to expect of the new employee, and the graduate will not be in the position of having to meet unreasonable expectations.

In the same vein, be realistic in appraising difficulties that exist on the job that did not exist in the training setting. Usually, equipment adaptations, workplace modifications, and special aids that were adequate to overcome problems during training will suffice, perhaps with slight alteration, to overcome similar problems on the job. Occasionally, however, you may encounter tasks which present problems that are unreasonably difficult, if not impossible to solve. For example, electronics technicians who construct prototype equipment on the basis of engineering drawings have to be able to read and understand complex, unfamiliar wiring diagrams. This is a substantial obstacle for blind technicians who may be quite able to perform troubleshooting or other tasks of great intellectual complexity on equipment with which they are familiar. There are two ways one might attempt to get around the obstacle: prepare raised-line drawings, or provide the technician with an aid, such as the OPTACON (see Chapter 6) for reading the ink version of the diagram. Neither is really practical in some situations. Preparing raised-line drawings is an art form and very time consuming. Even if someone could be found to do the drawings, delays would necessarily occur while the drawings were being prepared, to say nothing of the expense of an extra salary. In a discussion with one of the authors, a blind equipment specialist likened the difficulties attending the latter approach to one that would face a sighted person who tried to figure out a complex diagram by peering through a hole in a sheet of paper one letter in size. In other words, it's possible, but many blind people will not always be successful using this approach.

If problems arise that you cannot solve, tell the

employer this and call in rehabilitation or other specialists with whom you have contacts. If no solution is found, it is far better not to place the student with that employer. This approach will avoid an unnecessary failure for the student and will build employer trust in your earnestness to find good matches between the candidate and the job.

Concern: Handicapped employees will not be able to work well with others, or will put excessive demands on them.

Often, supervisors and coworkers will have had little or no experience in working alongside the handicapped. Their needs for new skills, information, and understanding will probably be similar to those of vocational teachers with handicapped students in their classes for the first time.

Some specific concerns in this area are based on simple misunderstandings, such as the fear that the blind will be forever getting lost or crashing into things unless they have someone to guide them around. Others are more legitimate, such as the fear that a retarded worker may not understand a supervisor's instructions if given in the usual way.

You can overcome concerns in this area by providing training and information to supervisors and coworkers before the handicapped student arrives, by providing on-site assistance during the transition to work, or both. The variety of specific methods that might be useful is too large to attempt to enumerate fully. Some things you may suggest are:

- Instruction for coworkers in basic tips for communicating with deaf workers.

- Assistance in familiarizing the blind worker with the new environment.

- Provision of tips for workers with the retarded (Figure 7-5).

- Assistance in familiarizing the retarded worker with new duties, responsibilities, plant layout, and work rules.

- Meetings between the vocational teacher and the prospective supervisor to discuss any interpersonal problems the student had in class, ways that such problems were solved, and how the teacher feels they can be avoided.

- Meetings between work/study or on-the-job training site personnel and the prospective employer to discuss any problems that developed and how they were solved. Of particular interest, when relevent, will be the quality of the students' interactions with customers.

- "Ice-breaking" introductions of the student to supervisors and coworkers before employment begins.

Specific points related to individual students

Some handicapped students will no more need "primed" coworkers than will nonhandicapped students. The best approach is the one that fits the individual in among his or her coworkers with the minimum amount of fuss.

SMOOTHING THE TRANSITION TO WORK

In this step you carry out the plans of action made with employers in previous steps. The activities you undertake in worksite or equipment modification, or in preparing supervisors and coworkers follow directly from the plans developed in response to employer needs and concerns. The skills you have developed in serving handicapped students, in preparing teachers, and in tapping outside sources of assistance should be directly applicable in undertaking these activities. The procedures suggested in earlier chapters of this book will help in overcoming any new problems that arise.

These activities will suffice for placing most handicapped students. However, more specialized programs may be desirable in some circumstances. This is particularly true if students require very close supervision and guidance by special staff as they move into the competitive labor force. Two models are presented below. One model is being used by a vocational program, the other by an advocacy group. They suggest operating procedures that you may be able to adapt to needs for closely supervised transition that arise in your

so you're
going to
hire the

mentally
retarded

memo for employers

So you have decided to hire a mentally retarded worker. Here are a few "Do's" to keep in mind. And remember: You are gaining not a "retardate" but a human being who happens to be mentally retarded, and who can become your devoted, loyal, hard-working employee.

DO talk to him on a person-to-person level, as you would to anyone else. Only try to be more specific, more precise and crystal-clear—as if you were speaking to someone in the upper levels of grade school. Don't "talk down" to him as though he were a small tot. He's not.

DO speak in concrete terms, not abstractions. If, for example, you want him to put the pail away, show him exactly where "away" is.

DO demonstrate what you want him to do; don't just tell him.

DO show him where things are—time clock, lockers, restroom, cafeteria or lunch area, drinking fountain, supply room—same as you would for any new employee. Only DO take your time, don't rush, and be sure he understands.

DO take extra care to explain about working hours, proper clothes on the job, his work station, whom he reports to, what his pay will be, where the bus or streetcar stops. It's doubly important for him to know these six points.

DO ask a question now and then to make sure he's keeping up with you.

DO "Now show me your work station," or "Where does the bus stop?" or any kind of question that checks his understanding.

DO introduce him to his fellow employees and supervisors. He may seem a bit withdrawn at first, but he'll warm up once he gets to know the people. He'll warm up faster if he can find one coworker at first with whom he can feel free and easy; someone to answer questions and listen to problems.

DO let him know he's one of the work-a-day family. He may learn to mix with others at work, but tend to be by himself after work. After-hours friendships shouldn't be forced; he may be vocationally ready but not quite socially ready.

DO be ready to give him a guiding hand should new situations and new problems arise which he needs help in coping with.

DO make note of his on-the-job strong points. When he turns out to be a good employee, pass the word on to other employers that . . .

IT CAN BE GOOD BUSINESS TO HIRE QUALIFIED MENTALLY RETARDED WORKERS.

Strong points that most mentally retarded men and women show on the job:
• They want to make good. They will work particularly hard to make good.
• They want to stay put on the job. They're not anxious to job-hop. They're happy to learn the job and remain with it.
• Their attendance record usually is better than average.
• They are willing workers, and will stay at routine tasks.

FIGURE 7-5.

program. The key thing in each program is that the need for careful transitional supervision and integration is met by staff skilled in working with handicapped students. This not only puts these tasks in the hands of those best able to carry them out, but avoids placing extensive extra demands on the employer's staff.

Two Specialized Approaches

Group Employment and Training Program

In this program, conducted by the Nassau County, New York BOCES, supervision of new employees is undertaken by BOCES staff, as described in the following excerpt from a report dated 1976.

A total of 234 adults with special needs, ages 18 and up, were placed in either individual or group employment situations in 43 firms under the surveillance, evaluation and support of professional program staff.

Clients are placed in entry-level jobs in industry under partial or full supervision by BOCES instructional and counseling staff.

Once a placement in an entry-level position is effected and the employee has reached a point of independence and self-sufficiency in his employment, every attempt is made with the employer to arrange a plan for upward mobility and upgrading of job skills and responsibilities. With the employer's cooperation, BOCES instructional resources are contracted to assist the employee in attaining the necessary skills for upgrading.

To date, 88 of these special needs adult employees have "graduated" to unsupervised, independent employment. Sixty-eight of these employees have since received promotions or other advancement to positions of greater responsibility.

In the group employment and training program, groups of from 3 to 12 employees were employed under regular supervision of in-plant BOCES instructional staff in a total of 12 firms. All employees are salaried by their employers. However, some employers elect to apply for 50% reimbursement of salaries through BOCES liaison with the Nassau County Departments of Labor and Office of Manpower (CETA). In cooperation with these employers, the BOCES in-plant instructional personnel work side-by-side with the special needs employees and assist them in learning job skills, acceptance of supervisory direction, work attitudes, and relationships with fellow employees.

During the two previous years of operation, 234 adults with special needs have been successfully inserted into Long Island's work force in such jobs as plastic forming operator, health aide, food service worker, drill operator, switchboard operator, office worker, auto mechanic, elevator operator, order processing clerk, computer console trainee, computer operator, packaging, printed circuit assembly, maintenance, housekeeping, laundry operations, machinery and mechanical inspection operations.

In addition to the employment success of these individuals, 45 adults with special needs voluntarily participated in after-hours programs of job upgrading, adult basic education and Saturday morning driver education classes. Serving this population were contracted BOCES professional personnel who provided specialized occupational skills training, remediation of skills, reading, computational, and communications remediation, life skills education, Civil Service preparation, psychological assistance, specialized employability instruction and counseling services.

The importance of the role played by these projects within the county were significantly reflected by the wide range acknowledgment, recognition, and support given by some of the major agencies in the county. Evidence of this was a total of 210 referrals made to these programs by more than 38 agencies and organizations including the Office of Vocational Rehabilitation, the Association for the Help of Retarded Citizens, the Association for Children

with Learning Disabilities, the Epilepsy Founda-
tion, North Shore Hospital Vocational Rehabilita-
tion, Human Resources Laboratory, the Nassau
Medical Center, New York State Employment
Service, Division of Special Education of Nassau
BOCES and various local school districts.

"Community Work Stations"

This approach is designed to help mentally retarded
students make the step from skill training to competitive
employment. The following excerpt from *OJT Information*
published by the National Association for Retarded Citizens
describes the approach:

> Often, there is little opportunity in local business
> and industry for the "almost ready" worker who
> needs to sharpen his skills before meeting the
> challenge of full-time employment.
>
> Development of the "Community Work-Station"
> concept is now providing employment to increasing
> numbers of mentally retarded persons—adding a
> valuable stepping-stone between training and com-
> petitive employment.
>
> The essence of this concept is a crew of mentally
> retarded workers who are under contract to perform
> services throughout the community. Ordinarily, the
> crew works on a continuing basis, each member
> specializing in a specific skill. Areas especially
> suited to this concept include janitorial services,
> factory projects, service station work and landscape
> maintenance.
>
> The overall purpose of the work-station concept is
> the continual placement of trained personnel in
> competitive job markets. Already, mentally re-
> tarded workers who began as members of a contract
> crew have made successful transitions into business
> and industry.
>
> The work-station concept is mutually advantageous
> to both employer and employee. The employer gets
> a good labor force for a needed service, while the
> mentally retarded worker acquires experience in an

on-the-job setting. While the crew member is learning the job, he receives less than average wages—but once he reaches a stated level of proficiency, he gains entry into full-time employment. In many instances, such advancement would have been impossible without the work-station "stepping stone."*

CONDUCTING PLACEMENT FOLLOW-UPS

Many vocational programs conduct follow-up studies of their graduates as a matter of routine. These studies can help to overcome problems in individual placements; reveal areas in which existing programs should be improved; suggest courses of study that should be expanded, added, made smaller, or eliminated; and determine the long-term success of graduates. Such outcomes are as valuable for placements of handicapped students as of the nonhandicapped. Areas of special importance for the handicapped graduate are discussed below.

Purposes of Follow-Up

Overcome Immediate Problems

Notwithstanding the best efforts of all concerned, problems will sometimes arise. Maybe the graduate is slow to pick up detailed skills normally learned on the job. Perhaps the work station modifications are not satisfactory. Or the graduate may be having trouble getting along with the supervisor for one reason or another. Whatever the problem is, you should find out about it as soon as possible and take steps to eliminate it.

This is much more critical for handicapped placements than for others. First, the handicapped student is more likely to have confronted failures, rejection and disappointment than other students and may well see an unhappy first

*Reprinted from *OJT Information* in *Programs for the Handicapped*, May 20, 1977, with the permission of the National Association for Retarded Citizens.

placement as yet another example of rejection by society. Thus, a lot of the good that the program has done for the individual's self image may be undone. Second, the employer may generalize from a failure with one handicapped person and reject future overtures to hire the handicapped. This is particularly likely if the employer has no other, or only a few other, handicapped employees.

Build a Favorable Reputation for the Program

If you conduct careful follow-up to overcome problems that arise, this information will be passed between employers. If an employer feels left in the lurch, this word will spread, too. As in business, word of mouth advertising is the most effective, and word of mouth criticism the most destructive. High-quality follow-up will assure your reputation with employers and make them more willing to accept other handicapped graduates.

Find Out How Well Handicapped Employees Are Progressing

Follow-up is concerned not only with success in entry-level jobs, but also with job advancement. If handicapped graduates are not progressing as rapidly as others, you will wish to find out what stands in their way, to work with the graduate and the employer to determine if advancement is desirable, and to help work out a plan for further training or other actions to make advancement practical.

Occasionally, too, an employer will attempt to take advantage of a handicapped worker, for example, by excessive scheduling on undesirable shifts, or by keeping wages low. The handicapped worker may not realize that this is happening, or may fear the consequences of standing up to the boss. If this happens, you may have to serve as an advocate for the handicapped person or encourage him/her to press the issue.

Identify Needed Program Improvements

In conducting follow-ups, you may find areas in which the training program has fallen short. Program graduates may not have some of the job skills required or behave inappropriately toward fellow workers. Consistent problems in any area would suggest program modifications or improvements.

Similarly, you may discover that worksite modification or training given to coworkers were inadequate. This outcome may point to improvements needed in placement procedures.

An Example Showing the Importance of Follow-Up

This example comes from the Brainerd [Minnesota] Area Vocational and Technical Institute (BAVTI). BAVTI is one of 30 such schools in Minnesota. It is basically a post-secondary institution, although it has an "open-door" admissions policy so that a high school diploma is not required for entrance.

The student of interest in this example, while not classified as retarded, was definitely a slow learner whose second-grade level in reading and math, and low scores on a mechanical ability test indicated that he would need substantial help from BAVTI's Supportive Services Department to succeed in the welding program. Welding and Supportive Services staff developed a program for this student, including special instruction in life skills, basic math, and reading in addition to technical instruction in welding. Substantial effort went into developing this program on the part of BAVTI staff, and the student himself worked very hard to succeed. After a year in the program, Mr. Jesme, head of the welding department, decided that the student was a competent production welder and had reached his maximum potential. He arranged for the student to have an interview with the personnel director for a company in a town 100 miles from Brainerd. The student was offered the job and given a week to make his decision. He came back to BAVTI scared to death! This meant leaving familiar situations, friends, and family; and he had decided by the next morning that he wanted no part of this. The staff of the Supportive Service Department talked and talked to the student. They encouraged him to try out the situation, telling him not to be afraid and trying to build up his confidence. He finally decided, after much prodding, to try the job. He went for the first week and came back on his first day off, very disgusted! He hated the job, the town, and everything connected with it. The Supportive Service staff talked again. They told the student not to give up, to keep on trying, and he returned. Almost one year has passed. The student returned to visit the Supportive Service Staff. He really enjoys his work, looks well, and is getting married. He is going to be made a supervisor over one small section of the plant. BAVTI had three special education students in the modified welding programs in 1975-76. Two of them were failures as far as a vocational program goes—but—how do you measure the success of the student who made it?

In this case, all of the efforts to prepare the student might have been for nothing but for the timely intervention of Supportive Services staff. Obviously the student succeeded on the job once he had adjusted. Without counseling support he may very well have quit early causing all of the program efforts to be written off as a failure.

Planning Systematic Follow-up

There are two key factors for successful follow-up: (1) rapport established with the student and with the employer during training and placement contacts so that either party feels confident in calling; and (2) an active policy of contacting the employer and the former student. In the example just given, the student felt adequate confidence in BAVTI staff to confide in them when he became unhappy on the job. To be maximally effective, follow-up programs should be designed to include procedures to detect trouble as soon as it starts and to take corrective action, as former students or employers may not bring problems to the attention of staff.

In his influential book on vocational preparation of the retarded, Brolin (1976) recommended follow-up with both the employer and the employee after the *first day* on the job, and weekly for the first month. After that, he suggests monthly follow-ups should be made until the employee has enjoyed six straight months without significant problems on the job. While you may wish to adjust this schedule to fit local circumstances, the important features of *early* and *frequent* contacts with the employer and the *graduate* are critical.

Personal contacts, either over the telephone or face to faces, are far better than mail contacts. Be ready to probe to be sure that no problems have come up. A general question, "How is it going?" may simply get the answer, "fine," when more careful questioning will uncover small problems that should be looked into before they become big ones. Use your information about job demands uncovered during job analysis and of steps taken to smooth the transition to work to guide your questions. For example, if communication tips were given to the supervisor of a deaf graduate, find out how well the supervisor and the employee feel they are getting messages across to one another. Similarly, if a retarded worker must read sales orders, find out from the supervisor if the performance is satisfactory, and from the employee if the reading is harder than expected or not.

If hints of trouble appear in interviews, you should immediately make a visit to the work site to find out more details and to work out a solution. In some cases the "solution" may simply be reassurance. "Oh yes, teachers had trouble understanding his speech at first, but they started getting used to it in about a week." Or, "The other employees don't really know you yet, they'll open up more once you've been there a little longer."

At other times the problem may be more substantial. The new employee may be having trouble using the equipment, getting along with coworkers, or may not seem to understand instructions. Whatever the symptoms, try to find out in detail the circumstances under which the problem arises. For example, if the problem is in the area of equipment usage, try to ascertain exactly what aspect is causing the problem (e.g., set up operation monitoring) and why it is difficult (e.g., the operator's arm must be extended for continuous periods during operation, thereby fatiguing the person) and work out a solution for that problem (e.g., providing an arm support).

Similarly, your former student is probably not having problems with *all* coworkers all the time. The difficulties are probably with a few workers some of the time, and it is these situations that you should identify and attempt to remedy.

The root of the problem may become readily apparent in conversations with the handicapped worker and the employer. For example, they may both readily recognize that they are having trouble getting information across to each other. In other cases, your own observations or those of another expert may be required. In any case, the early identification of problems and their effective solution is a crucial factor in assuring a high percentage of successful placements.

CHAPTER REFERENCES

Ball, Neil. "Electronics Plant Offers New Job Opportunities," *San Diego Union,* August 19, 1975, page B-3.

Board of Cooperative Educational Sciences, Nassau County, New York. *Programs of Supervised Industry Based Occupational Preparation for Adults With Special Needs.* Mimeo, 1976.

Board of Cooperative Educational Services, Nassau County, New York. "Strategies and Techniques: Assisting Clients with Job Finding Skills." Mimeo. No date.

Brolin, Donn. *Vocational Preparation of Retarded Citizens.* Columbus, Ohio: Charles E. Merrill Publishing Company, 1976.

Campbell, L. Wayne, Todd, Medford & O'Rourke, Everett V. *Work Study Handbook for Educable Mentally Retarded Minors Enrolled in High School Programs in California Public Schools.* Sacramento: California State Department of Education, 1971.

National Association for Retarded Citizens *OJT Information.* Arlington, Texas: Author.

National Center for a Barrier Free Environment. "The Reasonable Cost of Reasonable Accommodation." *Report.* May/June, 1976, page 3.

President's Committee on Employment of the Handicapped. *Application for Employment to American Industries from the Physically Handicapped.* Washington, D.C.: Author, 1965.

William Cochran Associates. "The Cost of Accessibility," Mimeo available from Mainstream, Inc., 1156 15th Street, N.W., Washington, D.C.: 1977.

Wolfe, Joe. "Disability is no Handicap for DuPont." *The Alliance Review*, Winter, 1973-74.

8

Full Circle

So now we come back to the beginning. The point of this chapter is the same as the point of Chapter 1: handicapped people can succeed, and you can be a major factor as they gain the skills needed for that success. Between the first chapter and this, we have tried to give you a wide variety of practical steps you can take as you go about imparting those skills:

- *Chapter 2* discussed the development of positive attitudes, so basic to the success of any educational endeavor.

- *Chapter 3* described desirable architectural features of a vocational facility to make it more useable by handicapped.

- *Chapter 4* presented methods for assessing handicapped students and showed how to use assessment results to prepare an individual plan for handicapped students.

- *Chapter 5* showed how to modify the curriculum and teaching methods so that handicapped students could be taught in a class with their nonhandicapped peers.

- *Chapter 6* listed a variety of problems that might arise in the use of tools and equipment, and showed how these problems can be overcome with equipment modification or the use of aids and devices— some as simple as a long-handled wooden spoon, some as complicated as the OPTACON which "converts" ink print to an array that can be read by touch.

- *Chapter 7* showed how handicapped graduates can be placed on the job.

You, in your role as a teacher, counselor, placement officer or administrator, have the most immediate impact on your students, and it is upon you that the success of any program depends. This is as true when the program includes the handicapped student as when it exclusively enrolls the nonhandicapped. Therefore, we would like to say just a few final words about using this book in playing your role effectively.

FOCUS ON LOCAL NEEDS

We have tried to cram this book full of examples and helpful suggestions. Still, we could not cover every situation that might arise. Nor did we try to. That would have been as futile as trying to prepare a vocational program which included every last conceivable circumstance that might arise for a person in a given occupation. Inevitably, the vocational graduate must deal with situations that differ in one way or another from those used in training. So it is as you use this book.

You will have to adapt the procedures or modifications suggested in this book to fit the situation in your school or classroom and the individual capabilities of the particular students you serve. This volume will be most useful if used as an "idea book" to spur your thinking and that of your colleagues. It will be least useful if used as a manual of solutions to all problems, for it is no such thing.

Also, remember that things do not happen all at once, so don't feel that you have to implement every idea in this book immediately. We meant to provide information that you can use to meet the needs of your handicapped students, not to present a list of things-you-must-do-or-else-feel-guilty. Some of the assessment techniques, teaching strategies, and equipment and facilities modifications may never be necessary. Often, you will be able to develop less elaborate approaches than some mentioned in this volume. Similarly, many attitudinal problems may never arise, and certain employers will turn out to be quite willing to hire the handicapped and sophisticated enough to require little or no effort to overcome some of the concerns discussed in the placement chapter. In sum, this book is a professional too. Use it with creativity and imagination.

HAVE REALISTIC EXPECTATIONS

We hope that you meet with success in teaching handicapped students. We are confident that you will in a great majority of cases. But, should things go wrong with one student, don't let that discourage you with the next.

Throughout this book we have taken an upbeat tone emphasizing success and not failure, because success is the goal. Still, things sometimes go awry. Teaching handicapped students, no less than teaching in general, is a very human undertaking. And, like any human undertaking, it will have its ups and downs.

The slow learner welding student discussed in Chapter 7 was successful, but two other handicapped students were not. As it happened, all three students were enrolled during the same year, so the staff had a success to offset failure. Still, if it had happened that the unsuccessful students were the only ones enrolled during the first year, it would have been a shame to give up in discouragement and miss out on a success for staff and student alike.

If things are going poorly with a particular student, seek the advice of other professionals, try a new approach, or arrange for additional support or materials. Most often, you can overcome problems that arise in teaching handicapped students just as you overcome problems that arise in teaching nonhandicapped students. Moreover, as your experience grows, your proficiency will increase, as in any other undertaking.

Perhaps most importantly, do not prejudge the potential for success of one handicapped student on the basis of experience with another. You don't do this for students in general, so don't do it for the handicapped in particular. One student may sail through where another fails. Which leads again to the oft repeated point: it is the capabilities and limitations of the individual student and the suitability of the program provided for that student that lead to success or failure. Use this book as a tool in identifying the needs of your handicapped students and in meeting those needs, individual by individual.

HAVE A GOOD TIME

In this book we have included examples of vocational educators who teach handicapped students in their regular programs. They have found their experiences very rewarding. In all likelihood, you will find youself rewarded as well—not only in providing students with skills valuable for making their way in the world, but also in discovering skills in yourself that you may not have suspected.

Appendix A
Handicapping Conditions*

HEARING IMPAIRMENT

Although this invisible disability is seldom recognizable, 13 million Americans are estimated to have some loss of hearing in one or both ears. There are approximately 250,000 deaf adults, or 1 out of every 500 adults, in the United States whose hearing cannot be restored by medical treatment.

The nomenclature related to hearing impairments differentiates between hard of hearing, which refers to a partial loss, and deafness, which implies a total loss. The term "deaf mutism" has traditionally been used for persons who were congenitally deaf and who, never having heard speech, were unable to produce it. If, however, there is no impairment of the speech organs, it is no longer assumed that a child who is congenitally deaf is unable to speak. Advanced technology and modern teaching techniques make it possible for children to speak even though the child may never hear his or her own voice. The term "deaf and dumb,"

---

*Adapted and reprinted with permission of the San Diego County Human Relations Commission.

while originally meant to express that an individual could not speak, carries the connotation of stupidity rather than the inability to talk. "Deaf" or "hearing impaired" are the terms used by the deaf themselves.

Deafness is classified as either conductive or sensorineural (nerve deafness), the former being a failure in the transmission of sound waves occurring in either the outer or middle ear, and the latter being a failure in receiving the vibrations because of a defect in the inner ear. In some instances, a person can have a mixture of both types of hearing loss.

Most cases of sensorineural deafness are irreversible, and efforts on behalf of the individual must be directed toward rehabilitation measures which minimize the disability. In conductive deafness, however, a number of restorative procedures may be employed.

VISUAL IMPAIRMENT

Approximately 2 out of each 1,000 persons are blind. Of this blind population, 10% are under 20 years of age and 50% are over 65. Blindness is more prevalent among men than women and among the non-white population than among the white. Cataract and glaucoma are among the principle causes of this disability. Approximately 10% of blindness is caused by injury, with occupational accidents figuring significantly in this category. A number of persons have blindness of congenital origin often associated with brain damage and defects of speech and hearing. An individual whose vision is so impaired that optimum visual acuity in the better eye of 20/200 is considered to have statutory or legal blindness. Not all blind persons are totally sightless. There are varying degrees of visual impairment, including the need for corrective lenses, color-blindness, tunnel vision, and lack of visual acuity.

MENTAL RETARDATION

Mental retardation is a condition in which the individual functions with less than normal intellectual capacity.

It is estimated that approximately 3% of the total population can be diagnosed as mentally retarded. Of this total, 85% are mildly retarded and are capable, with proper education and training, of becoming self-sufficient citizens. Twenty-five percent of all cases of mental retardation can be ascribed to a biomedical cause. In all other cases, either the cause is unknown or it is assumed that the retardation is the result of environmental deprivation. There is a high correlation between premature birth and the incidence of mental retardation.

PHYSICAL DISABILITIES

Individuals with physical disabilities include those whose locomotion, according to the diagnosis of a competent physician, has been severely impaired due to birth injuries, congenital anomalies, traumas, tumors, infections, developmental diseases, or other such conditions as fragile bones or muscular distrophy. In many cases, a physical disability may be the aftermath of such a disease as poliomyelitis. Many students with physical disabilities need special equipment in the classroom, motorized wheelchairs, and physical therapy as part of their total program. Physical disabilities include:

Congenital conditions and deformities

These include a variety of physical problems affecting the individual from birth, ranging from heart defects to club feet to dwarfism. The physically evident deformities have relatively clear-cut implications for what can be attempted, but less evident are internal defects, which, although unseen, may prove to be more serious limitations on stamina and the effort to be expended in school or on the job. Congenital defects are apt to be fairly stable, although they can sometimes be alleviated through operations.

Traumatic conditions and amputations

These include the physical disabilities resulting from accidents and operations. While the conditions are usually stable and self-evident, psychological damage is a special consideration.

Muscular dystrophy

This is a progressive disease of the voluntary muscles such as the arm, thigh, and calf muscles. Small muscles in the hand are usually last affected. Weakness results from the replacement of muscle with fatty tissue. Consequently, persons having this condition should keep active since disuse of the muscles may accelerate deterioration.

Arthritis

This is an inflammation of the joints for which no present medical treatment seems to be effective. It is generally progressive and painful. Over time it sharply reduces dexterity and the ability to perform manipulative tasks.

Hemophilia

This is a disorder of the blood which impedes coagulation. This "bleeder's disease" is a congenital defect which requires constant caution against rupture of the blood vessels. Ruptures can result from sudden twists or pressures as readily as from cuts.

Poliomyletis

Infantile paralysis is a disease in which the spinal cord is damaged by a virus, paralyzing the limbs. Fortunately, the availability of Salk vaccine (in 1956) has greatly reduced its prevalence among the school aged.

Cerebral palsy

This neurologic disorder (not a disease) results from brain damage or incomplete development. Unfortunately, while polio has been on the decline, the palsied seem to be in greater proportion among the school aged youngsters—on the order of 30% of the physically handicapped population. In brief, cerebral palsy results in mascular malfunction, either being spastic, rigid, jerky, uncontrolled, uncoordinated, or some combination of these. Perhaps the most disturbing agent of cerebral palsy is that in the *majority of cases* not only is there a primary motor disability but there are secondary handicaps. These secondary handicaps can be of serious consequence, for they can include mental retardation, visual defects, speech defects, hearing defects, or combinations of several. More than half of the cerebral palsied students will have speech defects which, coupled with poor facial muscle control (drooling, etc.), can give a false impression of mental retardation. *In spite of all these complexities,* the cerebral palsied represent a physically handicapped group with considerable vocational potential and who continually surprise those around them with what they can do.

Spina bifida

This is one of the most common birth defects causing disability in early childhood. While operations have been increasingly able to correct this defect in the spinal column, it is not uncommonly encountered. Its effects are generally paralysis of the legs and (of more severe consequence for vocational purposes) lack of control over the elimination of body wastes. In some instances, hydrocephalus (enlargement of the head) is also present. Excepting the latter complication, most persons with spina bifida function normally in intelligence.

Other health impaired

Among these are the *diabetics* (who can function effectively given a proper diet and insulin treatment), the *respiratory disordered* (e.g., asthma, a difficulty in breathing is most common), those with *nephrosis* (a degenerative kidney condition), and those with *osteomylitis* (a spreading inflammation of the bone).

A more detailed description is provided here of some of the common physical disabilities likely to be encountered by vocational educators in mainstream classrooms.

Paraplegia

Paraplegia is a condition of loss of function in the lower extremities (legs). The most common cause of paraplegia is injury to the spinal cord at the thoracic or lumbar level. Most injuries to the spinal cord are sustained as the result of motorcycle, automobile, sporting, and shooting accidents. The term "paraplegia" may be used to identify varying degrees of paralysis in the lower extremities. The degree of paralysis an individual sustains as the result of a spinal cord injury is the result of (1) the level of injury, and (2) the extent of the injury to the spinal cord.

If a person's spinal cord is completely severed, there will be total loss of muscle and sensory function from the level of injury down. Thus, a person with an incomplete injury may be able to lift one leg, move one foot, or have feeling below the level of injury. The degree of paralysis will also depend upon the level at which the injury takes place. Assuming a total transection of the spinal cord, the higher the level of injury the more extensive the paralysis. If a person injures the spinal cord at a higher level, he or she will probably find it necessary to rely on a wheelchair for mobility. If the person injures the spinal cord at a lower level, he or she may be able to walk with the aid of canes, leg braces, crutches, or a body brace.

Paralegia can also result from various muscular atrophies such as poliomelitis or muscular dystrophies. The damage here is to the muscle, not the nervous system.

There is no connection between paraplegia and mental impairment. A person with paraplegia has the ability (dependent on the individual capacity) to perform in the same occupational areas as the ambulatory, except for those occupations which require the use of the legs.

Quadriplegia

Quadriplegia is a condition in which all four extremities (arms and legs) are affected by paralysis. The most common cause of quadriplegia is spinal cord injury at the cervical (neck) region of the vertebrae (spinal cord). The most common causes of spinal cord injury are motorcycle, automobile, and sporting accidents.

The degree of paralysis which exists in the quadriplegic state caused by trauma is determined by two factors: (1) the level of injury to the spinal cord, and (2) the extent of the injury to the spinal cord. If an individual suffers an injury which results in a total transection of the spinal cord, the result will be complete paralysis from the level of injury down. If the individual's spinal cord is not completely transected, paralysis will be incomplete, with muscles and sensory function occurring patchily throughout the affected body parts. Thus, persons with quadriplegia can differ greatly in the degree of their paralysis. A person with a high cervical injury may have total paralysis from the neck down, requiring the constant use of a respirator, while a person with a low cervical injury may have movement in and control of the upper extremities, except for the absence of finger grasp. All persons with quadriplegia do have in common some degree of paralysis in the upper extremities.

The most common levels of injury among spinal cord injured persons is at the sixth and seventh cervical vertebrae, which allows for almost total use of the upper extremities except for the grasp function of the fingers.

In addition to spinal cord injury, quadriplegia may be caused by poliomyelitis, Guillian-Barre syndrome, or various dystrophies of the muscle.

Amputation

Amputation is, by definition, the surgical removal of a limb or portion of a limb, with disruption of the continuity of the bone, when bone is involved. The term amputation may also be applied to any projection such as a breast or the nose. When an amputation involves the removal of a limb at a joint, it is called disarticulation.

Amputation may be performed for a number of reasons. Specific indications are (1) trauma to the extent that reconstruction is impossible or in which the intra-tissue and the loss of blood threaten the life of the patient; (2) vascular disease in which the blood supply is lost, the blood vessel changes, and gangrene occurs often as the result or a complication of diabetes, or as a result of frost bite, or a vessel occlusion; (3) infection of the bones and joints; (4) soft tissue injury, infection, or contracture, particularly when the condition is long standing; (5) tumor; and (6) deformities and paralysis.

A person with an amputation whose remaining limb portion is free from postsurgical complications and who has been fitted properly and trained to use a prosthesis can take care of all daily needs, drive a car, and handle virtually any kind of job. Among persons under the age of 50 who have had a single extremity amputated, 75% have returned to their former occupations. Precautions are advisable in making vocational plans for amputees, but none impose serious limitations. The person with an upper extremity amputation should expect a prosthesis to function in vocational activities where the work done does not solely depend on the prosthesis. A lower extremity amputee should, for example, be dissuaded from undertaking a job which involves climbing a vertical ladder. Amputees are currently holding jobs in virtually all vocational fields— industrial, clerical, services, and professional.

Epilepsy

Epilepsy affects four million people in the United States, or 1 out of 50 persons. Epilepsy is a neurological disorder characterized by some type of seizure varying from slight to severe, depending on the individual. Epilepsy is as common as diabetes and twice as prevalent as stroke. It affects more people than cancer, cerebral palsy, multiple sclerosis, muscular dystrophy, and tuberculosis combined. It is not an emotional, psychological, or social disturbance. The symptomatic "seizure" is a sign indicating part of the brain may have been injured at some time by a blow, an infection, a stopped up blood vessel, lack of oxygen or impaired circulation, accidents, prenatal or birth injuries, the after effects of anoxia (lack of oxygen) at or following birth, infectious diseases, tumors, or bodily disorders. Some cases are of unknown origin.

Approximately 50% of persons with epilepsy have their seizures completely under control through the use of medication, while another 30% have minimum effects from their condition.

Twenty-seven percent of persons with epilepsy are professionals, businesspersons, and college students. Clerical and skilled workers comprise 28% of the workforce of this group. Twenty percent of persons with epilepsy are sales and service workers and 25% are unskilled laborers.

Appendix B
Agencies and Organizations
Serving the Handicapped

The agencies and organizations listed below can often assist you to teach handicapped students better. The list is far from exhaustive. Consult with local special educators or rehabilitation personnel to identify locally available services and to determine which agency is most likely to be able to supply the resources you require.

GENERAL SERVICE PROVIDERS

The Council for Exceptional Children
1920 Association Drive
Reston, Virginia 22091

- Provides materials on the education of exceptional children

- Conducts research concerning education of handicapped children

Library of Congress
Division for the Blind and Physically Handicapped
Washington, D.C. 20542

301

- Provides braille, large print, and recorded books for the blind

- Provides listings of aids for handicapped readers

President's Committee on Employment
of the Handicapped
1111 20th Street, N.W.
Washington, D.C. 20210

- Encourages employers to hire the handicapped

- Disseminates information on how to open employment opportunities for the handicapped

- Encourages barrier-free designs

United States Office of Education
Bureau of Education for the Handicapped
400 Maryland Avenue, S.W.
Donahoe Building
Washington, D.C. 20202

- Sponsors research and demonstration projects to improve the education of handicapped persons

- Supports resource centers to provide assistance in teaching handicapped students

United States Office of Education
Bureau of Occupational and Adult Education
7th and D Streets, S.W.
Washington, D.C. 20202

- Sponsors activities intended to enhance the occupational status of handicapped persons

SERVING THE VISUALLY HANDICAPPED

American Foundation for the Blind
15 West 16th Street
New York, New York 10011

- Library services for the blind

- Provides special aids and devices

American Printing House for the Blind
1839 Frankfort Avenue
Louisville, Kentucky 40206

- Provides a wide variety of instructional aids

Braille Institute of America
741 North Vermont
Los Angeles, California 90029

- Conducts job development for the blind

Science for the Visually Handicapped
919 Walnut Street, 8th Floor
Philadelphia, Pennsylvania 19107

- Develops and manufactures aids, special instruments, and materials

National Braille Association
85 Godwin Avenue
Midland Park, New Jersey 08432

- Prepares braille, large type, and recorded materials

National Society for the Prevention of Blindness, Inc.
79 Madison Avenue
New York, New York 10016

- Provides information about aids for those with poor vision

Recording for the Blind, Inc.
499 West Charleston Road
Palo Alto, California 94306

- Provides free recorded educational material

SERVING THE DEAF, HEARING IMPAIRED, AND SPEECH IMPAIRED

Alexander Graham Bell Association for the Deaf
3417 Volta Place, N.W.
Washington, D.C. 20007

- Provides information on speech and hearing problems

American Speech and Hearing Association
9030 Old Georgetown Road
Bethesda, Maryland 20014

- Professional association of speech and hearing pathologists

Junior National Association of the Deaf
Gallaudet College
Florida Avenue at 7th Street, N.E.
Washington, D.C. 20002

- Provides opportunities for deaf youth to develop their full potential

- Provides information about instruction of the deaf student

National Association of the Deaf
814 Thayer Avenue
Silver Springs, Maryland 20910

- Advocates for the deaf in education, jobs, and legislation

- Provides job information for the deaf

National Technical Institute for the Deaf
One Lomb Memorial Drive
Rochester, New York 14623

- Designs and develops devices and techniques to improve communication skills of the deaf

- Provides technical training for deaf students in conjunction with the Rochester Institute of Technology

Registry of Interpreters for the Deaf
P.O. Box 1339
Washington, D.C. 20013

- Provides lists of interpretors for the deaf in the United States

SERVING THE ORTHOPEDICALLY HANDICAPPED

Center for Independent Living
2539 Telegraph Avenue
Berkeley, California 94704

- Encourages independence for handicapped persons

- Serves as an advocate for the rights of the handicapped

Mainstream, Inc.
1156 15th Street, N.W.
Washington, D.C. 20005

- Provides technical consultation on facility modifications

National Association of the
  Physically Handicapped, Inc.
6473 Grandville Avenue
Detroit, Michigan 48228

- Undertakes activities to improve the economic and social status of the handicapped

National Center for a Barrier-Free Environment
7315 Wisconsin Avenue, N.W.
Washington, D.C. 20014

- Encourages barrier-free buildings and transportation

- Disseminates newsletter (NCBFE REPORT) keeping up with technical and legal developments

National Institute for Rehabilitation Engineering
Pompton Lakes, New Jersey 07442

- Designs and builds aids and devices for the handicapped

- Provides extensive training for handicapped purchasers in use of the devices

National Paraplegia Foundation
333 North Michigan Avenue
Chicago, Illinois 60601

- Disseminates information regarding rehabilitation, job placement, and legislation

United Cerebral Palsy Associations, Inc.
66 East 34th Street
New York, New York 10016

- Supports research and education related to cerebral palsy

SERVING THE MENTALLY RETARDED

American Association on Mental Deficiency
5201 Connecticut Avenue, N.W.
Washington, D.C. 20015

- Professional organization of researchers and practitioners

Joseph P. Kennedy, Jr. Foundation
719 13th Street, N.W., Suite 510
Washington, D.C. 20005

- Supports research on the prevention of mental retardation

- Develops programs to benefit the retarded

National Association for Retarded Citizens
2709 Avenue "E" East
Arlington, Texas 76011

- Advocacy group to promote the well being of the retarded and to encourage public understanding and acceptance

Appendix C
A Suggested Guideline Model for LEA/RLA Use Both in Developing and in Reviewing Individualized Educational Programming as a Process*

Described in this section is a process-oriented guidelines model which may be utilized by Local Education Agencies (LEAs), Responsible Local Agencies (RLAs), and any other types of organizations offering special education and related services in their development of individualized educational programming procedures. This process model may also be useful as an internal monitoring and review guidelines document to describe and ensure compliance with state and federal statutes related to Procedural Safeguards, Least Restrictive Alternative, Nondiscriminatory Testing and Confidentiality Assurances.

This model may be utilized in compliance with P.L. 93-380; P.L. 94-142, P.L. 93-112, Sec. 504 (Rehabilitation Act of 1973) and current state laws and regulations. Certain references to the California Education Code (EC), Sections 56300-56367, and to EC Sections 49060-49078, and significant others are included for the convenience of those LEAs or RLAs wherein these apply. Federal regulations (FR) references are to Title 45, Part 121a.1-121a.754 (P.L. 94-142 regulations), to Title 45, Part 84.1 - 84.64 (P.L. 93-112, Sec.

---

*California State Department of Education.

504 regulations), and to Title 45, Part 99.11 - 99.39 (P.L. 93-380 regulations). References to the California Administrative Code, Title 5 (CAC, T 5) are also indicated. "LEA" is used throughout in the broadest sense to refer to any organization which is offering special education and related services to individuals with exceptional needs.*

SUGGESTED PROCESS MODEL

I. *Identification, Location, and Screening*—at least two approaches should be employed

A. *Formal* Processes
Formal procedures for use with the in-school population is the responsibility of the LEA-wide administration. Both regular and special education personnel should be appropriately involved. Protection of the confidentiality of personally identifiable data and parental consent are included here. (PL 93-380, 513; & EC 49060-49078)

Formal processes include:

1. Required communitywide SEARCH and Serve procedures (PL 93-380, 613 (b) (1) (A); FR 121a.560-573; EC 49060-49078)

2. Any other formal processes such as district-wide screening which involves the total school population

B. *Informal* "Awareness" Process
In conjunction with communitywide SEARCH and Serve procedures and any other formal processes, an "awareness" process should be developed and implemented by the local education agency for all teachers and support staff, and for parents in the local communities, to enable them to make informed judgments as to possible educational needs of children

---

*Similar cross-referencing to state and federal codes and regulations should be used to assure compliance with legal mandates when guidelines such as these are updated or adapted for use in other states.

within their purview. Personnel development activities include ongoing training in this process as indicated. (PL 94-142, 614 (a)(1)(A) & (B); FR 121a.128-129; P.L. 93-112, 504; FR 84.35, 36 & 39; P.L. 93-380, 513, FR 99.11-99.39)

1. Teacher, parent, or individual him/herself identifies problem or need

2. Other professional identifies problem or need at "awareness" level (no written individual assessment information has yet been collected on the individual)

II. *Consultation* (informal, oral)

Prior to a formal referral, a consultation between the referring agent and an appropriate resource at the local school level (i.e., principal, counselor, resource specialist), may result in modification of the regular program or referral to other program options.
This possibility should be protected as a safeguard of the individual's right to a least restrictive educational environment, including only that degree of assessment which can be justified as necessary in the best interests of that individual. Any assessment intended to be used to establish eligibility for special education and related services must have the written, informed consent of the parents. (PL 93-380, 613 (a))

III. *Procedures for Implementing the Assessment-Placement-Reassessment Process*

The following discussion includes procedures for referrals, procedures for assessment planning, due process hearings, interim placement, and surrogate parents. (PL 93-380, 613(a); 121a.341(b); CAC (T 5), 3155)
As a result of the ongoing formal and informal activities in I and II, above, those individuals who warrant additional concern should be identified. (PL 94-142, 615; FR 121a.500-583; CAC (T 5), 3155 (c), 3156)

To ensure procedural safeguards and equal opportunity at this point, a formalized process should be available in each LEA which includes:

A. Provision for immediately accepting direct referrals from a parent, physician, teacher, the individual himself/herself, or other responsible citizen, which includes:

　　1. A written statement (referral) including a functional description of the problem or need, and a request for further consultation. (CAC (T 5) 3153, 3154(a) and (b))

　　2. A routing of written referrals through an administrator or designee who logs each case and assigns responsibility for developing an assessment plan for the pupil. The assessment instructional planning process and initiation of the IEP must be completed within thirty-five (35) school days from receipt of parents' written informed consent for the assessment. (See an exception for SAT-EAS procedures.) (CAC (T 5) 3311-3314)

　　3. Analysis of the referral by the referred individual's teacher(s) and the staff person responsible for initiating the assessment process. Not all pupils who are referred will necessarily become eligible for special education services. Modification of the regular classroom or other program change, for example, may more appropriately meet the described needs. Only that level of assessment deemed necessary and sufficient for that individual should be implemented.

B. Establishment of a procedure to be followed in developing an assessment plan for each referred individual:

　　1. Define responsibilities for an assessment team which should include those personnel who can best determine the individual's needs, including the teacher and an in-

formed representative of the pupil's cultural/language background (when and as appropriate).

2. Define the assessment plan model to allow for gathering sufficient and appropriate information on each individual, while at the same time protecting due process and confidentiality rights, respecting the "least restrictive environment" concept, and ensuring protections in assessment. (PL 93-380, 513 and 613(a); PL 94-142, 612(5) (c), 615(b) (A-E); FR 121a.530-534; CAC (T 5) 3152-3153; EC 56330 (a) thru (i))

C. Implementation of an Individual Assessment

1. When an individual assessment is planned, *written communication* of their child's referral is sent to the parents, in ordinary wording and in the primary language used in the home, including an invitation for them to attend a meeting with staff personnel to provide them information to ensure their "informed consent" and to provide an opportunity for parent input. (FR 121a. 500, 502, 504, 505; CAC (T 5) 3158-3159; FR 84.34, 84.35, 84.36)
If the parent is unable to attend, the following items should be presented in writing or through documented telephone calls or, possibly, a home visit:

a. description of the problem

b. assessment needs and procedures, including any anticipated referral of records and to whom (based on the individualized assessment plan prepared for that pupil)

c. identification and explanation of all tests, records, and information-gathering procedures to be used

d. possible uses of the information to be gathered

e. notification concerning due process, procedural safeguards, confidentiality, and
parent access to records (PL 93-380, 513;
FR 121a.561, 562, and 567; EC 56336;
CAC (T 5) 3312-3314)

2. The following items should be sought from
parents at the invitational meeting or in
another feasible manner:

a. written informed consent for the assessment before it begins (FR 121a.501-505)

b. written consent for obtaining and sharing information regarding their child

c. parental perception of problem as related
to school's performance

d. identification and explanation of any
language and/or cultural factors which
may affect the child

e. home expectancy and goals for the child,
and perceived learning strengths

D. Parents shall be informed of these procedural
safeguards immediately upon written referral,
and these safeguards shall be carried through
consistently for each individual. (PL 93-380,
613 (a); PL 94-142, 614(a)(1)(B); FR 121a.530-
534, 560-574; EC 56337-56341; CAC (T 5) 3152
(c) (1-9), 3157-3159, and 3313-3314; FR 121a.
500-506; CAC (T 5) 3159 (d))

1. The LEA shall:

a. inform the parents of the right to present
a complaint relating to the identification,
assessment, or placement of their child;
and other procedural safeguards, including confidentiality of records.

b. provide knowledge of a formal procedure
for parents to submit a complaint (CAC
(T 5) 3160)

2. The opportunity for informal consultation

regarding a parent complaint shall: (CAC (T 5) 3163)

a. be extended by the LEA superintendent within 10 days

b. precede a legal due process hearing at the LEA level, and

c. be made available to parents in a written statement including time limitations, school contact person, etc., in accordance with CAC (T 5) regulations. (CAC (T 5) 3157 and 3159)

3. Legal due process hearing procedures shall be established, providing for:

a. conduct of the meeting by a fair hearing panel (persons who are not involved in the education of the child nor having a personal or vested professional interest in the hearing) (EC 56340-56341; PL 94-142, 615(b)(2); FR 121a.507-512; CAC (T 5) 3166-3170)

b. right of the parents to representation (PL 94-142, 615 (d); PL 94-142, 615(c)

c. local procedures (school district, county, etc.)

d. appeal to state level, if decision is unsatisfactory

e. civil action

4. During the due process proceedings, the individual will remain in the current placement or will enter public school for the first time, pending due process appeal, unless parents and LEA argue otherwise. (PL 94-142, 615 (e)(2) and (3); EC 56340(a); FR 121a.513)

5. Federal regulations require that surrogate parents be assigned for a child when parents or guardian(s) of the child are not known or are not available, or when the child is a

ward of the state. (PL 94-142, 615 (b)(1)(A);
FR 121a.514)

    a. The LEA will determine which indi-
viduals need surrogate parents and assign a surrogate parent to each of those
students in accordance with predetermined criteria approved by the school
board.

    b. The surrogate parent(s) must have no
vested interest that would conflict with
his/her primary allegiance to the individual he/she represents; and must demonstrate competencies predetermined
and approved by the school board that
assure adequate representation of the
child.

The LEA should develop and describe
these procedures during the planning
period, secure local school board approval, and make knowledge of these avail-
ablt to assessment teams and others.

IV. *Assessment*

In order to assure identification of each individual's
"unique needs," the individualized assessment
plan shall be based on a continuum of assessment
methods and procedures corresponding to perceived
problem(s) of the individual. (FR 121a.530-534 and
550)

Decisions on the assessment procedures shall be
made by the participants in the individual assessment team, and interpreted to and approved in
writing by the parent(s) before written assessment
activity is begun.

The individual continuum may encompass the four
phase levels described in the following charts;
however, not all individuals referred will need to
proceed through all four phases. Assessment should
be halted at the earliest point at which the team
agrees adequate information for planning has been
obtained. However, it is necessary to develop an
individualized education program (IEP) for each

individual who is found eligible for special education and related services *before* that person is so placed. (CAC (T 5) 3154 (a))

NOTE: In addition to the federal and state regulations already discussed, Education Code Sections 56500-5642, 56600-56619, and 56700-56729 require further specific steps in assessment, placement, and instruction of pupils placed in categorically designated special education programs (i.e., mentally retarded, autistic, etc.), which are more detailed than is included in the above discussion.

NOTE: This discussion continues with item V on page following the charts of the four-page assessment model.

A. *Phase I*—Environmental Considerations

  1. School Observation

    a. demands the learning environment places upon the child, including a description of cultural/ethnic variables

    b. description of child's behavior including available learning modality, strengths, and any useful learning strategies

    c. child/teacher/peer interaction

    d. teacher style (individual difference in approaches to the instructional task)

  2. School History

    a. prior educational history including interventions, special services or programs and results, test scores (no more than two years old)

    b. Hearing and vision data (no more than one year old) and any other medical problems relevant to defined educational needs

  3. Interview with child, parent, teacher, and/or others as may be thought useful
     Phase I leads to adjustment of the regular school program (change of teacher, class

section, etc.), or referral to other regular program options (remedial reading, ESL, etc.) with possible future referral for further assessment a remaining option.

B. *Phase II*—Educational Considerations

   1. Assessment of language development, and if indicated, language dominance

   2. Intensive review of academic performance record

   3. Vocational/career assessment as indicated

   4. Intensive assessment of social/affective functioning with attention to cause-effect relationships

   5. Assessment of specific need for specialized designated instruction and services
   Phase II may lead to adjustment of the regular class program and modified regular class placement, designated instructional services (DIS), and/or resource specialist program or equivalent. The IEP would so specify.

C. *Phase III*—Adaptive Behavior/Medical Considerations

   1. Formal assessment of adaptive behavior is undertaken

   2. Medical assessment/developmental history (may require conduct of a physical examination by authorized medical practitioner)

   3. Intensive assessment of need for designated instruction and services (perhaps in more than one area)
   Phase III leads to same possible placements as in Phase II with the addition of special class or itinerant assistance and possible additional designated instructional services.

D. *Phase IV*—Ability Variables—Formal assessment in one or all of these:

1. Formal assessment of sensorimotor functioning

2. Psycholinguistic assessment

3. Psychological adjustment

4. Intellectual functioning

Phase IV may lead to special class placement on a regular school campus, or special center, if more appropriate; referral for further assessment to state residential schools; or private/public institutional/ agency placement with due consideration of the least restrictive educational environment.

E. Further Suggestions for Consideration in Asessment:

1. All assessment procedures shall be selected so as not to be racially or culturally discriminatory. In meeting this requirement, professional staff may find exploring the following questions for each case helpful:

   a. Can the procedure or test be expected to provide an adequate sample of the behavior or the characteristics of concern for the individual whose assessment is proposed?

   b. Does the instrument make underlying, possibly unstated assumptions with regard to generalization of acculturation patterns? If so, what are those assumptions? Are these assumptions credible and appropriate for the individual with whom its use is proposed?

   c. Are reliability and validity data available? How were they determined? Are the criteria pertinent to this individual?

   d. Do the items included in the test or procedures evidence different psychometric characteristics for individuals from different economic or cultural groups? If not, how can its use be justified with such individuals?

e. In assessing abilities other than language, does the test or procedure rely heavily upon receptive and expressive language abilities in English for mediating the examiner's direction and the individual's response? If there is a parallel form for languages other than English, are the language characteristics used consonant with those of the individual to be assessed?

f. Does the individual evidence characteristics that might match some in the examiner in order to create a better environment?

g. Are the testing environment and techniques or procedures utilized conducive to the individual's optimum responses?

h. Can the data obtained by the particular assessment techniques under consideration be directly related to instructional interventions for the individual?

i. In obtaining this information, is the privacy of the individual protected?

j. Are there potential future dangers to the individual in obtaining the information? What safeguards can you guarantee to any possible future misinterpretations of the data?

2. Assessment is provided and administered in the individual's primary language or mode of communication. FR 121a.532(a)(1); CAC (T 5) 3152 (C) (2)

3. Cultural background differences of an individual are taken into account in selecting, administering, and interpreting the assessment information. (CAC (T 5) 3152 (C) (1); FR121a 430;EC 56337 (e)

4. Assessment results accurately reflect the dividual's performance in the area tested rather than reflecting the possible impaired sensory, manual, or speaking skills, or lack of skill in Standard American English, unless a determination of the child's primary language is being made. CAC (TS) 3152 (c) (4); Fr 84.35 (b) (3)

5. Individual intelligence test scores shall not be used as the sole basis for program placement; also included shall be a behavioral description and interpretation of functioning on the various subtests by the qualified examiner who administered the test; and an expression of the results in terms of the student's strengths, weaknesses and needs. CAC (TS) 3152 (c) (6) FR 84.35 (b) (c)

6. No single test or procedure shall be used as the sole criterion for determining the individual's program placement.

7. Interpretation of the assessment data and subsequent determination of the individual's educational placement are made by a team of persons including the parent(s), who are knowledgeable about the individual, the meaning of the evaluation results, the placement options, and the personnel available to provide special education and related services. In California, this step is combined with the development of the IEP. (CAC (T 5) 3152 (c)(8); FR 84.35(c) (b) (2))

NOTE: The prime consideration in gathering assessment data and in selecting assessment instruments and procedures should be the determination of factors and conditions which will lead to the individual's optimal demonstration of competence. Furthermore, in keeping with the stipulation for placement in the least restrictive educational environment, the assessment process should be limited to the least restrictive assessment phase necessary and sufficient for the development of an optimal individualized educational program with maximum interaction in the regular school program as appropriate. All assessment data should relate directly to instructional goals and objectives, and have the capability of evaluating the achievement of those objectives.

V. *Writing the Individualized Education Program (IEP)*: Generalized Procedures for Instructional Planning*

The instructional planning process requires the continuing involvement of the local school (or regional or district) assessment team, the parent, and the individual when appropriate, in the instructional planning conference, which should focus on: (PL 94-142, 614 (a)(5); FR 121a. 340-349; CAC (T 5) 3152 and 3154; FR 121a.346)

A. Pinponting the individual's needs, based on the assessment data, and establishing resulting eligibility for special education and services.

B. Developing a written plan called the Individualized Education Program for each individual based on his/her needs, with, at least, the following required components: (PL 93-380, 613a; PL 94-142, 614(a)(4); FR 121a.346; CAC (T 5) 3154 (b) (1) & (2))

    1. The individual's present levels of educational performance

    2. Annual goals and periodic objectives (within the time period of the IEP)

    3. All specific educational services to be provided, including specification of instructional strategies, special materials and/or media and any environmental considerations, and adaptations necessary for placement

    4. Listing of those individuals responsible for implementing the IEP at the time it is initiated

    5. Extent to which the individual will participate in the regular education programs; and justification for the educational placement which the individual will have (least

restrictive educational environment rationale). (CAC (T 5) 3154(b) 3-9)

6. Projected dates for initiation and duration of special education and related services

7. Projected timeline(s) for any service(s) not immediately available

8. Type of special physical education and career and vocational education, if appropriate to the individual's assessed needs

9. Appropriate evaluation procedures and schedules for determining, at least annually, whether instructional objectives are being met

C. Assuring participation of parents at the conference to develop the written Individualized Education Program
If parents are unable to attend, other alternatives such as conference telephone calls must be attempted and documented. If a parent cannot attend, a representative or advocate should be sought. When no parent can be determined, a surrogate parent may be required. An interpreter must be provided by the LEA if a communication barrier (such as deafness or primary language other than Engligh) inhibits the parents' understanding. (FR 121a.344-345 CAC (T 5) 3154(a))

D. Reviewing and documenting alternatives for program placement which are compatible with the individual's needs, goals, and objectives in order to assure informed consent and least restrictive appropriate program placement. (FR 121a. 551-552 CAC (T 5) 3155(b) and (c); FR 121a. 242)

E. Reviewing any related services necessary to carry out the instruction and placement decisions.

F. Each LEA must maintain records and assure confidentiality of these individual educational plans, and document their review and revision. (FR 121a.560-573)

VI. *Placement*

A. *Least Restrictive Educational Environment*

    1. After alternatives for program placement have been reviewed with the parent(s), the least restrictive educational environment appropriate for the individual is selected. The placement will assure that, to the maximum extent appropriate, handicapped students will be educated with students who are not handicapped; and that special classes, separate schooling, or other removal of handicapped students from the regular educational environment, including extra-curricular activities, occurs only when the nature and severity of the handicap is such that education in regular classes with the use of supplementary aids and services cannot be achieved satisfactorily. FR 121a 552, 121a. 550, 301-307; CAC (TS) 3155; FR 84. 34, 84.35, 84.36 (Sec. 504; FR 84.34-37)

    2. Each LEA will identify the specific placement alternative appropriate for each individual in the written individualized education program, based on consideration of alternative possibilities both within the schools and in the community. Criteria may include:

        a. program name and location

        b. entry and exit criteria

        c. definition of the program's major goals and objectives

        d. indications of the program's appropriateness for the goals of the particular IEP (FR 121a.551; CAC (T 5) 3154 (E)(6); FR 84.33 (3), 84.38 and 84.39

B. When the selected placement is within another public or private education agency at public expense, that public or private education agency will implement and maintain an individualized educational program observing the standards set by state and federal regulations and by the responsible local education agency. (FR 121a.550, 554-556; FR 121a. 450-460; FR 84.33; CAC (T 5) 3155(a) and 3152(c) (9); FR 83.34(a))

C. Except where the student's individualized educational program requires some other arrangement, the student shall be educated in the school which he would normally attend if not handicapped.

VII. *Instruction*

A. When the written individualized education program including the placement decision is completed and consented to by the parents, the program is implemented and kept current by the teacher or specialist indicated in the IEP. Each receiving teacher or specialist should be directly involved in the IEP conference, but if that is not possible, then at least one member of the IEP conference team must confer with each receiving teacher or specialist to assist in developing the short-term objectives. These written, short-term objectives shall become a part of the IEP, and the teacher should record the individual's progress in these objectives for use in any subsequent review of that IEP. FR 121a. 340-349; CAC (T5) 3251 (9), 3154; FR 84.33 (b) (2)

B. Monitoring for revision of short-term objectives, instructional strategies, media, materials, environmental variables (keep parents informed)

C. Continuing progress checks to ensure that the individual education program is dynamic and may change to meet the pupil's changing needs (keep parents informed) (CAC (T 5) 3153 and 3154(a)(b) (2); FR 121a. 346(a) and (b)

VIII. *Evaluation of IEP: Reassessment of Individual with Exceptional Needs*

A. Each student's educational plan shall be reviewed at least annually by the responsible team, including at least, the teacher, parent(s), and administrative representative, using the IEP including the short-term objectives, any assessment results, and measures of achievement of the IEP goals and objectives. (FR 121a.531-533 and 534 FR 121a. 344-346; CAC (T 5) 3311(i), & 3313(j)

B. Each student's placement, as stated in the IEP, will be reviewed at least annually, and the parent(s) must participate, when possible, in these annual reviews, as suggested in VI, C and D, above. (FR 121a.504(a))

C. The student's parent(s) or teacher may request a review of the individual educational program at any time they believe such a review is indicated. (CAC (T 5) 3311 (j))

D. In case of needed reassessment, repeat the steps taken in the original assessment procedures as described in IV, above. (FR 121a.534(b))

Prepared by:
Eunice W. Cox, Ed.D.
Office of Special Education
Resources Development Section
Program Development Unit

Index